The Golden Age of the Luxury Car

AN ANTHOLOGY OF ARTICLES & PHOTOGRAPHS FROM "AUTOBODY" 1927-1931

Edited by

George Hildebrand

Dover Publications, Inc.
New York

Published in Canada by General Publishing Company, Ltd., 30
Lesmill Road, Don Mills, Toronto, Ontario.
Published in the United Kingdom by Constable and Company,
Ltd., 10 Orange Street, London WC2H 7EG.

The Golden Age of the Luxury Car is a new anthology of articles
and photographs from *Autobody* magazine, 1927–1931, edited and
with an introduction and design-drawings by George Hildebrand.

International Standard Book Number: 0-486-23984-5
Library of Congress Catalog Card Number: 79-56506

Manufactured in the United States of America
Dover Publications, Inc.
180 Varick Street
New York, N.Y. 10014

Introduction

Connoisseurs of fine automobiles consider the model years of 1928 to 1931 to have been the golden age of the coachbuilt luxury motorcar. In no other period, and in no other product of human endeavor, has that extraordinary combination of art, engineering and craftsmanship been realized to such perfection. The automobile salons and shows exhibiting these vehicles, with their superb handcrafted custom-built bodywork, likewise reflected the grandeur and elegance of a unique historical era in this country and abroad. Nowhere in America were these activities chronicled and pictured with greater authority, authenticity and affection than in the pages of *Autobody* magazine, whose tiny circulation was directed to the custom-body builders, their suppliers and to the top automobile executives in Detroit. *Autobody*, published monthly from 1922 to 1931 in New York City, was greatly respected for maintaining the highest standards of technical excellence and editorial integrity. It attracted the foremost figures of the world's coachbuilding fraternity as contributors, and the pages of *Autobody* were enlivened by fascinating disclosures of their most closely held ideas.

I was thirteen years old in 1928, imbued with the ambition of one day being an automobile body designer, when I first chanced upon a copy of *Autobody*. Excited by its ineffable delights, I ventured to their offices on Columbus Circle to see about getting other issues of the magazine. The editor, Richard Vail, not only presented me with a free subscription, but immediately arranged for me to show my drawings to Roland L. Stickney, the great designer-illustrator at Le Baron. That meeting led to my apprenticeship as a student designer with Stickney, and was the beginning of a cherished friendship spanning almost five decades. Stickney's considerable talents as a body designer were overshadowed by his reputation as the premier illustrator of the classic-car era. Nine of his remarkable renderings from the lush Le Baron salon catalogs are reproduced in this book (pages 3, 4, 7, 16, 17, 22 and 36).

The worldwide economic collapse of the early 1930s, combined with dramatic technological changes within the automobile industry, led to the ultimate demise of coachbuilding for the individually designed motorcar. The now-legendary classic designers were drawn into the mass-production design establishments of Detroit: Thomas L. Hibbard to General Motors (later to be director of styling at Ford), Raymond H. Dietrich to Chrysler and Alexis de Sakhnoffsky to Hayes Body. Stickney was the exception; refusing to "go West," he joined Henry Dreyfuss, a pioneer New York industrial designer, where he remained until his retirement.

My own design career followed a somewhat different course. With the closing of Le Baron's Fifth Avenue office in New York, I went across town to the Rollston Company, whose high-grade coachworks literally were on the other side of the tracks, in the neighborhood of Hell's Kitchen. I gained valuable experience as assistant to chief designer Rudy Creteur, but Rollston went into receivership just as I completed college. Having no alternative, I too became involved in production automobile design; first with Helen Dryden on Studebaker cars, then inevitably to Detroit, with the General Motors Styling section under Bill Mitchell and Harley Earl. However, being a confirmed New Yorker, I seized the opportunity to return as an aeronautical engineer at Republic Aviation (now the Fairchild Republic Company), where I was responsible for the engineering of pilot's cabins and ejection seat systems for numerous high-performance aircraft. Twenty-five years later, in 1965, my career came full circle. I established Fairchild's automobile safety research and development programs, and ultimately directed the design and manufacture of the first experimental safety cars, the Fairchild Safety Sedans, for the U. S. Department of Transportation.

Exactly a half-century has gone since my youthful ambitions were given their first impetus by Vail of *Autobody* and Stickney of Le Baron. In tribute to them, I gave thought to recording my viewpoint of the great, final golden years of custom coachbuilding, but found the literature already replete with far too many viewpoints of that era, authoritative and otherwise. Instead, I reached for my precious pages of *Autobody*, and reconstructed them into a definitive seven-part anthology of the design, the craftmanship and the exhibition of the great international classic luxury cars from 1927 to 1931.

The first part of the anthology reflects the glamour and excitement of the annual Automobile Salons and National Automobile Shows, which were so brilliantly mirrored in *Autobody*. The Automobile Salon was indeed a major social event of the season, but the motorcar world was concerned with its more lasting implications. Because the exhibitors were in the vanguard of automobile design, and the Salon, itself, preceded the National Automobile Show by almost two months, the unveiling of new trends and techniques was eagerly awaited every autumn.

The first Automobile Salon opened in 1904, on the top floor of Macy's department store in New York, exclusively as a showcase for foreign cars. When the outbreak of World War I abruptly ended luxury car production abroad, a selected few of the more costly and elegant American chassis were permitted to enter the annual Salons, now held at the Hotel Astor. When hostilities ended, the rule permitting custom-body builders to exhibit coachwork mounted on domestic chassis was continued; also, some luxury-class American automobile manufacturers were allowed to show complete cars if they made their own custom-built bodies. The Grand Ballroom of the Hotel Commodore, which had been equipped with a special automobile elevator, was chosen as the final setting for the New York showing of the Automobile Salon. In Chicago the Salon was held at the Drake. In California the settings were at the Biltmore in Los Angeles and the Palace in San Francisco—until it all ended in 1931.

The old Madison Square Garden was the site of the first National Automobile Show, which opened in New York in 1900. A board speedway, an obstacle track for car testing and a ramp to the roof were built at the Garden, enabling the forty exhibitors to demonstrate the handling and hill-climbing capabilities of their vehicles. From 1913 to 1940, the National Automobile Shows usually were held at the Grand Central Palace, which became the annual display center for America's burgeoning mass-production automobile industry.

In Europe, the significant salons and shows for luxury cars were those held in Paris, London, Monte Carlo, Brussels and Milan. The Paris Salon, originating in 1898, was enormously successful from the start, owing much to its timing and its setting. Held in early October, it was the first event of the annual series of great international automobile exhibitions. Also, no other city in Europe could offer a showplace of the magnitude and magnificence to compare with the Grand Palais in Paris. Given to the French automobile industry for only a token rental fee, it was a truly international gathering place, where all the world's languages could be heard in the hall. The London shows of the *Autobody* years were at Olympia, a huge architectural pile whose eclectic design stirred considerable controversy. The *Autocar*, published in England since 1896, called the Olympia shows, with their hundreds of exhibitors, the world's motor market, but the Paris Salons were regarded as the source of automobile fashion.

Fashion was indeed in full flower at the fabulous Concours d'Elégance held in France and Monte Carlo, where the combined chic of the owner and automobile were on display. The Paris Concours d'Elégance was inaugurated in 1922 under the auspices of the French publication *l'Auto*, with the great houses of haute couture and the grand carrossiers in the competition. Some of the most glamorous women of Europe lent further charm to the festivities by acting as models for these exotic creations. Costumes and car designs, stylishly matched, were judged individually and in ensemble by a jury composed of coachbuilders, artists and writers of the daily and technical press. The trophies and prizes awarded on these occasions were greatly valued on both sides of the Atlantic.

The majority of America's high-quality coachbuilders were located in the eastern part of the country—the worlds of society, finance, business and the arts being highly concentrated in the Boston–New York–Philadelphia corridor. Many of the famous custom-body shops evolved from the fashionable carriage works which, in an earlier time, had served the same clientele. Some eastern firms and much creative talent were moved to the Midwest when they were absorbed by the major production-body manufacturers located there. The motion-picture colony, and a handful of the old families, supported a small number of California coachbuilders whose work often was rather less inhibited than that of their eastern counterparts. Following is a list of American coachbuilders whose work appeared in *Autobody*, 1927–1931:

EASTERN STATES

Brewster (New York, N.Y.)
Brunn (Buffalo, N.Y.)
Derham (Rosemont, Pa.)
Fleetwood (New York, N.Y.)
 (Fleetwood, Pa.)
Holbrook (Hudson, N.Y.)
Judkins (Merrimac, Mass.)
Le Baron, Inc. (New York, N.Y.) (Bridgeport, Conn.)
Locke (New York, N.Y.) (Rochester, N.Y.)
Merrimac (Merrimac, Mass.)
Rollston (New York, N.Y.)
Walker (Amesbury, Mass.)
Waterhouse (Webster, Mass.)
Willoughby (Utica, N.Y.)
Wolfington (Philadelphia, Pa.)

MIDWESTERN STATES AND CALIFORNIA

Baker-Raulang (Cleveland, Ohio)
Dietrich (Detroit, Mich.)
Fleetwood (Detroit, Mich.)
La Grande (Indianapolis, Ind.)
Le Baron–Detroit (Detroit, Mich.)
Weymann American (Indianapolis, Ind.)
Murphy (Pasadena, Calif.)
Kirchhoff (Pasedena, Calif.)

The coachbuilding trade in Europe had its origins around 1450 in the Hungarian city of Kocs, where the carriage coach was invented, and from which it received its name. Although the antecedents of Rippon Brothers of Huddersfield, England, did build a coach for Queen Elizabeth I in 1564, most of the old-line classic-era coachbuilding names dated back to the nineteenth century. They were joined by dynamic new firms after World War I, bringing great vitality and originality of design to European coachwork, already well known for its elegance. Following is a list of European coachbuilders whose work appeared in *Autobody*, 1927–1931:

FRANCE

Belvallette	Kellner
Billeter et Cartier	Lavocat & Marsaud
Binder	Letourneur & Marchand
Busson	Marbeuf
Carrosserie S. P. C. A.	Meulemeester
De Viscaya	Million-Guiet
Felber	Muhlbacher
Fernandez	Ottin
Gallé	Proux
Grummer	Saoutchik
Henri-Labourdette	Weymann
Hibbard &-Darrin	

ENGLAND

Barker	H. J. Mulliner
Grose	Rippon Bros.
Gurney Nutting	Thrupp & Maberly
Hooper	Vanden Plas
Mann Egerton	Weymann
Arthur Mulliner	

BELGIUM

D'Ieteren Frères
Généraux
Gyselynck & Selliez
Van den Plas
Antoine Van den Plas
Vesters & Neirinck

ITALY

Castagna
Farina
Sala
Touring

GERMANY

Joseph Neuss
Papler

The stagecoach and commercial wagon were the forerunners of the deluxe motorcoaches and smart delivery cars described in *Autobody*. Long-distance motorcoach travelers were offered accommodations as luxurious as on first-class railways, and style-conscious merchants demanded impressive coachwork to advertise the character of the shops they represented. The designs of both commercial and passenger-car bodies were strongly influenced by the modern art movement of the 1920s. *Art moderne*, streamlining and other "modernistic" trends were becoming increasingly evident, in sharp contrast to the traditional offerings by the more conservative coachbuilders. The decade of the 1930s brought new advances in body-building technology, giving designers wider latitude in construction technique and greater esthetic freedom. The safety and aerodynamic characteristics of closed bodies were undergoing continual improvement. Open car bodies, now more rigid and rattle-free, featured ingenious new folding mechanisms to further reduce the bulk of the top in both the raised and lowered positions.

Motorcar design of the future is the final theme in the *Autobody* anthology. Leading authorities in the industry anticipated the challenges that would confront the automobile body designer in the years ahead. They called for more functional design configurations and better structural systems to provide increased comfort, safety and efficiency. The ensuing decades saw many false starts and wrong turns, but the best qualities of the modern automobile owe their heritage to the imaginative designers and skilled artisans of the great age of classic coachwork.

George Hildebrand

Heritage Village
Southbury, Connecticut
October 1979

Contents

IV
SELECTED EUROPEAN COACHWORK

V
DELUXE DELIVERY CARS AND MOTORCOACHES

VI
BODY DESIGN ART AND ENGINEERING

VII
MOTORCAR DESIGN OF THE FUTURE

I

The Salons & Shows of America

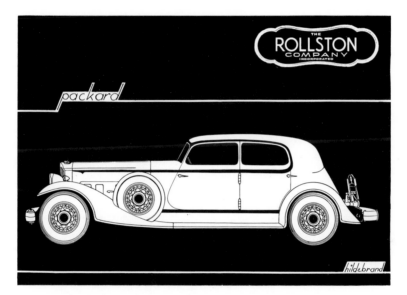

Custom-body designers, coachbuilders and chassis manufacturers combined their skills in the creation of "show jobs" for the annual automobile exhibitions. George Hildebrand designed this custom Packard club sedan for Rollston. It was proposed for display at the National Shows and the Chicago World's Fair.

Opening of the *Automobile Salon* New York Dec. 2

THE 24TH ANNUAL SALON, which will open in the Hotel Commodore, New York, on the evening of Dec. 2, gives promise of being the most interesting and successful Salon of the long series that have been held here; interesting because of variety in design and the excellent workmanship, and successful because of the general prosperity prevailing in the country. The new features are too varied to be summed up briefly, unless it be said that designers have had a free hand and have made use of this freedom to develop new belt and color treatments and have incorporated features that have been used abroad but, only occasionally, in domestic coachwork.

GREATEST CHANGES IN EXTERIORS

The greatest changes are in exterior design, interiors having become more conservative and dependent chiefly on arrangment, fine workmanship and quality of materials. There are a few exceptions to this conserva-

builders stands include: Cadillac, Duesenberg, Franklin, Chrysler Imperial, LaSalle, Lincoln, Packard, Pierce-Arrow, Stearns-Knight and Stutz.

Coachwork exhibits will be made by: Brewster, Brunn, Castagna, Derham, Dietrich, Fisher, Fleetwood, Hibbard & Darrin, Holbrook, Judkins, Le Baron, Locke, Murphy, Rollston, Weymann and Willoughby. In addition there will be special exhibits of supplies and equipment by William Wiese & Co., Custom Built Tire Co., Para Tire Co., F. Schumacher & Co. and Triplex Safety Glass Co. of North America.

EXTERIORS

Referring again to the general trends indicated by the advance illustrations, it would appear that the formal cars are more conservative, while the sporting types overflow with innovations in color, line and disposition of units. Some of these features are imported ideas seen here for the first time, while others are

Aero-Phaeton by Le Baron on Lincoln Chassis

Aeronautical practice influenced this design, from front to tail. The radiator ornament is a miniature fuselage; front mudguards are of aerofoil section; bonnet and wheel disks are of polished aluminum; body streamlined without a break to the "aeronautical" tail; repetition of horizontal louvers accentuate the streamlining; rear cockpit has wind deflector of polished aluminum; seats in both front and rear cockpits are placed on floor which is recessed for footroom, passengers sitting deep in body and thus lowering center of gravity. Chassis, mudguards and body are in maple-leaf green, a leather of softer shade being used for the cockpits where the trimming is in the aeronautical style—plain plaits without bindings of any kind. Non-shattering glass is used in the windshield

tive trend in interiors and mention should be accorded especially to two modernistic interiors that will be seen at this Salon. In general the appeal will be to conservative tastes, with a judicious apportionment of striking or "show" jobs intended to attract more radical-minded clients. Sport cars will display many features never seen in production, and convertibles will be found on nearly every stand. There will be a free play of color on these sport jobs, and the color treatment of the more formal cars will embrace combinations of colors from the world's famous masterpieces of painting.

Before giving further details, it may be well to present a list of the exhibitors, who represent six different nations, include 14 prominent American custom-body builders and two from abroad; in addition it is expected that the imported cars will offer the latest creations of six more European carrossiers.

EXHIBITORS

The motor cars to be exhibited by their makers or importers at this Salon include: Cunningham, Isotta-Fraschini, Lancia, Mercedes, Minerva, Renault and Rolls-Royce. Other cars represented in the coach-

simply receiving a more general application. In the last class are such features as polished-aluminum moldings and wheel disks, and "engine-turned" bonnet and cowl panels; disappearing tops; flatter folding head fittings for convertible cars; adjustable seats; floor wells, etc. Belt moldings exhibit a great variety; they are swept, recessed and windsplit at the corner posts, but there are few straight "through" moldings. Window treatment evidences study and reveals and moldings are being modified, in painting if not in form. Non-shattering glass is progressing in its adoption, and clear vision is featured in a number of cars, not only at front corners, but also at the center pillars. Many splayed fenders are in evidence this year, because of the predominance of the sporting cars. Spare wheels or tires are more often carried in the front-fender wells than at the rear.

In body types the phaetons and the convertibles seem to have received the most attention and bristle with changes in design, equipment and color. Other body types have likewise been under study, but the changes are not so striking, unless one excepts the "lady's town brougham" on Stutz chassis by Le Baron which is intended as an abrupt plunge from the conventional into the modernistic era. It is wholly different in treatment, but preserves the essentials of the classic town-car type. Le Baron's "aero-phaeton" on Lincoln chassis is another novelty with a timely motif that was handled with noteworthy success. In the convertible field, many builders having been improving the early models, rather than revert to the "sunshine" car which has been engaging the attention of Europe for several years. Dietrich has concentrated on convertible types and presents flatter folding head fittings for his coupes and sedans and also shows an intermediate convertible type designated as a "convertible victoria." This seats four inside, using bucket seats in front and folding seats in the rear, extending the Brunn idea introduced last year by adding center-

Chapeau de Poil"; Gainsborough's "Blue Boy"; Velasquez' "Philip IV"; Sorolla's "Swimmers," and a dozen others. The painting of several of the Willoughby cars will be noteworthy for the use of color as a part of the "silhouette" design, color being an integral element of the design rather than subsequent decoration. Another interesting treatment is the "lady's town brougham" by Le Baron in which the entire car is painted Poilu Bleu, with the exception of the wire wheels which are bright red like the lining of the *poilu* coat. The inside window moldings being in the same bright red, a hairline of this color is visible in the exterior view and enlivens the softer blue effect; the modernistic interior trimming is in soft tones of blue, silver and sand, the cabinetwork repeating these colors.

Variety Features Phaeton Design

Stutz "roadster-phaeton" by Le Baron. This design has a disappearing top. When rear seat is not in use, the opening in the tonneau may be closed by swinging the rear seatback forward, making a conventional deck lid. The front windshield is unframed except at sides; wings open with the doors. Rear windshield may be lowered into tonneau. The body is finished in cream, set off by black moldings windsplit at the windshield pillars

Chrysler Imperial phaeton designed by Locke & Co. The wide beading around the tonneau is painted light-primrose yellow which is also used for the under side of the fenders, chassis and brake drums. Valentine's Dustproof Gray, deep, is used for the body, upper side of fenders and chassis aprons. Center folding armrests are provided for both seats; secondary windshield disappears completely, being raised and lowered by a crank regulator

Sporting design by Le Baron for a phaeton on Duesenberg chassis. It has a long rakish raised panel swept from the radiator back into the front door where it is swept forward to the base line, leaving a long depressed panel done in a lighter finish and containing a novel grouping of bonnet louvers, each of which are swept and slightly longer than the preceding one. There is another light-finished depressed panel around the rear. A conventional secondary cowl and windshield are provided

folding and side armrests, smoking and vanity cases so that these passengers enjoy practically the comfort of the standard closed car.

PAINTING

Advance information indicates the considerable use of the all-black car, but color will be the dominant note at the Salon because of the numerous sport cars and the adoption by Fisher and Fleetwood of color combinations based on some of the world's masterpieces of painting, this suggestion coming from the art-and-color section of General Motors. These color schemes will present the original colors of the masterpieces and give to each color the same value that it has in the painting; included are such subjects as: Leonardo da Vinci's "Mona Lisa"; Ruben's "Le

INTERIORS

The dominant note in the interiors is the conservative treatment adopted in most of the bodies. The plain-stretched style continues in the ascendancy, and a noteworthy feature is the considerable use of narrow leather piping. Leather will also be considerably used in the sporting bodies in combination with fabric seat covering. Another interesting feature noted in the advance reports is the use of bedford cord for the seats in combination with broadcloth head and side lining. Numerous doeskins and bedford cords will be seen this year although broadcloths, both plain and figured, will continue to be the principal upholstery fabric. Novelty in upholstery materials will be the reptile skins and the rayon fabrics; the latter will be seen especially in the modernistic jobs by Fleetwood

Convertibles at the Automobile Salon

Fleetwood Body Corporation's convertible coupe on Cadillac chassis. This has the lancehead raised panel on the cowl and the wide rolled belt characteristic of Fleetwood's new convertibles

Derham coupe-roadster on Lincoln chassis. It has high body sides and an extremely low top, folding as closely as that of an ordinary roadster. Finish will be entirely in black except window reveals, under side of fenders and chassis, gasoline tank, brake drums and striping which will be in Matador Orange. The top is Burbank and the interior is trimmed with bright-finish black leather

A 2/4-passenger convertible coupe by the Holbrook Co. on Franklin chassis. It is finished in a combination of Pastelle Cream for the body, and black for the moldings, superstructure and wheels. The top is of Burbank and the seats are trimmed in black Colonial-grain leather

Everyone is inside, out of the rain, in this 4-passenger convertible coupe by Brunn & Co., on Stearns-Knight chassis. The interior is trimmed with an imported bedford cord and the top is of Burbank. The body is finished in Golden Wheat Tan, set off by dark-brown moldings

Dietrich's 4-passenger "convertible victoria" also seats all passengers inside, two on standard bucket-type seats in front and, in the rear, two on individual spring-cushioned folding seats, with center-folding and side armrests. When extra passengers are not carried, this space accommodates golf clubs, guns or luggage, although a trunk is also provided behind the body

Mercedes 4-passenger "torpédo transformable" by J. Saoutchik of Paris. This is mounted on the Model K chassis and is capable of 100

mi. per hr. The bonnet and wheel disks are of polished aluminum "engine-turned." Interior trim is in genuine lizard skin

and Le Baron. Needlepoint medallions which have been used for several years on the backs of town-car seats will be conspicuously absent or in small number. Broadlace will be used to some extent, but will be by no means general. Most of the trimming on the doors will be simple, set off by stitching or welts and in some cases, piped with leather.

Numerous adjustable seats will be in evidence, and the rear folding seats used in the Brunn and Dietrich convertibles permit emergency passengers to ride inside, or golf bags and luggage to be stowed, when no passengers are carried. In a number of sporting jobs the seat cushions have been set directly on the floor, and wells have been provided to afford footroom; this European practice has been employed occasionally heretofore, but not so frequently as this year. Interior fitments will be in considerable variety, ranging from butler-finish silver to hand-hammered bronze and from color-plated knobs to cloisonné enamel or ivory. Cabinetwork, where used, will be interesting and the most elaborate examples will be found in the modernistic jobs of Le Baron and Fleetwood in which numerous kinds of hardwood will be used. A Brewster 7-passenger enclosed drive, with fitments in green bronze and bright-green cloisonné, will have the interior woodwork in a greenish-toned curly maple.

Data received from exhibitors prior to the opening of the Salon are summarized below:

BRUNN & CO.

Brunn & Co., Inc., will have three exhibits on Stearns-Knight and Lincoln chassis. One of the most interesting will be the Stearns convertible coupe for 4 passengers, all of whom will be carried inside, instead of using a rumble seat. This body is illustrated elsewhere in this issue and is finished in Golden Wheat Tan, trimmed with dark brown. The top will be an English Burbank, and the seats are upholstered with an imported bedford cord. Duplicates of this job will be shown at the other three Salons. The other body on Stearns-Knight chassis will be a 5-passenger landau with all-weather front; duplicates of this will also be shown at Chicago, Los Angeles and San Francisco. The entire car is finished in black, with a light-blue stripe on the moldings. The interior is trimmed with a plain powder-blue De Luxe broadcloth and the fitments are in a butler-finish design executed by Mac-Farland. The other Brunn exhibit is a Lincoln town car, with all-weather front and coupe-pillar molding. The main body panels and window reveals are finished in Valentine's Zircon Brown, the rest of the car being black, including the moldings which are striped with ivory. The interior is upholstered with a Wiese plain gray doeskin and there is a center armrest in the rear seat. Hardware is supplied by the Sterling Bronze Co. All glass in this job is of the Triplex non-shatterable type.

DERHAM

Derham Body Co. will feature a Lincoln convertible roadster and a Franklin "gentleman's sedan." The convertible roadster (illustrated in this issue) has exceedingly high body sides and low top which is made to fold as low as the ordinary roadster top. The entire body is black except the Burbank top and the under side of the fenders, gasoline tank, exposed parts of the chassis, brake drums and window reveals, which are in Matador Orange. The striping is also of the latter color. The seats are trimmed with bright-finish black leather. The Franklin sport sedan is featured by narrow pillars, both at the front corners and at the center where both doors hinge on the same pillar. Besides clear vision, ventilation has been given special attention by the use of small rear-quarter lights that open outward, instead of lowering. The body is finished in black, striped with Carribean Red which is also used on the chassis frame, though not on the splashers. The interior is trimmed with broadcloth and tan leather.

DIETRICH

Dietrich will feature this year his convertible jobs and will have not only convertible coupes and sedans, such as were shown last year, but also a special model, intermediate between the foregoing types and designated as a "convertible victoria" in which four passengers ride inside on individual seats. The front seats are of the bucket type and tilt to admit the passengers to the rear seats, which are fully upholstered, the cushions folding up against the backs to permit the space to be used for golf bags or other luggage when desired; there is a folding armrest between these seats, as well as side armrests; spring cushions, armrests and companion cases provide as much comfort in this convertible as in the usual closed car. Improvements have been made in the former convertible sedan and coupe, allowing the tops to fold exceedingly flat. A slanting windshield is now used with these jobs and the omission of outside head joints on the coupe permits the top to be lowered readily from the inside.

FISHER BODY

Fisher Body and Fleetwood will display 18 Cadillac and LaSalle jobs, the coloring of 17 of which has been taken from masterpieces of the world's leading painters, including such subjects as: Leonardo da Vinci's "Mona Lisa"; Gainsborough's "Blue Boy"; Titian's "Flora"; Rembrandt's "The Noble Slav"; etc., these color combinations have been suggested by the art-and-color section of General Motors Corporation. It is stated that the colors used duplicate exactly those of the original paintings. The Fisher exhibit will include five bodies on LaSalle and three on Cadillac; upholstery in all of the open models is leather, with one exception; in the closed cars, broadcloth predominates and is trimmed with leather piping and broadlace, the coloring in the laces being taken directly from the paintings and given in each design, the relative value it has in the painting.

FLEETWOOD

Fleetwood will exhibit principally on Cadillac chassis, but will also have a Stutz "transformable cabriolet" (cabriolet-type town car, with all-weather front) and two bodies on LaSalle chassis, one a "transformable cabriolet" and the other an all-weather phaeton. A special feature of the Fleetwood exhibit will be a body on Cadillac chassis done in the style of *l'art moderne*. This will be a town car of about the lines illustrated elsewhere in this issue, but the exterior will be finished in a showy combination of sable and polished metal. The recessed bonnet and cowl panel will be of polished aluminum in Damascened finish; moldings around the windows and top and around the back, and the base molding will all be in polished aluminum; the lamps, windshield frame, wheel spokes and trunk rack will be chromium plated. A silver-leaf stripe on the black finish carries out this polished-metal effect. The modernistic motif is particularly carried out in the interior where a new rayon figured fabric is used on the seats and armrests, and piped with silver leather; a plain rayon lining is used for the sides and ceiling. The cabinet in the division has two recessed opera seats and is elaborately inlaid with 22 kinds of polished hardwood done in a modernistic design; the hardware is "color plated" in a 2-tone effect.

Other Fleetwood exhibits on Cadillac are in color schemes based on the masterpieces of painting and include the following body types: The convertible coupe (illustrated elsewhere); all-weather phaeton, with division; 5-passenger sedan, with small quarter window; "transformable brougham," with rear-quarter windows and metal back; 5-passenger "club cabriolet"; "transformable cabriolet"; 7-passenger "transformable cabri-

5-passenger Duesenberg berline (illustrated elsewhere) is finished in two shades of tan and trimmed with copper-striped gray broadcloth on the seats and a plain broadcloth headlining; the division glass lowers completely to permit owner or chauffeur driving. An all-weather town car on Duesenberg chassis (illustrated elsewhere) is finished in brown and the interior is trimmed in a gray suede broadcloth with elaborate panel design worked out with broadlace. A panel brougham with all-weather front, but retaining the classic coach lines, will be exhibited on a Packard chassis, finished

Town Cars for Both Conservatives and "Moderns"

← ⚞⚞
Brunn & Co. are building for each of the four Salons a 5-passenger, all-weather landau on Stearns-Knight chassis. The finish of the New York Salon car will be entirely in black, except the molding stripes which will be light blue. The interior will be trimmed with a plain powder-blue De Luxe broadcloth and will have special MacFarland butler-finish hardware

⚞⚞→
The "Moderns" have it in this "lady's town brougham" by Le Baron on the Stutz Black Hawk chassis. The entire car is finished in Poilu Blue, except the wire wheels which are in the bright red of the lining of the poilu's coat; this is also used for the inside window moldings, a narrow line of the bright red showing from the outside and enlivening the exterior color. The modernistic design in the interior includes both the woodwork on the door and division panels, and the upholstery fabric

← ⚞⚞
Holbrook town car, with all-weather front, on Duesenberg chassis. This has the long Duesenberg front fenders, the new arrangement of bonnet louvers, extremely high body sides and shallow windows. The interior will be trimmed with a gray suede broadcloth and have an elaborate panel design worked out with broadlace

⚞⚞→
A Fleetwood town car of this general type will be finished in the modernistic manner. The exterior is a showy combination of sable and polished metal. Side panels of bonnet and cowl are of polished aluminum in "Damascened" finish; moldings around windows, top and back are polished aluminum and other exposed metalwork is chromium plated. The interior will exemplify "l'art moderne" in a full marquetry cabinet on the division, in the "color plated" fitments and in the rayon upholstery

olet"; and a 7-passenger "imperial limousine." Hibbard & Darrin, of Paris, sent over an enclosed cabriolet on Cadillac chassis.

HOLBROOK CO.

The Holbrook Co. will exhibit four bodies embracing: A 4-passenger convertible coupe on Franklin chassis (illustrated elsewhere); it will be finished in Pastelle Cream, with black trimming; a tan Burbank will be used for the roof covering and the seats will be trimmed with black Colonial-grain leather. A

in a combination of black and maroon and trimmed with a plain tan De Luxe broadcloth.

LOCKE & CO.

Three Locke bodies are mounted on the Chrysler Imperial chassis. These include a convertible coupe, a convertible sedan and a sport phaeton. The last mentioned is illustrated elsewhere and is characterized by wide beading around the tonneau; the seats are trimmed with Radel's black leather in the smooth-stretched style and there are folding armrests in the center of both the front and rear seats; the side trimming is carried up on the edge of the body rail and finished off with a small bead molding covered with the same leather; the secondary windshield is operated by a crank regulator and may be lowered into the tonneau out of sight; the exterior is done in Valentine's Dustproof Gray, deep, and light Primrose Yellow. The collapsible coupe is featured by a deeply rolled belt and the absence of outside head joints; access to the rumble seat is provided by a special door on the curb side; the body is finished in Opal Brown and Mica Schist Gray and the seats are trimmed in a fine-grain gray leather. The convertible sedan has a special arrangement of the glasses for the rear doors; these open or shut with the door, but can also be swung horizontally and with a small center glass constitute a secondary windshield that can be raised or lowered by means of a regulator handle; a single color, a deep Ceylon blue, is used for this car, though the wheel spokes are left in the natural-wood finish; the seats are trimmed with Wiese's Channel bedford cord

partment are trimmed with a Wiese imported novelty fabric No. 3275 (illustrated elsewhere) and the lining is Wiese's drab doeskin. The Pierce-Arrow coupelet for two passengers is finished in Alpine Green, with wheels, body moldings and crest panels in Wood Bark Buff. The chassis and the landau leather of the collapsible rear quarter are in black. The interior is trimmed with a Wiese green-and-tan, pin-check worsted.

LE BARON, INC.

A number of the most striking Le Baron jobs are illustrated and described elsewhere in this issue. These include: The modernistic "lady's town brougham" on Stutz chassis, the "aero-phaeton" on Lincoln chassis, the Stutz roadster-phaeton and the rakish sport phaeton on the new Duesenberg chassis. Other Le Baron exhibits include: A Lincoln cabriolet-type town car, with all-weather front and rolled belt which differs from the Hibbard & Darrin type which has been so widely copied in this country. Packard all-weather brougham, with glass quarter and forward-facing extra

Willoughby "Silhouette" Sedans

Willoughby's 4-passenger "town sedan" on Lincoln chassis. This design, developed to give a proper silhouette or "flash effect" of the car in motion, has been adopted by Lincoln for a standard model. The exterior is a solid background of gray green. The oval belt, the drip moldings and window reveals —constituting the silhouette and the suggestion of motion—are in a darker Reseda Green. The color schemes is repeated in the interior, the darker green being used for the bedford-cord seats, in combination with a plain broadcloth lining

A Packard "sedan-limousine" for chauffeur or owner driving; partition-glass channels are flush with the lining. The main exterior is Cracker Buff and the picture-frame effect is done in Geneva Blue, striped with the body color. A new belt treatment is achieved by the wide, dark convex belt being recessed and having the indented panel in the body color. Interior is trimmed with a Wiese heather broadcloth in plain-stretched style, with broadlace to match

in two tones of blue and the side lining is of a special blue leather to match the exterior color; the top is a gray Burbank.

J. B. JUDKINS CO.

The J. B. Judkins Co. will exhibit four bodies on Pierce-Arrow, Stearns-Knight and Lincoln chassis. Two will be on the last named chassis; one is a 6-passenger berline in two tones of brown, but with black chassis and black landau-top leather; the seats in both compartments will be trimmed with a 2-tone tan bedford cord and the lining is a plain tan De Luxe broadcloth. The Lincoln coupe for two passengers will have the main body in Blue Fox Gray, medium, the moldings and superstructure in Blue Fox Gray, dark, and the window reveals in Evenglow; the chassis and top leather are black. The seat is trimmed in a 2-tone gray bedford cord, with lining of matching broadcloth. The Stearns-Knight 7-passenger enclosed limousine (illustrated elsewhere) is finished in University Blue, with black superstructure, moldings and chassis, except wheels which have the body color. The window reveals are in Ostrich Gray. The seats in the passenger com-

seats which are extra wide and permit the carrying of three emergency passengers; the rear seat is upholstered in the tufted style, well adapted to a large car of this type and in contrast with the prevailing vogue of simplicity. A Packard all-weather cabriolet-type town car, with opera seats and a folding armrest in the center of the rear seat; the driver's canopy is arranged to roll and fold into a box over the division window. A Packard cabriolet-type sedan arranged for owner or chauffeur driving; the channels of the division window are practically invisible when the glass is lowered.

ROLLS-ROYCE-BREWSTER

Rolls-Royce exhibits will be chiefly with Brewster coachwork, but there will be two cars with bodies by Walter M. Murphy Co. The Brewster coachwork will be on a 4-passenger "Speedster" phaeton; a town brougham, with canework aft of the door pillar; Wimbledon 4-passenger coupe; Newmarket 4-passenger convertible sedan, with engine-turned finish on the top of the bonnet, cowl and moldings, the interior being trimmed with tan broadcloth and brown leather, and the fitments being done in hammered French bronze; Salamanca de Ville 4-passenger "sport enclosed drive" with the interior done in bedford-cord seats and broadcloth lining; St. Alban 7-passenger enclosed limousine with interior woodwork in greenish curly maple and bright green inlay matching cloisonné inlay in the green-bronze hardware; a St. Stephen 7-passenger landaulet, with all-weather front; a Lonsdale 7-passenger enclosed limousine. The sport phaeton by Murphy is trimmed with a combination of leather and bedford cord. The disappearing-top coupe with rumble seat by the same builder has seats trimmed with bedford cord and lining of Baronial-grain leather.

ROLLSTON CO.

Rollston exhibits include two bodies on Minerva chassis and two on Packard. The latter comprise a roadster finished in argent and black, with chrome-plated wheels and a special ebony running board with chrome-plated protection bars. The Packard semi-collapsible cabriolet with all-weather front is finished in

WEYMANN AMERICAN

Weymann American Body Co. will exhibit two Weymann bodies on Stutz chassis. The 2-door Deauville will be mounted on the 127½-in. Black Hawk chassis and will have unusual interior trimming; the side wall and headlining will be of a Wiese fabric, but the seat cushions and backs will be trimmed with watersnake skins, while the front seatback and the sides of the rear-seat armrests will be in lizard skins. The other Weymann job will be a 7-passenger limousine on the 145-in. Stutz chassis and has been designed to approximate the interior appearance of American cars; the trimming, a Wiese fabric, covers the door locks and other hardware typical of the flexible bodies; the exterior is covered with a black Zapon fabric leather. The Deauville is also sheathed with Zapon.

WILLOUGHBY

Willoughby will exhibit four cars in which the color effects are closely interwoven with the body features such as panel contours, moldings, belt panels, reveals, etc. Two outstanding examples, the Lincoln 4-pas-

Berlines by Holbrook and by Judkins

← A 5-passenger berline, by Holbrook, on Duesenberg chassis with horizontal arrangement of bonnet louvers. It is finished in specially made light and dark tans, and the interior is trimmed in a gray copper-striped broadcloth with plain headlining. The division glass disappears completely when an owner-driven effect is desired

Judkins' 7-passenger enclosed limousine on Stearns-Knight De Luxe chassis. The main body panels and wheels are finished in University Blue; the superstructure, moldings, splashers and fenders in black; window reveals are in Ostrich Gray. Front compartment is leather trimmed, while the seats in the rear are upholstered with a Wiese imported Italian novelty cloth with wool-velours finish and small sunken green-and-purple figure →

two shades of gray, with silver striping. The driving seat is trimmed in gray calfskin and the passenger compartment in a gray De Luxe broadcloth; this job has a V-type windshield and the special ebony-and-chrome running boards. On the Minerva chassis, Rollston has mounted a sport roadster finished in Surface Green and Opex Gray, dark, striped with silver; there are armrests on both front doors and the trimming is in a special grain Eagle-Ottawa leather; the windshield is of Safetee glass and the door hardware is of the Tilbury design in platinum finish. The other Minerva is an all-weather, 5-passenger "stationary cabriolet" finished in Pastelle Cream and black, with striping in the opposite colors; non-shatterable glass is used in all windows and the curtain over the driver is concealed in the recess over the division window; a black turtle-grain leather is used for the top and for the trimming of the driving seat; the rear seat is trimmed in a plain tan De Luxe broadcloth and has a center folding armrest; the hardware is of Tilbury design, supplied by MacFarland.

senger town sedan and the Packard "sedan limousine" are illustrated and described elsewhere. The other exhibits include: A 7-passenger enclosed limousine on Lincoln chassis with Brewster angular-type windshield in which is incorporated a Neutralite glass visor. This is an extra large body with 38-in. headroom over the rear cushion and 14 in. between the rear seat and the spacious forward-facing, armchair auxiliary seats, which fold into the division recesses and are concealed by flush-fitting flaps. The rear compartment is trimmed in a Wiese English fabric of cream and light-tan shades, supplementing the exterior color scheme. The other Willoughby job is a Franklin all-weather town car with the main body panels in Mulberry Maroon; the molding, the belt and upper framing are in Beige Beaver-pelt; the roof and back leather in black; the interior repeats the exterior colors with a Wiese mulberry-and-tan heatherweave and matching broadlace; the upholstery is in the one-button tufted style; interior hardware has a platinum-nickel finish and is in a plain Puritan pattern.

Review of the National Automobile Show

TWO SERIES of cars presenting design features of exceptional interest were released only with the opening of the National Show. These were the new Willys-Knight 66B models designed by Amos E. Northup, and the White Prince series, designed by Hibbard & Darrin, for the Windsor division of Moon Motors Corporation. Jordan and Peerless each exhibited a new series that had not been previously released, but these were more conventional in design than the first two groups.

OTHER NOVELTIES

Dietrich's sport sedan on Franklin chassis in aluminum finish, with gold trimming, was of course one of the most striking novelties, but this was an individual design and not intended for a standard series as were the other jobs. Another individual novelty was the Auburn "Cabin Speedster"; an illustration of this "airplane" model, by Griswold, was published last month. Reference was also made last month to the use by Pontiac of concave moldings, and depressed cowl-and-bonnet panels. A distinctly new molding and belt treatment was noted on Studebaker Commander models, the central feature of which had a horizontal-V

LOW-PRICED CARS ATTRACTIVE

In general design there was improvement in nearly every make of car, but the betterment was chiefly noticeable in the low-priced cars; improved designs make their appearance scarcely distinguishable except by size, from the luxury cars. Chevrolet may be cited as a particularly good example of this improved designing. Its exterior compares favorably with any of the cars in the high-priced field so far as sweep of line and proportion are concerned, and its design is distinctly better than several of its higher priced sisters. A specially noteworthy feature is the panel that has been provided between the front frame members. It is one of the few attempts to "clean up" the fronts of the cars. This panel has a chrome-plated cap in the center, for the crank-handle opening, and on each side are groups of transverse louvers.

In the du Pont exhibit were two interesting bodies, one noteworthy as a super-sport type and the other an extremely attractive close-coupled sedan with sloping "V" windshield. This body, built by the Waterhouse Co., was finished in an extremely dark blue, with light-blue window framing and a recessed polished-

"White Prince" coupe-roadster for the new Windsor Motors. This was one of the novel designs of the recent National Automobile Show and was developed by Hibbard & Darrin for this new division of Moon Motors Corporation. The radiator shell is painted in the body color but has chromium-plated beading fore and aft. Long horizontal bonnet louvers accentuate the car length. A tapering molding is generously swept over the cowl and adds to the graceful effect of the car, which has four speeds forward

section, with narrow moldings above and below, the whole combination being swept at the cowl and at the rear quarters. The new Peerless models continued the use of a wide belt molding which divided as it passed around the back. Jordan introduced a variation in its belt molding, using a "split" type. There were several cars with polished-aluminum moldings, and one of the du Pont sedans, by Waterhouse, had a recessed polished-aluminum belt with a "spot" of the polished metal swept on the cowl toward the lower corner of the windshield.

PAINTED RADIATOR SHELL ON WHITE PRINCE

One of the novel features of the Hibbard & Darrin "White Prince" design was the painting of the radiator shell and the use of bright-metal beading fore and aft thereof. The military visor had a beading on its lower edge, painted in the lighter body color. Long horizontal louvers in the bonnet panel accentuated the length of the car. The swept molding and raised-panel framing of the windows followed the characteristic H. & D. design for this company. The Northup design for the new Willys-Knight series was the most revolutionary of any that has lately appeared for a production car; the new features were so numerous that they will be discussed and illustrated later.

aluminum belt; there was a touch of this polished metal on the cowl, swept toward the lower windshield corner. The upperworks had an unusual and attractive roof line. The first and second window were rectangular, but the rear-quarter window was D-shaped, corresponding with the upper back panel; the back light was a long oval, and a trunk continued the curve of the back. This body had the characteristic sweep below the belt that has been found on du Pont bodies in recent years. The du Pont roadster was extremely sporting, with an insect tail and continuous fenders set high along the body sides after the manner of some European sport models.

NEW WILLYS-KNIGHT SERIES

The new Willys-Knight 66B series was noteworthy for its high degree of originality and the pleasing effects obtained exteriorly with the use of line and proportion and in the interior with the restrained use of a modernistic motif. Three models were shown in this new series: A rumble-seat roadster, a 6-passenger coupe and a 4-door sedan. The accompanying views give an idea of these interesting designs but do not reveal fully their good points. The side view of the roadster presents a graceful treatment of high relief and panels, the side being reminiscent of carriage days but with a daring departure from the old cane or conventional basket weave; the wide squares are repeated on the leather trim on the inside door panels. The deck is designed to obtain extreme length without overhang beyond the rear fenders, and a width surpassing that of the usual deck without the observer being aware of it: instead of the two traditional moldings at each side, this deck has a generous central molding which, growing out of the seatback molding, tapers down toward the end of the deck into the other offsets of the rear view. The radiator shell, cap and the headlamp tiebar are of special design; the nameplate, and the shield on the headlamp tiebar, are part of the modern decorative scheme of the car, rather than identification plates.

Returning now to the closed models, these have similar frontal features but the remainder of the bodies naturally call for different treatment, especially in the interior where the modern decor was carried out in exceptionally good taste. The proportions of these closed cars are unusual for the length of wheelbase, 120 in.; the width across the front is more than 49 in., providing excellent vision and comfort. One result is that three passengers may sit with comfort on the front seat of the coupe, and by an ingenious adjustable seat unit and a wide door, the front-seat passenger need not leave his seat to permit other passengers to get into the rear seat. At the rear of the coupe an unusually capacious trunk is mounted.

The 66B sedan, like the coupe, can carry six passengers when necessary but it is assumed that ordinarily not more than four will be carried. As on the coupe, the division line of the two main colors marks also the offset of the main cowl and body panels; the raised effect on the cowl and bonnet has a distinctive line and the length of this section is accentuated by omitting the usual bright-metal cowl band and mounting the parking lamps on the front fenders. Another feature of the design that adds to the length is the treatment of all the side windows as a unit, omitting reveals for each window and using moldings to encircle and accentuate the framing of the group; the painting supplemented this effect.

MODERNISTIC INTERIOR TREATMENT

The interior of these closed models were pleasing examples of the application of modernistic treatment in keeping with our machine age. The elaborate and complicated forms of the Gothic and Renaissance periods are omitted, and the simpler straight-line motifs of the present are employed. This is particularly noticed in the door treatment and in the interior hardware which was in bronze ornamented by offsets and plain reliefs. The seats were trimmed in an unusual manner with a 2-toned bedford cord; there were four plaits at the center, the remainder of the seat being plain stretched; the armrests of the rear seat were also covered with bedford cord, the whole having the appearance of a divan in comfort and looks. On the doors the plain broadcloth was enlivened by a 6-in., bedford-cord panel, adorned at the top by a small embroidered panel with shaded silk squares; the vertical fluting of the walnut garnish rail caps suitably this simple but pleasing door treatment. Around the back window was a walnut fillet that extended down around the corners of the seat. The corner lights were triangular in shape, with the vertex at the bottom; angularly cut translucent glass gave a soft light for the interior. On the front seatback was a walnut rail and at the center a smoking set was concealed by

a bronze cover fluted to correspond to the decoration of the garnish rails.

THE FOREIGN CARS

The five foreign exhibits by Austin, Daimler, Mercedes, Renault and Vauxhall attracted considerable attention, though much of this was doubtless mere curiosity as some of the cars were not for sale. Austin showed its "Baby Seven" in a phaeton and three closed bodies, one of which was fabric covered; while these looked like toys, there was a surprising amount of seat room. Daimler showed a Royal limousine, with enclosed driving compartment and "V" windshield. It was finished in Royal Scarlet and black and was extremely high as cars come nowadays; a thin roof of exceedingly good line contributed to this effect; the interior was trimmed with a silk-and-mohair brocade of unusual texture. Mercedes exhibited three attractive bodies by Saoutchik. Renault showed two bodies of its own construction, a convertible coupe and a sedan on the Monastella chassis, and two custom bodies on the Reinastella chassis. Both of the latter were exceedingly good looking; one was a glass-quarter brougham by Arthur Boulogne and the other a Hib-

The unusual interior of the Willys-Overland 66B sedan. A 2-tone whipcord is used for the seats which have four rather wide plain plaits at the center and are plain stretched on both sides thereof. The lining was a matching broadcloth and an unusual feature is the use of the bedford cord as the central feature of the door decoration which is capped by a small embroidered panel and an unusual walnut garnish rail. Unfortunately this pleasing effect is but faintly seen in the engraving. The instrument panel conforms to the rectangular effects used in the door decoration

bard & Darrin berline-landaulet with all-weather front; this had a sloping windshield and the new type window regulator which permits lowering of the glass in the door without leaving a gap between the glass and the side frame of the door. Vauxhall exhibited a good-looking convertible coupe of composite construction, with exposed metalwork in copper, and a semi-Weymann fabric sedan.

STRIPING IN GREAT VARIETY

In painting there was no changed tendency to report, unless it be the great and varied use of striping. As in the case of the Salon exhibits, blue shades predominated, with greens, browns and grays also in much favor. Black was by no means neglected, and there were several cars entirely or partly finished in satin aluminum and then lacquered. Striping was extremely varied and was applied almost without exception on belt moldings. It was also usually carried out around the windows, and on a few jobs, on the base molding as well as on the molding aft of the rear-quarter windows. In one instance the striping on the molding aft of the rear-quarter window was carried forward to the front corner post where it ended in an arrowhead; the latter treatment also applied to the through molding which ended a little aft of the radiator. On one job striping and double-belt molding were so arranged that the upper molding had a sag, but this treatment is not one that is apt to be imitated.

NEW CORNER-POST CONSTRUCTION

More attention continues to be given to securing narrow corner posts. Most of the Chrysler jobs had such clear-vision posts and a Packard De Luxe sedan was equipped with a special clear-vision corner within

angled hooded type and were of steel usually with an embossed panel for combined stiffening and decorative effect. Several of the higher priced cars used colored glass visors which permit traffic lights to be observed without the necessity of the driver bending. A few cars had hinged inside visors with colored-celluloid or coated-fabric panels.

Most fenders were of the full-crowned type and often had embossed ends and less frequently an embossed longitudinal line down the center. The continuous fender on the side of the du Pont roadster was set extremely high, after the manner of some of the European sport cars of this type.

New 66B Series Designed by Amos Northup for Willys-Overland

Different and pleasing were the new designs developed by Amos E. Northup for the Willys-Knight 66B series. This roadster, finished in black and light green, had the un- *usual molding treatment shown and on the rear deck, a longitudinal center molding. The square decoration on the doors was supplemented by piped squares on the interior trim*

← ⫸

The new 6-passenger coupe in the Willys-Knight 66B series has an unusually wide door which permits easy entrance to the rear seat. The front seats are both adjustable and folding and the backs so arranged that three persons can be accommodated comfortably if desired. The interior treatment in the modern manner is similar to that of the sedan shown on the opposite page

⫸→

The Willys-Knight 66B sedan presents many novel features both exteriorly and interiorly. It has an unusual raised panel on the bonnet and cowl and the molding and window framing is also worthy of note. The treatment of the window framing as a unit accentuates the length of the body. The interior is equally novel, the treatment being in the modern manner as will be noted in another illustration

the limits of the "interpupilary distance"; a special cast-aluminum distance piece was affixed to the front of the pillar, thereby permitting a contour harmonizing with the general design without interfering with the manufacture on a production basis of the forged pillar, which was depended upon for structural strength. The removable frontal piece is an interesting development for front corner posts, as it permits changing of designs without interfering with the general manufacture on production basis of the drop-forged or pressed-steel pillar. Another feature of this pillar was the use of a piano hinge for the upper section of the door pillar; this fitted against the corner pillar in such a manner as to be concealed and take up no vision space.

The great majority of the visors were of the sharp-

REGROUPING OF LOUVERS CONTINUES

Regrouping of louvers was one of the marked features of 1929 cars. This custom is a carry-over from last year, but it is worth noting that a large proportion of the cars had new grouping of this feature on the bonnet panels. Some groups were placed vertically and others horizontally and a great number had the louvers pressed in embossed panels. Gardner used louvers on the cowl sides as well as the bonnet panels of its "130" series. Several makers who used single vertical groups had these extended so as nearly to fill the panel. Chevrolet, however, had a small chaste group of vertical louvers positioned with good effect slightly aft of the center of the panel and harmonizing well with the sweep of the fender. Several makers used a single group of long horizontal louvers which tended to accentuate the length of the car. Stutz had one of the best arrangements of this kind in which the lower louvers were stepped off to correspond with the fender sweep; the Black Hawk division also used horizontal louvers in a rectangular group, but the rectangular grouping was relieved by a plain lozenge-shaped panel in the center.

MOLDINGS FREELY USED

Moldings are being used in great profusion, generally wide at the belt and swept at the front corners and at the rear quarters. At the front corners, they often

split three ways: Across the cowl, up the corner post and aft into a wide belt. At the rear quarters, a branch usually runs up behind the window and joins the drip molding or an upper window molding thereby framing the windows as a group. The use of moldings around each window, however, is still general; sometimes moldings are used at the bottom of the windows and taper, as they go up the sides, to nothing. Moldings at the base of the body are generally wider this year, occasionally being as much as 2¼ in. in width. Polished-aluminum moldings were employed on a few sport cars.

Besides the new molding and belt treatments already referred to, mention should be made of the LeBaron innovation on some of the larger Stutz cars; on these a single through molding was split in the center of the body to embrace the door handles converging aft therefrom to form the single molding again; the small panel thus formed by the split of the molding around the

ings outlined a rather deep belt in which there were raised panels of a different color from the remainder of the belt.

The tumble-in belt was more used this year than heretofore, and a new roof line was noted at the back of some of the Graham-Paige models, the roof meeting the back panel at an angle instead of the more common curved effect. The Reo smaller series, designated as the Mate, has an interesting "air line" effect similar to the compass-bottom carriages of the pre-motor era. This sweeping effect was more pleasing when no spare wheel was carried.

"Le Pirate," a striking exhibition model designed and built by Dietrich, Inc., on Franklin chassis. The entire exterior was in aluminum, trimmed with dull gold. Note the unusual bonnet "louvers" or decorations, repeated on the special housing of the rear wheels; also the parking light positioned on the upper rear quarter. Another striking feature of the design was the curved lower skirt of the doors which were extended to the running board

A ventilating feature used on some of the Gardner closed bodies was a short cutout along the upper edge of the glass of the front door window. By using a deep channel at the top of the window, the opening was completely sealed when desired, but lowering the glass about an inch permitted the slot to act as a suction ventilator, this slot being located next to the corner posts so that the air current from the windshield would draw out the vitiated air from near the ceiling of the car.

A new steel spare-wheel housing was provided on the 1929 Hupp cars; the upper shell of these housings were secured by two threaded pins. Trunks were much in evidence this year and were generally of steel, sometimes built into the body, but in nearly all cases conforming to the contour of the back or rear deck. A Nash built-in trunk had recessed panels, with ⅛-inch striping as on the body. A steel trunk used by Hupp on its black sport roadster had light-

Jordan's new 8-cylinder sedan with horizontally grouped bonnet louvers and unusual molding treatment. The "split" molding is swept across the cowl and has a branch running up the concaved front pillar, and aft of the rear-quarter window a branch molding is swept up from the belt to meet the drip molding. The body has a wide base molding. The new nameplate is now displayed on the cross bar between the headlamps. The front seat is not fastened to the body sides and is adjustable by turning a handle at the heel board

handles was painted in the striping color, contrasting with that of the body. An unusual molding treatment was presented on one of the Elcar sedans which was finished in cream and black. This body had a wide belt outlined by double moldings which converged at a point just forward of the corner pillar; the molding aft of the rear-quarter window was swept across this belt to join the lower molding as it went around the back. A bonnet-hinge molding on this car was swept down on the cowl to join the molding at the base of the body. On a Reo Flying Cloud sedan, double mold-

green moldings attached in about the position that the leather straps of former days would have occupied. The lid of the deck seat of this roadster had no exterior fitments. Graham-Paige and one or two other makes had deck lids without fitments, but the majority had an exterior lock at the center and usually a handle. A special Essex roadster, finished in a reddish chrome and black, was unusual in having a deck seat for one, instead of the more usual provision for two emergency passengers.

Pre-View of Chicago Automobile Salon

THE 25th Annual Automobile Salon will open in Chicago on Nov. 9 at the Drake Hotel, where the addition of a new ballroom will permit the largest showing of luxury cars ever offered by this exhibition. These enlarged quarters put the Chicago Salon on a numerical par with New York and make it possible to include the two new American front-drive cars and to afford room for body builders who have not been in this exhibition previously.

INTERESTING VARIATION IN EXTERIORS

Advance illustrations indicate that body designers have not been idle during the past season. There are evidences of conscientious striving to develop new effects that would be practical and acceptable to the discriminating public interested in these high-priced cars. Some of these effects are illustrated in this issue, but lack of space or balance prevents the use of others that are equally interesting. Enough are presented to show what is for this country a great variety in exterior treatment. At this writing, no predominant trend

for the first time: it will present two interesting bodies, a roadster and a town car, on the new Ruxton chassis.

BRUNN & CO.

Brunn & Co. will exhibit three types of town cars and a 5-passenger convertible coupe. The last named will be mounted on the new Pierce-Arrow chassis and has a close-folding top, so that the full sporting effect of the car is retained when it is operated as an open car. The seats are leather trimmed and the top is covered with English Burbank. On Lincoln chassis Brunn will show an all-weather brougham and a semi-collapsible cabriolet, the latter being a duplicate of the job exhibited by Lincoln in Paris. The body panels and reveals will be finished in Valentine's Bolivian Calcite Gray and the remainder of the car in Bolivian Gray, deep. The rear compartment is trimmed with a fabric by Wiese, an Eagle-Ottawa leather being used in the driving compartment. On the 145-in. Stutz chassis, Brunn will mount a 5-passenger semi-collapsible cabriolet which is illustrated on another page. It has a V-

Locke & Co.'s design for a 5-passenger sedan on the new Ruxton front-wheel-drive chassis. This body will be entirely in black and without striping. The extremely low and flat chassis permits an unusual design with ample headroom. The customary moldings and running boards are omitted and the body sides are carried well down on the chassis side members

is indicated. Salon changes are generally conservative, but this year there seems to be more radical departure, injecting numerous elements of recent European practice, such as, the sportsman's coupe with sliding roof, use of the coach sill, carrying of body panels down below the chassis level, omission of running boards, and the use of chromium-plated protection beading on fenders. Interiors continue simple with a preference for the plain-stretched style of upholstering and a modicum of decoration. Colors are generally conservative at this exhibition, with a liberal sprinkling of all-black cars, but an ample display of color may be expected from the sport jobs.

EXHIBITORS

Coachbuilders exhibiting at this Salon are: Baker-Raulang, Brewster, Brunn, Derham, Dietrich, Fisher, Fleetwood, Holbrook, Judkins, Le Baron, Locke, Murphy, Rollston, Weymann and Willoughby. The chassis to be exhibited at the Chicago Salon this season include the following: Cadillac, Cord, Cunningham, Duesenberg, Franklin, Isotta, La Salle, Lincoln, Minerva, Packard, Pierce-Arrow, Rolls-Royce, Ruxton and Stutz.

Baker-Raulang Co., which is one of the oldest of our body-building companies, appears in the Chicago Salon

type windshield and is equipped with safety glass throughout. A folding-type canopy is provided for enclosing the driving compartment.

DERHAM BODY CO.

Four bodies, all of different type, are being offered by the Derham Body Co.: A convertible roadster on Stutz chassis; a convertible phaeton on Lincoln; a 5-passenger sedan on Duesenberg and an all-weather town car on Franklin chassis. The Stutz roadster is a low smart-looking car, with slanting windshield and door window of unusual shape, swept at the upper rear corner, the angle of the rear edge complementing that of the windshield. The car is finished in black except the wheels, window reveals and striping, which are in Moonstone. The top is covered with a Haartz fabric and the interior is trimmed with black Colonial-grain leather. The Lincoln convertible phaeton also has windows and top of unusual shape, being of the Hibbard & Darrin type. The bulbous rear provides a luggage compartment accessible through the back squab of the rear seat. The Duesenberg sedan is an extremely low job; to provide ample headroom, cushions are built up from the floor and are extremely soft. The moldings are unusual, as will be noted by the illustration on another page. The trimming and finishing are being done by the chassis maker. The Derham town car on Franklin chassis is a low body of good proportions, with transformable front and doors of unusual shape. The front compartment is trimmed in black Colonial-grain leather and on the rear seats and backs an imported Wiese tan novelty cloth is used, the lining being a fawn broadcloth.

across the fore door where it flows into a cowl molding swept into the base of the body, after the manner of a coupe pillar. Another interesting Franklin job is the Deauville sedan with high body sides and a striking molding treatment in which the cowl molding after following the line of the windshield pillar is swept aft into the base molding; the coach lamps on the rear

Bodies by Leading Builders on Pierce-Arrow Chassis

←⟪⟪⟪

An all-weather town car, by Willoughby, on Pierce-Arrow chassis. This has an unusual molding treatment and the transformable front is fitted with a solid detachable deck made of a light aluminum casting, providing a perfect roof line when the deck is in position. The front seat is trimmed with a tan Colonial-grain leather and the rear with a light-colored Wiese bedford cord, done in plain panels but with a center folding armrest

⟫⟫⟫→

A gentleman's sport sedan, by Locke & Co., on Pierce-Arrow chassis. Door construction above the belt is replaced by chromium-plated glass channels and the top is a Haartz Jonarts fabric, which is also used for the trunk cover. The interior is of conventional arrangement, except that there is a luggage space behind the rear seat, accessible by pulling the back squab forward

←⟪⟪⟪

A 5-passenger convertible coupe by Brunn on Pierce-Arrow chassis. Windows, of Duplate non-shattering glass, drop and the top folds compactly; when down the appearance is that of an open sport car. The top is covered with English Burbank and the cushions, backs and armrests are trimmed with leather

⟫⟫⟫→

An enclosed limousine by Judkins, on the 143-in. Pierce-Arrow chassis. The main body is finished in Deep River Blue; window reveals and wheels in Embassy Blue; superstructure, moldings and chassis in black. The front compartment is trimmed in a Colonial-grain leather and the rear in a Wiese sand-finish broadcloth done in the plain-stretched style

DIETRICH

In the Dietrich stand there will be eight bodies, embracing both formal and sport types. On Franklin chassis three bodies will be mounted. One of these is a formal town car of good lines, having two unusual features, the mounting of coach lamps at the rear quarters and the carrying forward of the belt panel

quarters and the use of horizontal louvers arranged en echelon suggest derivation from the Pirate model of a year ago. The other Franklin body is a convertible sedan with the angle of the slanting windshield complemented by the angle of the rear-door window. On Pierce-Arrow chassis, a convertible sedan of more conventional lines is mounted. A convertible sedan and a convertible coupe will be mounted on Lincoln chassis, the latter having individual folding chairs for all four passengers. On Packard chassis there will be the new 5-passenger Lido coupe and a convertible sedan; the Lido is also convertible and the folding front seats have a special mechanism that facilitates entry to the rear cross seat.

cars with transformable fronts, a glass-quarter brougham with transformable front and 5-passenger and 7-passenger berline-landaulets; on La Salle chassis, the Fleetwind, a sedan model with sport top; Fleetshire, a phaeton and Fleetway, an all-weather phaeton. No details have been received concerning these exhibits, nor of the Fisher exhibits which will probably be on Cadillac and La Salle chassis as heretofore.

Duesenberg Gives Designers a Free Hand

A Le Baron torpedo, on the Duesenberg chassis, suggests a buoyant freedom of movement with its one long flowing panel in tan and an Auburn Brown raised panel which flows into the body rail. This color effect is enlivened by the introduction of Nile Green striping, brake drums and trimming leather. The V-type windscreen is noteworthy for its simplicity and is set in a light chromium-plated bronze frame

A 5-passenger sedan-limousine by Willoughby, with a special belt treatment. The basic conception of this car is that it is built chiefly for the owner driver, with the division.glass dropping completely and being concealed by a flap. The windshield is set stationary, ample ventilation being provided on the top and sides of the cowl. A Neutralite glass visor is set in a chromium-plated frame

This Murphy town car is finished entirely in black, with polished-aluminum moldings. The door hinges are made of heat-treated duralumin and polished. The upper part of the division pillars are of bronze, chromium plated. The rear compartment is trimmed in silver cloth, each back squab being decorated with a bird done in black needlepoint. Ebony friezes on the doors and the partition are inlaid with silver birds

An interesting sedan by Derham on Duesenberg chassis. The body is exceedingly low and the molding treatment is somewhat unusual, with a touch of foreign practice in the chromium-plated protection strips on the rear mudguards. To give ample headroom the cushions are built directly on the floor and are extremely soft. The interior is to have special fixtures and cabinetwork supplied by the car maker

FLEETWOOD

Fleetwood will have 11 exhibits, principally on Cadillac and La Salle chassis, but will also exhibit a town car on Stutz chassis. On Cadillac chassis there will be a roadster, an all-weather phaeton, two cabriolet-type town

HOLBROOK'S G-E BODIES

The Holbrook Co., Inc., will exhibit at Chicago three bodies, mounted on Packard, Franklin and Ruxton chassis. These will be of the Gordon-England lightweight type, with the patented 3-point suspension, and all will have the body sides carried down to the running boards in accordance with European practice. On the new Packard 745 C chassis, Holbrook will show a 7-passenger all-weather cabriolet. The body panels will be finished in Miami Brown; upperworks, fenders and chassis will be in Beaver Brown, deep. A cross-grain leather in the same shade is used for the top and the leather on the front seat is finished to match. The passenger compartment is trimmed in a De Luxe broadcloth, the seat being done in the 2-button tufted style. On the Franklin 147 chassis is mounted a Speedster sedan, having a sloping front swept into the roof line without any projecting peak or visor. The entire car is

of Josef Urban. The front seat will be trimmed in plaited style, with a special tan leather harmonizing with the fabric used in the rear compartment, Schumacher's No. 33701 silver rayon; the rear seat is trimmed in plain style with a 2-cushion effect.

JUDKINS

On Duesenberg chassis, Judkins has mounted a particularly commodious 7-passenger enclosed limousine. The apparent lowness and length of the car result from the use of a high belt and shallow windows, accentuated by the lift of the moldings at the back and the raised V-panel on bonnet and cowl. Valentine's Russian Ruby, deep, was chosen for the body and bonnet panels, black

New Town Cars on Stutz, Cord and Franklin Chassis

←≪≪

A 5-passenger semi-collapsible cabriolet, by Brunn, on the 145-in. Stutz chassis. The clean design of the rear is noteworthy and the transformable front has a V-type windshield with mono-control. Exterior metalwork is chromium plated and all windows are of non-shatterable glass

≫≫→

A French panel brougham, by Le Baron, on Cord chassis. The body is finished in maroon with black upperworks and top. Silver striping and chromium-plated exposed metalwork enliven pleasantly the sober coach colors. The interior is trimmed with a tan doeskin in "bolster style." Besides vanity cases and ash trays, there is a small glove compartment, covered with the trim material and lined with velveteen

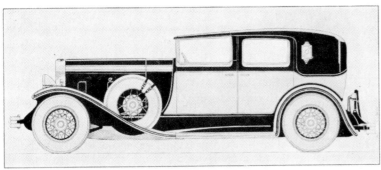

←≪≪

Town car by Dietrich on Franklin chassis. This has a transformable front, the canopy folding into a compartment over the division. Coach-type lamps are positioned on the rear quarter. The car is finished in two shades of gray and the wire wheels are painted a third shade. The rear compartment is trimmed in a Wiese modernistic broadcloth, piped with "gunmetal" leather

finished in black, with a cream stripe. The top is a light-gray Haartz material. Slender corner pillars give excellent driving vision and the forward flaring of the front doors promotes easy entrance to the front compartment. The car is upholstered throughout in a Wiese sand-finish broadcloth. Garnish moldings are of walnut and there are two walnut niches for smokers' requirements in the front seatback. The silk curtain at the rear can be controlled from the driver's seat to eliminate headlight glare of overtaking cars. On the Ruxton front-drive chassis Holbrook will mount a 7-passenger enclosed limousine, finished in a combination of Pine Manor Green and pastel under the personal supervision

being used above the belt. Narrow corner pillars and a non-glare visor set in chrome-plated frame provide excellent vision at the front, and at the rear there is a window of ample proportions set in a cast-aluminum frame. The driving seat is upholstered with a plain broadcloth and the doors trimmed with an unusual fan paneling. The rear seat is trimmed in plain style with an all-over embroidered fabric of different tones of brown. The entire division is paneled with marquetry made of American walnut inlaid with imported boxwood, ebony, amboyna and bubinga; the same treatment in miniature is carried out in the vanity and smoking cases positioned in the rear quarters. On the new

Pierce-Arrow chassis is another enclosed limousine finished in two shades of blue, with black superstructure, moldings and chassis; the front compartment below the belt is trimmed with Colonial-grain leather; the remainder of the interior is done with a Wiese sand-finish broadcloth in plain-panel style. The other two jobs in the Judkins stand are on Lincoln chassis. A 2-passenger coupe is finished in two shades of gray; the seat is upholstered in tufted style with a stone-gray Channel cord and a "pebble-grain" broadcloth is used for the wall and headlining. For the bindings, laces and lining of the cowl, Johnson's 542 Morocco leather was employed. The Lincoln 6-passenger berline has the lower body panels and window reveals finished in Rich Loam; superstructure, moldings, chassis and top leather are in Lanvin Maroon; both front and rear seats are trimmed with Wiese's 3440 basketweave and the lining is a sand-finish broadcloth of mahogany cast. The leather bindings are of Johnson's Morocco.

of green, a slightly deeper shade being used for the roof and chassis; bright-green striping along each edge of the chromium-plated bead molding enriches the whole effect. A beige interior forms a pleasant contrast. Two convertibles of quite different character, one on Lincoln and one on Stutz Blackhawk chassis, will be found here and on a Duesenberg chassis, Le Baron has mounted a 4-seater torpedo of flowing design. It has a light and graceful V-type slanting windshield and is finished in tan and brown, this color scheme being heightened by the introduction of bright Nile Green for the trimming leather, brake drums and striping. In the Le Baron, Inc., stand, there will be a sedan-limousine and two town cars, all on the new Packard 745-C chassis. The larger town car will seat five or even six in the rear compartment but does not appear larger than normal. The exterior has a minimum of bright metalwork and is finished in a 2-tone green combination. The trimming material for the interior is a Wiese doeskin done in the traditional

Two Interesting Weymanns on Cord and Stutz Chassis

Weymann "Elysée" model for the new Cord front-drive chassis. The exterior is sheathed in a smooth Zapon Liss in a color combination of light blue and light gray. Interior trimming is of light-blue leather, with gray sycamore cabinetwork. The front seat accommodates three; the rear seat is a side-facing occasional seat and faces a sycamore cabinet convertible into a writing desk

An interesting new model for the Stutz chassis by the Weymann American Body Co. This is a 5-passenger sedan known as the Chaumont model and has the fashionable coach sill and a graceful and effective molding treatment. The entire body is sheathed in black Zapon and the moldings are painted argent

LE BARON

In the Le Baron-Detroit stand will be found a noteworthy job on the new Cord. This is a panel brougham of the modified French type, set lower than on the conventional car because of the front-drive-chassis conditions. The line of the sloping windshield pillars is continued by a cowl molding swept to the base line. The painting is conservative, maroon body panels and black upperworks enlivened by silver striping and chromium-plated wire wheels. The rear compartment is trimmed in "bolster" style with a tan doeskin; in addition to vanity and smoking sets, a small compartment for gloves is covered with the trim material and lined with velveteen. Another body of pleasing composition is the Le Baron-Stutz sedan-limousine with sloping windshield; this has a mild suggestion of the modern with plain panels, absence of wide belt molding and window reveals; instead there are narrow chromium frames around the windows, a bright beading at the belt and at the top of the doors. Graceful streamlining at the back of the cowl carries it up and into the windshield pillar. The entire body is painted a soft medium-light shade

tufted style. The smaller town car is a smart-looking job of low appearance but having ample headroom, due to the new Packard construction, and long front fenders. A European touch is given by the chromium-plated protection strips on the fenders.

LOCKE & CO.

The Locke 5-passenger sedan on Ruxton chassis will of course come in for a great deal of attention both because of the special lines selected for this design and because of the interest in the new front-drive chassis. The body is finished entirely in black, without striping, and its general lines are presented in an accompanying engraving. The interior is trimmed in plain style with a Schumacher beige extra-heavy rayon bedford cord, and the interior hardware is enameled to match the cloth. Another striking design by Locke is the gentleman's sport sedan on Pierce-Arrow chassis. The body is finished in two shades of green, with a touch of Coronado Tan on the window reveals and wire wheels. The tan top and trunk cover is a Haartz Jonarts double-coated material. The interior is of the conventional sedan type except that the luggage compartment in the bulbous rear is reached by pulling forward the back squab of the rear seat. The interior is trimmed with a De Luxe broadcloth, piped with green Samurai leather. The appointments are painted to match that leather. Locke will also have a sport roadster on Lincoln chassis, a feature of which will be the disappearing top and a newly designed compartment in which it is stowed. On Franklin chassis, this body builder will show a convertible close-coupled sedan finished in Rich Maroon, with fenders, brake drums and reveals in Devonshire Cream; the seats are upholstered with a Wiese buff bed-

windshield and slanting front door windows which lower without gaping. The Regent, a 2/4-passenger convertible coupe, finished in tan and cream, with polished-aluminum moldings, is shown at the bottom of the page. Other exhibits include the Huntington, a 7-passenger enclosed limousine finished in black and green and trimmed with a green figured broadcloth; fittings are of green inlaid bronze and the cabinetwork of green stained burl maple inlaid with green stripes; the St. Andrews, a 7-passenger limousine in black and maroon, with brown broadcloth upholstery, mahogany trim and

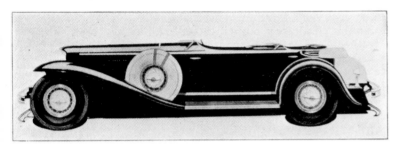

←≡≡

This interesting phaeton by Murphy on Cord front-wheel-drive chassis is finished entirely in black and has polished-aluminum concave moldings. The seats are trimmed in a special soft black leather and the secondary cowl is mounted with an unusual hinge that allows it to be opened without interfering with the low-top construction

ford cord and the rest of the interior is trimmed with Radel's mottled-maroon leather. The center pillar of this convertible drops into a well between the front and rear doors, when not required.

Walter M. Murphy Co.

In the Murphy stand will be found an interesting Cord phaeton, if completed in time for the Chicago Salon. This is to be finished in black, enlivened by polished-aluminum concave moldings; the secondary cowl has a special hinge and will open without counterbalance under an extremely low top. A Murphy disappearing top coupe, on Duesenberg chassis, is finished in satin aluminum below the belt line and in polished aluminum above; a special Barcelona Blue is used on fenders and splashers. The cross seat is trimmed with a soft blue leather and there is a single emergency seat in the fish-tail rear. A metal flap covers the window wells when windows are lowered. A Murphy-Duesenberg town car has chromium-plated center pillars, door

bronze fitments with red inlay; St. Martin, a 5-passenger brougham finished in dark and light brown, with cream striping, and trimmed with brown broacloth; the Dover, a 5-passenger sedan finished in Oxford Blue and black, the upholstery being a brown Heathertone and the fitments of French bronze; the Newmarket, a 4-passenger convertible sedan; a special sport roadster, with polished-aluminum moldings, and the Ascot, a 4-passenger sport phaeton. The last is one of the most dashing in the exhibit; it is finished in gunmetal lacquer and has sunken moldings of polished aluminum running from the radiator shell to aft of the rear doors.

Rollston

A Packard glass-quarter brougham with all-weather front will be mounted by the Rollston Co. for its Chicago exhibit. It will be finished in black and have gold-leaf striping. Special running boards are provided and the V-shaped windshield, and all other windows, will be glazed with non-shatterable glass. The rear

⟹→

The Regent, a dashing 2/4-passenger convertible coupe by Brewster on Rolls-Royce chassis. It is finished in tan and cream, and has polished-aluminum moldings

hinges of polished duralumin and polished-aluminum moldings which contrast with the black body. The interior is trimmed in pillow style with a silver cloth and the back squabs of the seat are decorated with a bird done in black needlepoint. The division and door friezes are of ebony inlaid with silver birds. Running boards are of ebony with chromium-plated protection strips.

Rolls-Royce

Eight Rolls-Royce cars, with coachwork by Brewster, will be exhibited ranging from formal town cars to flashing sport models for the younger generation. A feature of all the closed bodies will be the use of the slanting

compartment is trimmed with a De Luxe broadcloth, the cross seat being done in buttoned plaits. The wide forward-facing auxiliary seats can accommodate three in emergency. The hardware is of the MacFarland Puritan design enameled to match the cloth.

Weymann American

A number of interesting designs are included in the Weymann American exhibit which embraces seven cars. Four of the bodies are mounted on Stutz chassis and one each on Cord, Duesenberg and Pierce-Arrow. The new Elysée model on Cord chassis is interesting in several particulars, being sheathed with a smooth Zapon Liss in a color combination of light blue and light gray.

The seating is unusual, the front seat accommodating three and in the rear there is a side-facing occasional seat opposite a hardwood cabinet which is convertible into a writing desk. The interior is trimmed in blue leather with cloth headlining and all of the cabinetwork is of gray sycamore, trimmed with light blue. A striking model on the Stutz chassis is the Chaumont, a 5-pasenger sedan covered with black Zapon and having contrasting moldings painted argent. Another sedan on the Stutz chassis will be the Versailles model, a 4-door sedan with sloping windshield and soft rear quarters. The body is sheathed in a smooth cream-colored fabric, the mudguards, chassis and molding being painted in Boatswain Blue. The Monte Carlo model, with sloping windshield and rear, is sheathed with a combination of pebble-grain maroon and tan Zapon. The interior is trimmed with imported goatskins in the English style and has friezes of burl walnut. The other Stutz body is a Longchamps model—a 4-passenger sportsman's coupe with Pytchley sliding roof. The roof is readily operated from the driver's seat. It is the first presentation here at an approved exhibition of this popular English type of body. A stone-gray fabric is used for the roof and rear quarters and the rest of the car is sheathed with a black fabric. A Weymann Ostend model is shown on Pierce-Arrow chassis; this is a sporting 2-door sedan covered with pebble-grain gray Zapon, which contrasts with a blue chassis. On a Duesenberg chassis, Weymann will exhibit its St. Cloud model. The main body panels, including a coupe-pillar effect, will be sheathed with smooth Zapon Liss of cream color. The upperworks, bonnet and hood will be covered with light-green, seal-grain Zapon. The interior is trimmed in English style with imported goatskins, matching the top color. The elaborate cabinetwork is of burl walnut.

WILLOUGHBY EXHIBITS

Willoughby is exhibiting two bodies, each, on Duesenberg, Lincoln and Pierce-Arrow chassis. The Duesenbergs are 5- and 7-passenger enclosed limousines of the same general construction but differing in molding treatment and other details. Both have the windshield set stationary, ample ventilation being provided through top and side cowl ventilators. The 5-passenger body is intended primarily as an owner-driven car and has the front seat trimmed with the same fabric as on the rear seat, and the division glass disappears completely. Two opera-type seats fold flush into the division for theater use or similar brief emergencies. The larger body has forward-facing wide auxiliary seats, accommodating three in emergencies, and affording 10 in. of kneeroom for the rear-seat passengers. A Wiese fabric of modernistic weave is employed for the seats and for the walls a plain broadcloth. The 5-passenger body is illustrated in the Duesenberg group on another page, the larger car having been shown in a previous issue of AUTOBODY. On Lincoln chassis, Willoughby is showing a 7-passenger enclosed limousine with angular-type windshield, and a square-corner brougham which is a duplicate of the one exhibited recently at the Paris Salon. The entire exterior is in black, set off by silver striping. The interior is trimmed with a light dove-gray doeskin supplied by Wiese; the seats are done in the plain-stretched style and piped with silver leather. On the division and door panels are modernistic needle-point designs in two tones of gray and silver. The garnish moldings, finished in a gunmetal color, are of a peculiar gray wood showing the grain. The Willoughby all-weather town car on Pierce-Arrow chassis presents a novelty in molding treatment, the coupe-pillar

molding being extended under the front door, curving up the cowl and joining the bonnet molding. As shown elsewhere, the belt is of the semi-rounded type with an indented crest panel on the rear door and rear quarter. A special removable deck, made of light cast aluminum, provides a perfect roof line when the front is enclosed; an emergency roll-up canopy is also furnished. The front seat is trimmed with a tan Colonial-grain leather and the rear compartment has a light Wiese bedford cord on the seat and a plain broadcloth on the flat panels. The other Pierce-Arrow job is a sedan-limousine of sporting lines with V-windshield and a scalloped-molding effect somewhat similar to that used on the town car but extending in this case over the rear fender and to the belt molding, creating a 2-panel effect. In the color scheme, Desert Sand and Pyramid Gray, the moldings are not accented but only serve to give the high-light or flash effect. A semi-crowned belt panel stops windsplit on passing the slanting windshield pillar and curves back in diminished size across the front of the windshield, ending in a slightly pointed cowl panel. The novelty of the design and its boldness is certain to command attention whether the car stands in the Salon or on the street. The landau-type rear and top are in the darker color, no black being used on this job. The interior is trimmed in plain style with a Laidlaw novelty fabric on the seats and a harmonizing plain fabric for the lining.

Automobile Color Index

THE important autumnal color families are brown, green and maroon, according to the Automobile Color Index issued by the Duco Color Advisory Service. Brown continues to hold its position next to blue,

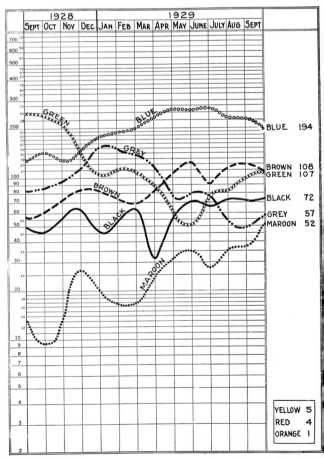

Automobile Color Index showing the popularity of the principal color families during the last 13 months

New York Salon Opens Eastern Show Season

Several Interesting New Productions Will be Seen at New York, but the General Trends of the Chicago Salon Will Apply to the Eastern Exhibition

THE 25th New York Automobile Salon will open its doors as this issue of AUTOBODY goes into the mails and will continue throughout the first week of December. Although the majority of the exhibits will duplicate those of the Chicago Salon, some interesting new productions will be on view at the Hotel Commodore, where seventeen of the leading American custom-body builders and two from abroad will have their own stands. It is expected that the latest creations of five additional European carrossiers will be mounted on the foreign-chassis exhibits.

THE EXHIBITORS

The motor cars exhibited as this Salon by their makers or importers are: Isotta-Fraschini, Lancia, Mercedes, Minerva, Renault, Rolls-Royce and Cunningham. American chassis to be exhibited on body builders' stands include: Cadillac, Cord, Duesenberg, du Pont,

senger collapsible body mounted on a 135-in. Stutz chassis is an extreme sporting type with special "parabolic" fenders and streamlined chassis valances and running boards. The body panels are carried below the chassis level, and the wheel disks and large trunk add to the sporting effect. The slant of the windshield is carried out in the door windows which are mounted in the special Hibbard & Darrin glass guides and leave no gap as the windows are lowered or raised. There are special panels in the top of the bonnet, with extensions covering felt-lined tool trays in the cowl. The entire car is in oyster gray, including the canvas top. The interior is trimmed with a natural-tan leather and the special front seats slide forward as the backs are tipped.

Other new exhibits at New York will include bodies built by Merrimac and Waterhouse on du Pont chassis, after designs of the du Pont body department. Merri-

A 7-passenger all-weather cabriolet of the Sylentlyte type to be exhibited by Hibbard & Darrin on a Packard 7-45 chassis. This aluminum-alloy construction is lighter than a composite body of the same size and is free from climatic troubles. The top is a beige alpaca material and has no seam at the header bar; when the front compartment is enclosed, there is no evidence of the conversion. The car is finished in two shades of sage green and a matching broadcloth is used in the interior. The rear seat is adjustable. Auxiliary seats are forward facing and the backs have an extra fold, giving them unusual height

Franklin, La Salle, Lincoln, Packard, Pierce-Arrow, Ruxton and Stutz.

Coachwork exhibits are being made by Baker-Raulang, Brewster, Brunn, Castagna, Derham, Dietrich, Fisher, Fleetwood, Hibbard & Darrin, Holbrook, Judkins, Le Baron, Locke, Merrimac, Murphy, Rollston, Waterhouse, Weymann and Willoughby. De luxe car equipment and accessories will be presented in special exhibits by William Wiese & Co., Triplex Safety Glass Co., Specialty Manufacturing Co., Martin Tires and William C. Reynolds.

THE NEW ALUMINUM-ALLOY BODIES

Among the interesting new coachwork are the Sylentlyte bodies on the Hibbard & Darrin stand. These aluminum-alloy bodies do not differ essentially in appearance from standard composite bodies, as will be noted in the illustration on this page of an all-weather cabriolet on the Packard 145-in. custom chassis. The other Hibbard & Darrin job is of unusual appearance, but not because of the Sylentlyte principle. This 5-pas-

mac will present a 4-passenger "speedster" of extremely sporting character finished completely in gray, except the wheels and bumpers, which will be in scarlet. The Waterhouse Co. will show a town car of interesting design, finished in sable, but with the wheels, bumpers and recessed door-belt panel in ivory which will also be used for striping. The body sides are carried down to the running boards, and swept up to meet the cowl molding at the dash. The cowl molding is carried diagonally downward as a continuation of the slanting windshield. The belt treatment is a slight variation of the Hibbard & Darrin design, and the outlines of the door panels are a departure from the customary lines for formal cars.

Dietrich will exhibit at New York a new convertible coupe of the Franklin "Le Pirate" series. Body sides and doors extend down and flare outward, concealing the running boards; the front pillars follow the inclination of the windshield and provide easy entrance to the driving seat. Le Baron, Inc., will also have a new job in its New York exhibit; this will be a close-coupled

New Body Models to be Shown at the New York Salon

A 5-passenger collapsible Sylentlyte body, by Hibbard & Darrin, on 135-in. Stutz chassis. It is finished entirely in oyster gray. The unusual steamlining of fenders, valan-

ces and running boards, the wheel disks, the large trunk and the extension of body sides below chassis level give the car an extremely sporting appearance

A town car built by the Waterhouse Co. on 141-in. du Pont chassis. The body sides are carried down to the running boards and swept up to meet the cowl molding that continues the line of the windshield. The car is finished in sable, with ivory wheels, recessed door-belt panels and striping

A 4-passenger "Speedster" built by Merrimac Body Co. on the du Pont "Speed" chassis with 125-in wheelbase. It is finished in gray, and has scarlet wheels and bumpers, and chromium-plated metalwork. Both compartments are trimmed with red-and-ivory snake-grain leather. The top is of Burbank

Le Baron, Inc., will exhibit a new sport cabriolet on Packard chassis. It is to be finished in black, with silver striping; the sloping "V" windshield frame and other exposed metal parts are chromium plated, carrying out the same color contrast. The top is a light-colored Burbank. The rear compartment is unusually close-coupled, for four passengers, and has the companion cases set in the division

Dietrich's "Pirate" model for a convertible coupe on Franklin chassis. Body sides extend down and flare outward, concealing the running boards. The front pillars follow the inclination of

the windshield, giving a wide easy entrance. The car is finished black and is trimmed with vermilion and silver. The top is a tan silk-mohair, piped with the same leather as used for the seats

sport cabriolet on Packard chassis and is illustrated on another page. Rollston has built, on Minerva chassis, a cabriolet-type town car with sliding roof.

Advance data on the foreign cars are not available in most cases, because of the uncertainty of the arrivals by steamer and the condition of the jobs when delivered to the importer. Mercedes-Benz Co., Inc., expects to exhibit two cars with Castagna bodies; one of these will be a 4-passenger "Country Club" sedan which will be finished in beige and have an aluminum molding; an imported novelty cloth will be used for the seats and a plain matching fabric for the lining. The other body will probably be a Dorsay limousine finished in Tuscany Brown with Malay Brown striping; the driving com-

attacks on this stronghold. Owner-driven convertibles were present in goodly numbers. The old composite construction was "attacked" by the Weymann and Gordon England methods, and in New York a third claimant for adoption will be the Sylentlyte aluminum-alloy body. The two front-wheel-drive cars may also be considered in the class of new constructions, as the body-building problem is changed by the opportunity of building on a flat chassis; however, the builders at present labor under the difficulty of rather short wheelbases which involve a big cut-out on the rear door. The conservative, conventional construction was adequately represented on the stands of all of the old established coachbuilders but many of them introduced changes on

Unusual Belt and Molding Treatments on These Cars

The "Clear Vision" sedan by Murphy, on Duesenberg chassis, has an unusual belt treatment done in polished aluminum. The interior is also refreshingly different with wood trim of plain green-stained maple, and instead of the usual carpet, a gunmetal leather is used on the lower half of the doors and front seatback. The chrome-plated protection beading on the rear fender is now standard on this chassis

A town car by the Baker-Raulang Co. on the Ruxton front-drive chassis. The painting of the belt is at once arresting, the old ivory standing out against the all-black car. The beading on the edge of the fenders and the embossed center line are also painted old ivory. The drip molding functions as a water shed and decorative feature, and eliminates the need of any other tack covering

This Deauville sedan on Franklin chassis, by Dietrich, has no molding around the back at the belt. The molding treatment emphasizes the door framing and particularly the sloping edge of the front door, which provides easy entrance to the driving seat

partment is trimmed with lizard-grain leather and the rear seats will have a 2-tone brown novelty fabric and a plain lining. The other alternative entry will be a berline with dark-green body, beige moldings and Beaver Brown chassis and wheels. The front compartment will be trimmed with a green-and-brown leather; the rear compartment will have a novelty wool fabric on the seats and a plain matching lining.

CONSERVATISM STILL REIGNS

The Chicago exhibits in general will be duplicated at New York and the few new models will probably make but little difference in generalizing from the trends of the earlier show. In body types and construction, conservatism was still dominant but there were numerous

some of their models, making the current Salon the most varied in design of recent years.

EXTERIOR CHANGES

In exterior design there were numerous changes in moldings and belt treatments without any dominant trend in these respects. The growth in popularity of the "V" windshield is noteworthy, especially in view of the fact that this trend seems to have been reversed at Olympia. Windshields with rounded corners were used by Le Baron on two sedans which were also noteworthy for their absence of reveals or offsets, their sole decoration being a narrow chromium-plated molding running through to the radiator shell. On the Willoughby-Duesenberg berline, the windshield was set stationary and the wiper installation concealed. The use of slanting windshields is now well established and a number of designers are carrying the front pillars down on the same angle of inclination, thereby providing greater footroom in getting in and out of the driving seat. Body sizes on numerous models were carried down below the level of the chassis and in some cases to the running boards. The adoption of steps has not gone as far here as it has abroad. The front-wheel-drive cars, because of their lowness, omitted the running boards. One example of a sliding roof was shown by Weymann and several bodies, notably those of Castagna, had glasses set in the roof ventilators, curtains being provided underneath to prevent the penetration of too much sunshine. These glass-lid ventilators make a considerable difference in the cheerfulness of the cars on drab days. On the Franklin "Avion" sedan, Holbrook used over the windshield a tubular ventilator of a type recently adopted abroad.

model has been changed to a berline by providing suitable panels at the side, or top, making the secondary windshield a division glass, and permitting it to embed itself against sponge rubber in the roof bow. Nearly every builder has made some improvement in his convertible during the past year. Several now provide for automatic loosening of the fabric at the rear quarters, but the disposition of the loose center pillar is not at all standardized. It may be snapped to the roof bow or pivoted downward and fastened against the lower pillar or division. Locke has provided an ingenious disappearing pillar which is made of stainless steel and consequently not subject to swelling or corrosion; it drops vertically into the body and is spring controlled so that when not in use it is flush with the surface. This Franklin berline also had lights set in the falling pillars, thereby giving better reading light and permitting the use of a narrower bow at the rear. Another feature of

Conservative Interiors by Brunn, Baker-Raulang and Willoughby

Interior of Brunn's semi-collapsible cabriolet on Stutz chassis. The seats were trimmed with a green bedford cord in plain-stretched style and the lining was a plain matching broadcloth. Hardware was in bronze of special design and the plain walnut door-belt panel was in keeping with the simple character of the interior

In trimming this Ruxton town car, Baker-Raulang Co. adopted the plain style with noteworthy success. The fabric was a rayon, as in all the other Ruxton cars. In this interior, a golden shade of a weave somewhat resembling a wide bedford cord was selected. The hardware was gold plated to match. Companion cases were set in the division on each side of the recess for the regulator handle. Note the clever utilization of the wheelhouse line in developing the armrest design

Rear compartment of Willoughby's French panel brougham on Lincoln chassis. The plain style is here relieved by "cordonnet" decoration of modern design on the door and partition panels; this was done in soft blues and grays that are exaggerated by the photo-engraving. The trim fabric is a Wiese French gray doeskin

There was a fair use of polished metal beading by Le Baron, Murphy and Brewster, the last named firm using concave polished-aluminum moldings on two of its bodies on Rolls-Royce chassis. Several builders used aluminum or chrome-plated drip moldings for the double purpose of a water shed and as a splash of color around the window. The tendency to mount window glass in chromium-plated metal sash continues as this permits the use of half doors and lightens the upper construction.

CONVERTIBLES IMPROVED

There were six open cars shown, two of which were roadsters and the remainder phaetons. The latter were especially interesting for their sporting character and the excellent workmanship they presented. Almost every builder showed one or more owner-driven convertibles. The coupes outnumbered only slightly the combined sedans and berlines. In several cases the sedan

the Locke convertible was the use of a stainless-steel header which fitted over the top material and was folded or rolled up with it.

GREEN MOST POPULAR COLOR

In painting, the most marked practice was the use of the duotone color scheme. Greens were the predominant color, followed closely by the all-black jobs. Maroons, blues, grays, yellows, beiges and browns brought up the rear guard, all rather closely together in point of numbers. Cars painted in chromatic sequence far outnumbered those in contrasting colors, but the black chassis still enjoys a good popularity.

Striping was so varied in character that it defies classification, but it is noteworthy that hairline stripes were used by a number of builders. Not a few cars omitted striping, this proportion being augmented this year by the increased Weymann exhibits, all but one of which were without striping and several without mold-

Rear seat and cabinetwork of the Judkins-Duesenberg 7-passenger berline. An all-over embroidered rayon fabric of various tones of brown is used for the seat, and a plain broadcloth for the lining. The cabinetwork by Linden is chiefly of American walnut, inlaid with imported boxwood, ebony, amboyna and bubinga. Another view, on the succeeding page, shows one of the auxiliary seats in position and the interesting "fan" treatment of the door panel

ings. Contrast in the Weymann exteriors was effected in some instances by the use of smooth-coated fabric for the main body panels and grained fabric for the quarters and upperworks. On several Weymanns, the engine bonnets were not covered with fabric, but the lacquer was grained in imitation of that of the fabric so that only a careful examination revealed this fact.

PLAIN AND TUFTED UPHOLSTERING

Interiors presented considerable variety this year, but the simple conservative type held the dominant position. The variants, however, were extremely interesting and attracted attention, if not custom. A number of examples are illustrated of both types of interiors. In general, there were but two styles of upholstery, the plain stretched and the tufted, the former being far in the lead. The plain-plaited style was found in only a few cars. Broadlace was sparingly used, but some cars had lace binding or piping instead of the more popular leather piping. In upholstery materials, the broadcloths led as usual, with bedford cords their

nearest rival as a seating material. Several printed broadcloths were observed. We noted three jobs trimmed in mohair plush, but a half dozen or more used rayon, sometimes with the rayon fibers predominating and on some of the imported cars, as a minor fiber mixed with wool.

Leather was popular for trimming the open and convertible cars but more than one-third of the convertibles at Chicago had fabric-covered seats, bedford cord being the most popular fabric. Only one car was trimmed with reptile skin, but several closed cars were upholstered with soft Italian goat skins. Sheepskin rugs, dyed a darker shade than the upholstery, were shown in many of the town cars.

MORE CABINETWORK

Door panels were generally treated with extreme simplicity; they were often plain, or the decoration limited to a welt or stitching in a simple geometric design. Door pockets were rare and usually of the flap type. With respect to cabinetwork and friezes on the doors

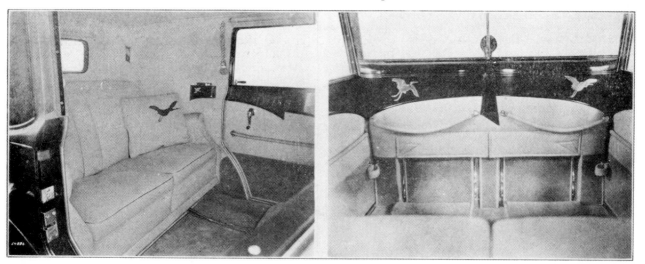

This modern interior, by Murphy on a Duesenberg town car, was one of the most daring and successful efforts at this Salon to create a different interior. The partition and door friezes are of ebony and of unusual shape; they are inset with silver cranes in flight and the same motif is repeated on the companion cases, the corner and domelights and in black needlework, on the loose pillows and laprobe. The trimming fabric is gray Silvercloth, done in plain-stretched style and piped with Silvertip piping leather. The telephone is concealed in a compartment with a spring-hinged flap covered with the trim fabric. Short curtains conceal the opening above the opera seats, shown in position on the succeeding page

and partitions, there seems to be two schools. The majority group eschews any decoration of this nature and the other uses it liberally. Among the outstanding recruits of the latter group were the Rolls-Royce exhibits, most of their formal cars having marquetry friezes or the entire division in cabinetwork. Several other builders employed cabinetwork more extensively than heretofore.

Companion cases swept into the friezes were numerous, but the separate type were in the majority. In a number of cars having solid quarters companion cases were recessed therein and a few of these had covers to keep out dust. There has been a tendency recently to use open pockets under, or forward of, the armrests. This practice has been improved upon by several builders who provide spring-hinged lids covered with the lining or seat fabric. Interior hardware was of noteworthy excellence; butler-finish silver predominated but there was a liberal use of bronze and several cars

support for the legs under the knees—a feature in which some builders' seats are lacking. The Weymann seating comprises a form-fitting back and a cushion having a soft, flat transverse section at the rear, and the remainder of the cushion, in plain plaits, rising at a rather sharp angle. This gives the necessary support under the knees. In a sport coupe in which a single side facing seat was used back of the driving seat, an air cushion was employed—something which has not been adopted in this country, although considerably used in England.

National Automobile Show

Forty-six makes of cars will be shown at the forthcoming National Automobile Show which opens at the Grand Central Palace in New York on Jan. 4. There will be 42 makes of domestic cars, two domestic cabs and two foreign automobiles — Mercedes-Benz and Voisin. The exhibition will close on Jan. 11 and will

At the left and right are additional views of the Judkins and Murphy interiors shown on the preceding page. The center view illustrates the unusual trimming of a Duesenberg sedan on the Derham stand; this body was trimmed by the customer with a brown "frise" supplemented with calfskin. Plain plaits were used on the seats, but on the doors and seatback, the trimmer was given carte blanche. Karvart panels, a decorative pressed wood, was used for the door friezes

had gold-plated, enameled or other special fitments. Radio receiving sets were fitted in a few jobs.

Nearly all driving seats were adjustable and several builders provided adjustable rear seats. Some front seats moved forward when the back was folded, thus automatically providing room for the rear-seat passengers to descend or enter easily from 2-door bodies. In most bodies there was no special effort made to provide more comfortable auxiliary seats, these being regarded as purely emergency equipment. There were several exceptions to this, some of the auxiliary seats being comfortably upholstered and sufficiently wide so that the two seats would carry three passengers in an emergency. The majority of the auxiliary seats folded flush into the division panel.

Weymann's Anatomical Seating

The Weymann interiors presented features that are rare here but considerably used in Europe, such as inlaid friezes on the doors, swept smoking or vanity cases, pockets with plywood lids in the back of the front seat, and European exterior features such as the coach sill, carrying the body sides down to the running board and the sunshine roof. The Weymann "anatomical" seating is also noteworthy as it provides a soft

re-open in Chicago on Jan. 25, continuing until Feb. 1. The domestic cars to be exhibited are listed below:

Auburn, Black Hawk, Buick, Cadillac, Chevrolet, Chrysler, Cord, Cunningham, De Soto, Dodge Brothers, du Pont (New York, only), Durant, Elcar, Erskine, Essex, Franklin, Gardner, Graham-Paige, Hudson, Hupmobile, Jordan, Kissel, La Salle, Lincoln, Marmon, Marquette, Nash, Oakland, Oldsmobile, Packard, Peerless, Pierce-Arrow, Plymouth, Pontiac, Reo, Roosevelt, Studebaker, Stutz, Viking, Whippet, Willys-Knight and Windsor White Prince (Moon). Taxicabs: Checker and Yellow.

The Calendar

Some Foreign Interiors at the New York Salon

Illustrations are Presented of Interesting Foreign Cars, and of Several Domestic Interiors, not Previously Available

THE general features of the 25th Automobile Salon at New York were adequately covered in the December issuse of AUTOBODY, but no illustrations were then available of the foreign-built bodies. Some of these were interesting as classic examples of conventional coachwork, while others presented interior features that were stimulating in their departure from the trite. One or two domestic interiors, not previously illustrated, are also now presented because of novelties in their upholstery or woodwork.

Several of the foreign bodies were noteworthy for their careful adherence to classic standards, combined with a clever adaptation of recent improvements. Lack of space prevents more than passing mention of some of these, such as the admirable cabriolet-type town car by Van den Plas, on Minerva chassis, with a delicate tan broadcloth interior done in the plain-

the body to be an enclosed limousine. The interior was extremely simple, trimmed throughout with a drab broadcloth set off by dark mahogany friezes which were gracefully swept, but without carving or inlay. It was admirably designed, both interiorly and exteriorly, but was unfortunately placed on the mezzanine floor of the Commodore and a large percentage of visitors probably missed seeing it. A more elaborate example of Farina craftsmanship, however, was observable on the Isotta stand in the main ballroom; this all-weather landaulet was trimmed with a novelty fabric in plaited style, with bolster-type armrests, and lace-covered piping instead of the prevailing leather piping. The friezes were of dark mahogany, plain on the doors but with toilet cases swept in the division frieze; these cases were sumptuously appointed, the accessories including bottles and other glass articles by Lalique.

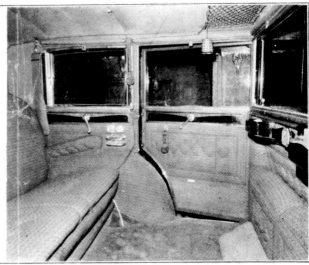

Castagna interiors always offer an interesting change from our conventional designs. These two interiors of semi-collapsible town cars on Isotta-Fraschini chassis sustain the reputation of this Milanese coachbuilder for original interiors. In the above body the wood trim consists of natural-finish maple, veneered on the friezes with curly maple. Three "cantines" are swept into the division frieze. The central case, fitted with toilet articles, has a glass cover, but the adjoining compartments for gloves and small parcels are provided with wooden lids. The lozenge design on the spring-hinged door pocket is repeated on the auxiliary seats. Although a door pull is carved into the maple garnish rail, a small toggle is also provided on the door

Another Castagna interior, the maple friezes of which are veneered with burl walnut; the carving is in the natural maple and makes a pleasing contrast with the darker walnut. The companion cases, swept into the partition friezes, are left uncovered in this instance. A silver-trimmed glass ash receiver and Autofum are installed forward of the left armrest; on the right side are annunciator buttons for driving orders. The plain-stretched upholstery is unusual in having a plait at the center of the cushion to correspond to the plait in the back forming the folding armrest; another feature is the lines of almond-shaped tufts across the cushions, back, armrests, door pockets, partition panel, etc.

plaited style but given a distinction by its simplicity and by the harmonious panel treatment on the doors and partition where the plaited trimming was repeated, in narrower form, under a burl-walnut frieze inlaid with rosewood; the Minerva-D'Ieteren glass-quarter brougham with excellent cabinetwork on the division and, around the door panels, the wood fillets characteristic of this builder; a Kellner enclosed cabriolet on Renault chassis, with 2-paneled quarter window controlled by a single regulator; the Farina glass-quarter brougham on Lancia chassis with a dignified interior, calculated to appeal to the most conservative American taste, and with an all-weather front that fitted so neatly that many, who did not see it transformed, supposed

Castagna interiors always offer a refreshing change from our conventional trimming, often presenting novelties that might well be adopted as regular practice. Two of his all-weather landaulet interiors, on Isotta-Fraschini chassis, are shown on this page. One is noteworthy for its striking cabinetwork and variation of the plain-stretched upholstery, and the other for the orthodoxy of its plaited trimming and the comparatively plain but practical cabinetwork. The latter is shown at the left and requires little comment, except with respect to the wood trim which is of straight-grain maple in natural color, overlaid with curly maple. The central cantine, having a glass cover, contains toilet articles; the empty cabinets at each side, with wooden lids, are for gloves or small parcels. The electric push buttons near the right armrest give directions to the chauffeur through a lighted annunciator on the instrument board. Near the left armrest are the light switches, an ash receiver and an Autofum, as shown in the view of the other body.

The wood trim in the body at the right is more elaborate. Garnish rails are of natural-finish maple; the frieze is a combination of plain and carved maple, with a veneer of contrasting burl walnut. The swept companion cases in the partition frieze are left open in this instance. Almond-shaped tufts in the plain-stretched upholstery are an interesting novelty of this body; also the use of a plait at the center of the seat

of the upperworks. This gave an interesting effect, providing a sort of setting for the upperworks. Fenders had an exceedingly deep crown. The windshield sloped at a small angle and had rather long triangular wings in chomium-plated frames, opening with the fore doors. (This was one of the few, if not the only town car without an all-weather front.) On the division pillars were handles to assist elderly passengers in entering. A spacious trunk had a large 3-pointed star, the Mercedes emblem, embossed on the rear panel.

The interior was noteworthy for its wood trim in burl walnut. The polished friezes were swept, and where a fitment was positioned were carved and left in natural finish or only lightly waxed; this carved portion

The Castagna "Dorsay limousine" on Mercedes chassis exhibited a novel belt treatment. The upper molding extended around the body to the sloping windshield; the lower half of this molding was rounded, but the upper side sloped at an angle of about 25 deg. and formed a sort of setting for the superstructure. In addition to this novel effect, the triangular windshield wings in chromium-plated frames attached to the fore doors were swept to provide an unusual appearance. The large trunk had the Mercedes emblem embossed on the rear panel

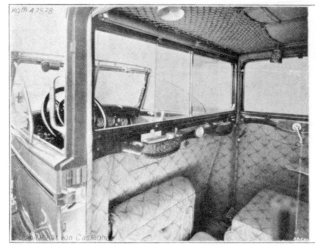

Interior of Castagna's "Dorsay limousine" on Mercedes chassis. This was noteworthy for the interesting carving of the burl-walnut friezes. The carving was left in the natural walnut while the remainder of the woodwork was polished in the customary manner. The swept companion cases on the partition frieze were open, as was also the case behind the clock which was encircled by a strip of carving. There was also a narrow strip of carving under the medallions on the face of the companion cases. Broadlace was used on the armslings and also on the heel-board of the rear seat which was adjustable by means of a crank handle shown in the view at the right. Lace-covered piping was used instead of the more usual leather piping. The wide auxiliary seats had a folding armrest on the outer side. The door panels have spring-hinged pockets and a toggle door pull. Package and hat nets were attached to the ceiling

cushion to correspond with the plait concealing the folding armrest in the back. The rear-quarter windows are in two panels, ingeniously controlled by the single regulator which actuates the upper panel first.

Another Castagna town car, on Mercedes chassis, was noteworthy for its carved burl-walnut friezes. This "Dorsay limousine" was also unusual with respect to its exterior belt treatment. A double belt molding is employed. The lower molding, into which the windshield pillar is swept, is carried through to the radiator. The upper molding extends around the body and stops at the windshield pillar; this upper molding is unusual in being rounded on the lower half above which it slopes upward at about 25 deg. until it meets the vertical plane

was surrounded by a plain polished "frame" and at the bottom, a narrow strip of carving was repeated, leaving a still narrower polished bead below. The door-latch handles were also of carved walnut, inset in the metal frame. The plain-stretched style of upholstering was used but, as on all Castagna jobs, presented variations from the conventional such as the use of lace-covered piping, broadlace on the heelboard but not on the door panels, wide spring-controlled flap pockets of unusual shape, toggle door pulls, etc. A novelty wool fabric of modernistic pattern was used for the seats and lower panels, with a plain broadcloth above. The rear seat was adjustable by means of a central crank. The auxiliary seats were wide enough to accommodate three

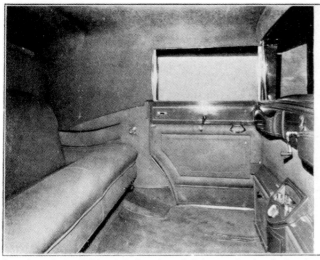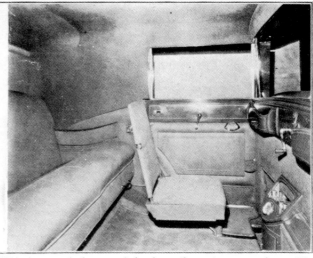

Interior of the Hibbard & Darrin cabriolet on Packard chassis. This is one of the new Sylentlyte all-metal constructions. The door and partition friezes are of cast aluminum and are painted in green fine lined with silver, matching the exterior; the friezes have plain rectangular offsets, except the last one which is curved. There are swept vide-poches on the division frieze, the toilet articles being placed in a case below, between the auxiliary seats, where a clock is set above a deep cabinet with double doors. The auxiliary seats have cast-aluminum bases, the center section being covered with cloth, while the edges are painted. These seats have an extra flap on the back to give ample support at the shoulders. There are wells for the feet of the emergency passengers, although the division glass lowers completely. The interior is trimmed with a gray-green broadcloth done in the plain-stretched style. The cushion of the rear seat is adjustable, "without any mechanism," dowels in the seat frame fitting into holes in the base, thereby giving three positions

passengers, and had a single folding armrest on the outer side. Parcel and hat nets were attached to the ceiling.

Above are presented two views of the interior of Hibbard & Darrin's Sylentlyte cabriolet on Packard chassis. These views show a conventional interior except for the treatment of the division; the latter is not a change due to the constructional system employed but merely the designers' interpretation of the present mode in Paris. The interior is trimmed with a gray-green broadcloth in the plain-stretched style; the curved armrests have flat tops and tight flap pockets in the sides for gloves; there are no other pockets here or on the doors as ample package space is provided by *vide-poches* in the division frieze. The rear-seat cushion is adjustable, "without any mechanism"; dowels provided

in the seat frame fit into holes in the base and give three positions, the adjustment being made by lifting up the cushion by the handles on the heelboard, one of which is visible in the engraving. The back is stationary but adjustment of the cushion gives passengers an opportunity to change position on a long ride, and the absence of complicated mechanism is considered desirable. The auxiliary seats, which have an extra flap on the back to give support to the passenger's shoulders, are not concealed in the partition but appear on the contrary to be a part of it. The seats have cast-aluminum bases, the center section being covered with cloth, while the edges are painted. There are wells for the feet of the emergency passengers, although the division glass lowers completely. Between the seats is a rather deep cabinet or cellarette, above which is the

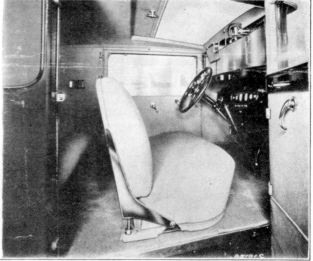

Two interesting Weymann interiors presenting numerous features characteristic of European bodies. At the left is the Weymann Monte Carlo model on Stutz chassis. It is trimmed with imported goatskin leather to the belt, the door panels having the plaited effect much used abroad. The seating is the Weymann "anatomical" style with a sharply rising plaited cushion in front of a plain-stretched transverse section. In the back of the front seats are pockets with plywood lids, hinged at the bottom. A radio receiving set is fitted into the instrument board and under the windshield is a walnut frieze with swept-in smoking case. In the friezes of the rear doors there are similar swept cases. The door friezes also have carved door pulls. At the right is the Weymann Longchamps model with a Pytchley sunshine roof. The front seat, trimmed with bedford cord, is adjustable longitudinally and the angle of the back can also be adjusted. Both bodies have adjustable inside visors

clock and a toilet case. The division pillars are hinged at the belt and fold down on the division when the car is operated as a phaeton. The division frieze has a *vide-poche* on each side of the regulator handle. All of the parts, with the fine silver striping, are painted green to match the exterior panels. This interior trim

The Murphy "clear vision" sedan on Duesenberg chassis departed from the usual in its interior wood trim and the use of gunmetal-finish leather instead of carpet on the doors and lower part of the front seatback. The seats were trimmed with blue-striped Lusterweave in the plain-stretched style and piped with gunmetal leather. The Wiese fabric was also used for the wall lining and the upper half of the door panels and front seatbacks, below which the gunmetal leather was used. The friezes were of straight-grain maple, stained in light green. The door panels had fillets of the same wood

is not of wood but of cast aluminum; the door and partition friezes have plain rectangular offsets, except the last one which is curved. The door panel has an overstuffed border and the inner panel is decorated with stitched beading in a geometric design.

The Weymann interiors shown on p. 18 were produced in this country but have features that are more characteristic of European than of conventional American practice. The interior shown at the left is from the American company's Monte Carlo model. This has the Weymann "anatomical seating" with sharply rising plaited cushion in front of a plain-stretched transverse section; the back is done in plain plaits, and similar trimming is used on the doors. The trimming material is Italian goatskins up to the belt line, and a harmonizing fabric above. The individual front seats are adjustable, and in the seatbacks are pockets with plywood lids, hinged at the bottom. There are swept-in smoking cases in the walnut friezes on the rear doors and in the frieze under the windshield. The door friezes also have carved door pulls. A radio receiving set is installed in the instrument panel and there are small glove pockets at each end of this panel. An adjustable inside visor is provided above the windshield on the driving side. The Weymann Longchamps model is shown in the view at the right. This is a 5-passenger coupe with Pytchley sliding roof and is the first showing at the Salons of the popular British "sportsman's coupe." The seats are trimmed with bedford cord and a plain broadcloth is used for the wall and headlining. The driving seat is adjustable longitudinally, and also for the angle of the back.

The trimming of the Murphy "clear vision" sedan on Duesenberg chassis was an interesting departure

from convention, particularly with reference to its wood trim and the use of gunmetal-finish leather instead of carpet at the base of the doors and front seatback. The seats were trimmed with blue-striped Lusterweave in the plain-stretched style and piped with gunmetal leather. The same fabric was used for the wall lining, and for the upper half of the door panel and front seatback, below which the gunmetal leather was used. This was also employed for covering the robe rail and for the special door pull placed about midway on the door at the line of division between the fabric and leather. The wood trim was unusual in character and material—a straight-grain maple, stained a light green. Its use for the friezes and for the top of the front seatback is clearly shown in the engraving; note that it was also employed for the fillets of the doors.

Another illustration shows the unusual trimming adopted by Le Baron for a convertible coupe on Lincoln chassis. The seat is upholstered with a Wiese bedford cord, plain-stretched except for a narrow transverse plait across both cushion and back. The deep drop of the molding at the rear quarter and a special head fitting permit the top to fold so as to silhouette effectively with and become a part of the contour of the car.

A number of other domestic cars had interesting departures from tradition. The Rolls-Royce exhibits were characterized this year by an unusual amount of cabinetwork; one town-car interior was almost entirely of carved walnut, and several had marquetry friezes of light-colored or stained woods suggestive of French drawing rooms. On one of these, the marquetry friezes

Unusual trimming style used by Le Baron in the convertible coupe on Lincoln chassis. The narrow transverse plait across the cushion and back gave this seat a special character. The fabric is a Wiese bedford cord. The deep sweep of the molding at the quarter and a special head fitting permit the top to fold so as to silhouette effectively with the design of the car

were carried out on the driving doors as well as in the master compartment. The exterior canework of the rear compartment was likewise carried forward to the front where it was stopped by a chromium-plated "coupe pillar" extension of the slanting windshield frame.

Reflections of the National Automobile Shows

STANDARDIZATION of body design seemed to be the keynote of the "production" exhibits at the recent National Automobile Shows. At a time when a new sales appeal was most needed, the cars of the large-production manufacturers looked more alike than ever. Roof lines, window shapes, moldings and belts were monotonously similar. The slight changes made served chiefly to bring models into greater conformity with "family" lines or with conventional practice. A broadside of the large-production cars puts them into two general classifications: (1) Those having a medium belt swept at each end and (2) the group using a modified H. & D. belt treatment. The expert may distinguish a difference in the angle of the visor,

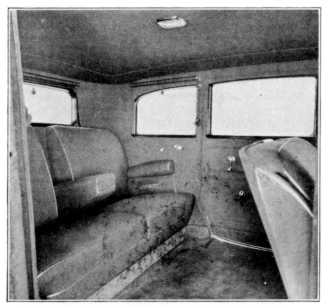

The Peerless Custom Eight sedan, designed by Alexis de Sakhnoffsky and built by Hayes Body Corporation, is characterized by extreme simplicity and comfortably deep upholstery. The trim fabric is a Wiese blue-gray broadcloth which is piped with a harmonizing Eagle-Ottawa leather. The 47-in. rear seat has bolster-type armrests underneath which is a small glove pouch. On the right side an electric lighter is attached at the end of the armrest and an ash receiver is recessed into the quarter. Note the uncommon framing of the back window

the width of the belt or sweep of a molding, but the average citizen will hardly be able to determine the make of a passing car of these groups; unless he sees the emblem, it will simply be another car.

MORE SAFETY BUILT INTO 1930 CARS

Though their body designs lacked special interest or appeal, these cars offered more than their predecessors in speed, comfort and reliability, thus fulfilling the industry's obligation to give progressively better individual transportation. Most of the bodies were wider and a number were longer or offered more legroom. Front seats were adjustable to accommodate the stature of the driver. Practically all windshields were of safety glass. In the higher priced cars laminated glass was used for all windows. As yet only a few cars embodied that other important safety feature—full driver vision at the front corners. All the cars on one stand, that of Packard, were equipped with this safety feature and most of the custom-built cars also had clear-vision

pillars. Production cars as a whole, however, still offer a blind spot that prevents the driver from seeing approaching cars at intersections of the road. The increasing traffic danger warrants greater consideration, by production manufacturers, of this driving hazard.

SOME INTERESTING NEW BODIES

For interesting new bodywork, one had to look to the smaller companies and to custom bodies exhibited on the stands of the higher priced cars. More custom cars were exhibited than at any recent National Show; these were interesting to the public, but had been seen by the "industry" at the earlier Salons. The majority have been illustrated in AUTOBODY and little further comment is required concerning their exteriors. No information, prior to the showing, was released respecting several interesting cars; among these were the Cadillac V-16 with an enclosed-limousine body by Fleetwood; a sporting roadster and an equally sporting sedan on Jordan chassis by the Facto Auto Body Co.; Elcar's new low "140" sedan and a group of unusual bodies on the du Pont stand. The two foreign exhibits, Mercedes and Voisin, also presented interesting and decidedly different bodywork.

Although previously illustrated, mention may here be made to some companies that were particularly successful with their new offerings. Among these were the Hayes bodies for the Marmon 69 and 79 series which were excellently proportioned and had just enough of novelty to be refreshing without shocking the conventionally minded buyer. The Peerless bodies, also by Hayes, follow similar precepts and give the new Peerless management a good sales opportunity for 1930. Another car that had "eye" appeal was the Cord front drive, exhibited at the National Show for the first time, although launched last summer. This quickly caught the public fancy, buyers hesitating only over the price and the novelty of the front-wheel drive.

Though not formally exhibited, the Gardner front-drive sedan, developed from engine dimensions given to Baker-Raulang Co. by the car manufacturer, was another example of unfettered designing that produced an original and pleasing embodiment of speed and comfort. An interior view in this issue supplements the exterior presented in the January AUTOBODY.

NEW JORDAN DESIGNS ATTRACT ATTENTION

The new Jordan bodies, built by Facto Auto Body Co., exhibited some of the old Jordan dash in their unusual lines and equipment. In consequence the Jordan stand was so crowded that it was necessary to go to the Show early if one wanted to make a leisurely and satisfactory examination. Exterior and interior views are presented of these interesting designs.

In a class by itself, of course, was the Cadillac V-16 mounted with an enclosed-limousine body by Fleetwood. This was dignified and conservative in character but incorporated a number of interesting features such as a V-front, an extra-wide belt, about $3\frac{1}{2}$ in. swept to $2\frac{1}{2}$ in. as it passed around the back of the body, chromium-plated window sills which, with the chromium-plated frames of the glasses, and a polished-metal drip molding, gave a bright framing for the windows and enlivened the black finish of the body. The interior was particularly spacious and was trimmed in plain-stretched style with a Wiese sand-finish gray broad-cloth, with small check design, and piped to mark the seat divisions. A narrow broadlace was used for paneling the doors and on the partition. The rear seat was adjustable—a feature that was embodied in several other high-grade bodies.

VISORS AND BONNET LOUVERS

One of the few features of the production cars in which there was considerable variation was the visors. Hooded metal visors were used by the majority and

Kissel interiors have always been noted for their excellent, and often unusual, upholstery work. This sedan is trimmed in a Chase cut mohair having a golden-brown pile and a reddish backing. The trimming is noteworthy for the use of a fold that was made in the plaits along the line of the buttons practically concealing the latter on both cushion and back. The door panel, which does not show to good advantage in this view, was really exceedingly well done; wide stitching outlined the panel and had an unusual effect on the deep pile; the shirred pocket was recessed and was practically flush with the panel. Another sedan was similarly trimmed with Wiese bedford cord on the seats and plain broadcloth lining. Both sedans had ventilating quarter windows, hinged along the forward edge

most of these were the sharp-angled type with embossed decoration and strengthening beading around the edge. On the Cord, the new De Soto and Dodge lines, the visors had an extremely sharp, deep drop which kept them close to the corner pillar. A fair proportion of cars used a hooded visor of medium angle, and an equally large group had no exterior visors. Some of these provided adjustable interior glareshields, generally made of plywood or covered with the lining fabric. Open-sided visors with colored glareproof glass were noted on the Lincoln and the Graham Special Eight. New bonnet louvers, have been adopted by Durant and Franklin who arranged their louvers horizontally, *en echelon*, Durant using a lance-head shape and Franklin the "Pirate" louvers introduced a year ago by Dietrich in a custom design for this chassis, retained in modified form for some of the Franklin bodies. The Graham, Hudson, and Peerless cars have followed Packard in adopting door-type ventilators on the bonnet.

OPEN CARS AND CONVERTIBLES

There was a fair proportion of open cars and convertible models, the latter type including both sedans and coupes. Roadsters outnumbered the phaetons 2:1, and had deck seats except in one or two instances where a tapering tail was used, as on the interesting Packard Speedster runabout. In place of the usual rumble there was a luggage compartment with a triangular deck lid, corresponding to the horizontal section of the tail. Considerable attention had been given to the design of the rear of this body which had aprons covering the chassis

and other units. A number of roadsters had 2-leaf deck openings instead of the more common single type. A Chrysler Imperial roadster of Locke design had a door on the right side for easy access to the rumble and used a 2-leaf opening, the forward leaf having glasses inserted so that it might serve not only as a windshield, but also to provide direct forward vision for these passengers.

SUBDUED COLORS FOR CLOSED CARS

Colors of the closed cars were more subdued than at any recent show. Many cars were finished entirely in black or in a single color. Contrasting color combinations were comparatively rare, chromatic sequence being more generally employed in duotone effects. Bright colors seemed reserved for the open cars where free play of color was generally to be found, although black was popular in this group. The surprising feature of this year's show was the return to black, more cars being so painted than at any time since the introduction of lacquer. The black cars far outnumbered (nearly double) those of any single color. Green was next in popularity, followed by blue, the maroons and the browns, which were about equally patronized. Gray enjoyed a moderate popularity, but the ivory-to-yellow group was slimly represented. One coupe was finished in aluminum, and several cars used this as the trimming color—executed rather crudely in one or two instances. However, the painting generally was of high order.

The Jordan "Speedway" roadster with door and deck panel opened to receive passengers for the deck seat. Note the right front seat both folds and slides forward; the hinged deck panel then gives ample passage to the rumble. The seats are trimmed in black leather piped with ivory leather, reversing the colors of the exterior. A folding armrest is provided between the front seats

Among the open and convertible cars, the color popularity differed, black, brown and grays being in the lead followed by green and blue. Most other colors, such as maroon, terra cotta, orange, ivory and aluminum were represented by a single car. Generally, but not universally, these open cars were painted in a single color with contrasting molding and wheels. The Chrysler open cars, with contrasting color in the concave moldings, were particularly effective.

STRIPING ASSUMES DEFINITE TREND

Striping for the first time in several years assumed a definite trend. Belt moldings generally carried two stripes, placed near the edges. A few cars used distant stripes and still fewer a single stripe in the center of

Two interesting Jordan exhibits with bodies by the Facto Auto Body Co. These striking designs put some of the old vim and vigor into the Jordan line which has been of indifferent character for several seasons. Note the sweeping lines, slat-type horizontal bonnet louvers, airfoil running boards unconnected to the fenders, and the downward sweep of the forward part of the fenders. The Woodlite headlamps and other fitments were also unusual. Interior views of the sedan are shown below. On the opposite page is another view of the roadster which presents an interesting solution for access to the deck seat

the molding. About half of the cars had striping around the windows and a moderate number striped the windows as a group. The tendency to make the reveals frame the windows collectively rather than singly was exemplified in the new Marmon 79 sedan, illustrated last month. Individual window reveals in contrasting colors were not so much used as heretofore; some cars, which had as many as three offsets from window to belt, painted these in the body color and depended merely on the high lights for the effect. The Castagna-Mercedes sedan and berline had belts about 2½ in. wide; running along the center was a small geometric decoration, apparently a transfer in the case of the berline. The belt of the sedan was of polished aluminum and in this instance the central geometric decoration appeared to have been etched and painted. Striping was omitted entirely on a number of bodies. Several bodies on the du Pont stand, a gray sedan and the all-black sporting phaeton, were without striping. There was no striping on the Le Baron sedan on Stutz chassis, the completely green car being relieved only by a small chromium-plated molding that encircled the body. A similar effect was to be noted on some Weymann bodies, though others had neither molding nor striping. An aluminum-finished Marmon coupe was set off with black moldings that were also without striping.

Light-colored fabric tops did not seem so popular for closed cars as heretofore, only nine of this type being observed. The majority had coated-fabric decking, usually with landau grain. Side roof panels were generally of metal, but a number of cars returned to the coated-fabric panel. An extremely neat side roof panel of fabric was to be noted on the Chevrolet club sedan, which has a soft rear; the coated fabric was carried forward, without joint at the quarter, to make the side roof panel, giving an attractive clean-cut effect. The landau grain was horizontal, instead of in the traditional vertical direction, but probably few moderns will notice this.

UPHOLSTERY FABRICS

Mohair continued to be the chief upholstering material, but it appeared to have lost ground. Slightly less than half the cars were trimmed with this material. The quality of the mohair also retrograded, the proportion of other fibers, such as cotton, wool and rayon, being notably high in the trimming of the cheaper cars. In medium- and high-priced cars broadcloths, bedford cords and other wool fabrics have replaced mohair to a considerable extent. Nearly as many cars were upholstered with this group of materials as with mohair. There was a moderate use of

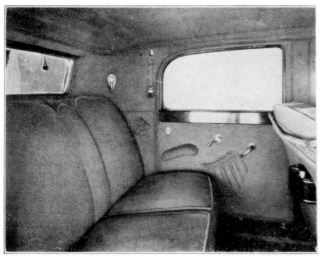

The interior of the Jordan Speedway sedan presents numerous novelties to supplement the striking effect of the exterior design. Passengers are seated forward of the rear axle and side armrests are placed on the doors of both compartments. Note the angle, suggestive of speed, at which the pockets and door fitments are placed. A smaller shirred pocket was set at a complementary angle on the quarter panel. Seats are trimmed in plain broadcloth piped with a matching, but striking, "cut" lace or beading which was also used to outline the doors, and in double form, at the junction of the wall and ceiling. Sconce-type corner lights were used, but no domelight. The plain rectangular door frieze had a transfer or marquetry medallion in the center, and a strip of broadlace was placed across the front seatback, beneath which the combined smoking-and-vanity case was mounted.

plain, printed and cut velours in the low-priced cars. A few cars were trimmed with straight rayon fabrics and several with wool-and-rayon cloths, the brilliant rayon being used in small designs to enliven the wool background; a particular effective interior with such material was to be found in the Waterhouse sedan on du Pont chassis. Leather was sparingly used except in its established positions in open and convertible cars and in the front compartment of chauffeur-driven types. Its position in the convertibles is being sharply contested by bedford cord.

BUTTONED PLAITS MOST POPULAR

Buttoned plaits were the most popular style of up-holstering, closely followed by plain plaits. Wide plaits were considerably used and were sometimes 6 to 8 in.

lined by unusually wide stitching which gave a pleasing effect on the plain mohair plush of the panel. Flap pockets were occasionally observed, usually on the higher grade cars. Many of these features will be noted in the interior views presented in this issue.

INTERIOR FITMENTS

The tendency in interiors continued to be toward the use of modern-art motifs, although the higher priced cars held aloof from this type of decoration. In the Waterhouse-du Pont sedan the fitments were in satin finish, but without decoration. Metal loops have been revived for door pulls, but some cars have door pulls pressed into the garnish rail or attached thereto. On several of the higher priced cars door pulls were carved into the walnut rails. Remote-control handles

The interior of the Cord sedan was interesting for its comfort and simplicity and the convenient placing of fitments. The seats were trimmed with a pin-striped De Luxe broadcloth done in buttoned plaits. Because of the flat chassis, the rear seat was made unusually deep and comfortable. Armrests were built up straight from the seat cushion and on top a flat squab was rolled over the front, a method that was used in several other cars. There was a strip of broadlace across the doors in place of a wood frieze. Open-face Metalcraft ash receivers were positioned in each armrest and in the front of the right armrest was a Casco lighter. Corner lights were of the sconce type and the new 4-cord toggles were used. Lace-covered beading was employed around ceiling, seat frame, armrests, doors and on the curve of the front-seat cushion

wide. About 20 per cent of the closed cars were trimmed in the plain-stretched style with the seat divisions piped, generally with the fabric or with a lace-covered beading. Leather piping was not used as much as it was in the Salons. Lace-covered beading was extensively used, frequently at the junction of ceiling and walls, and to make a panel in the ceiling, on the curved ends of front-seat cushions, and around door panels. The buttoned plaits in some instances were tightly drawn on the cushion so as to provide a flat rear section and a rising forward section somewhat after the manner of the Weymann "anatomical" seating, although in the latter the flat rear portion is not plaited.

DOOR PANELS

Door panels were generally simple, outlined merely by stitching, beading or an embossed center panel. Door friezes, either of genuine wood or the enameled-metal forms, were considerably used, but there was another school that omitted any decoration under the garnish rail; on a few cars a strip of broadlace replaced the frieze. On several Packard cars, there was a central plaited panel surrounded by lace-covered beading. On the Castagna-Mercedes sedan, a bottom-hinged flap pocket was used and across the panel was a series of diamond-shaped tufts, which also appeared on the backs and cushions of this car. Sometimes door fitments were set off in a separate beaded panel, as will be noted in the illustration of the Peerless Custom Eight sedan. Shirred pockets were generally placed on doors, but in several sedans they were positioned on the front seatback. In an interesting Kissel sedan the shirred pocket was recessed into a door panel out-

continued to be mounted on rear doors at a variety of angles; some operated in a forward direction and others in the opposite direction. Most of them were installed at an angle of about 45 deg. and on being pulled aft, lock the door; to unlatch the door it is necessary for the passenger, when in an awkward half-standing position, to push forward. Some cars adopted the plan of the taxicab makers and placed the handle in an upright position, but operative in the same direction as before. Checker cabs, which have been leaders in taxicab developments in recent years, had the handle mounted to operate in exactly the opposite direction; when the passenger takes hold of the handle to lift himself from the seat he unlatches the door in the same movement and is thus not in a forward-pitching position when trying to unlatch the door. Fitment knobs of "composition ivory" were installed by Packard and one or two other makers. Bronze hardware was used on a number of cars, but bright- or satin-finished silver was the rule.

ASH RECEIVERS ON BOTH SIDES

Companion cases in the better grade cars were sometimes recessed into the rear quarters, and occasionally enclosed. In the Packard Speedster sedan, the companion cases were set in the armrests and provided with a flap covered with the seat fabric and held, when not in use, by a snap fastener. This places the cases where they are ready for use, keeps out a large amount of dust and leaves the armrest as usable as ever. The positioning of ash receives this year takes cognizance of the fact that smoking is more or less universal. Numerous cars provided ash receivers on both sides.

Chicago Salon *Opens Show Season*

Owner-Driven and Sport Models Present Interesting Variations; Little Change in Formal Cars

ALTHOUGH changes in formal cars are chiefly in betterment of details, numerous interesting variations will be found in the aspects of owner-driven and sport cars which custom body builders will exhibit next week in the first of the official Automobile Salons. This annual exhibition of *automobiles de luxe* will be held in the Hotel Drake, Chicago, Nov. 8-15, and will be succeeded by the New York Salon, which opens on the last day of the month and continues through the first week of December, at the Hotel Commodore. In accordance with recent custom, the exhibition will be repeated on the Pacific Coast during February, at Los Angeles and San Francisco.

Some idea of the changes in the new custom cars will be obtained from accompanying illustrations and descriptions, which represent scheduled exhibits and of course, are subject to last-minute changes. Nevertheless, an approximate picture of the exhibition is ob-

TRENDS IN THE CUSTOM CARS

Before describing the exhibits in detail, it may be interesting to consider briefly some of the changing trends that are represented in the present illustrations: Noticeable among these luxury cars is the high proportion having narrow front-corner pillars, thereby eliminating the "blind spot" in driving. Visorless sloping fronts are numerous. Stationary setting of the windshield glass, though still rare, is increasing. Slanting V-type windshields continue in vogue here, contrary to the European trend. Front-door pillars often continue down on the rakish slant of the windshields, facilitating entrance to the driver's seat. The curved "coach" sill is popular, though not general. Weymann bodies will be shown this year in both the metal-paneled and the fabric-paneled types. Large trunks have definitely arrived. More sweeping tails and "designed rears" are also in evidence. Many convertible bodies are being

Dietrich, Inc., presents this interesting 4-passenger sedan on Packard chassis. It has many of the new lines of the current vogue, without being too radical for conservative tastes. Note the sloping visorless front, the narrow corner posts and the curve of the doors harmonizing with the lines of the coach sill. The two wide doors are hinged on the same pillar—a steel tee—with only two combination hinges which, with their secure foundation, are sufficient to keep the doors properly aligned

tainable from the advance data received from body builders and car manufacturers. The list of exhibitors follows, the names of the chassis on which the bodies are mounted being given in italics:

THE EXHIBITORS

Brunn (*Duesenberg, Franklin, Lincoln, Pierce-Arrow, Stutz*) ; Cunningham (*Cunningham*) ; Derham (*Duesenberg, Franklin, Lincoln, Packard*) ; Dietrich, Inc., (*Lincoln, Packard, Pierce-Arrow*) ; Raymond H. Dietrich (*Franklin*) ; Fisher (*Cadillac, La Salle*) ; Fleetwood (*Cadillac*) ; Judkins (*Duesenberg, Lincoln, Pierce-Arrow*) ; La Grande (*Cord, Duesenberg*) ; Le-Baron (*Chrysler, Lincoln, Marmon, Packard, Pierce-Arrow, Stutz*) ; Locke (*Chrysler, Duesenberg, Lincoln, Marmon*) ; Murphy (*Cord, Duesenberg*) ; Packard (*Packard*) ; Rolls-Royce and Brewster (*Rolls-Royce*) ; Rollston (*Duesenberg, Packard*) ; Walker (*Franklin*) ; Waterhouse (*Chrysler*) ; Weymann (*Duesenberg, Marmon, Stutz*) ; Willoughby (*Duesenberg, Pierce-Arrow, Lincoln*).

exhibited this year, convertible coupes predominating. A modified form of convertible coupe introduced last year is becoming popular under the designation of "convertible roadster"; this has a lighter superstructure than the usual coupe and the top folds exceedingly flat or is recessed into the body so that the passengers in the rumble are not cut off from the others. Most custom-built convertible coupes now provide for four, or five, passengers within the enclosure. Convertible sedans have been improved in detail and one "semi-convertible" sedan has a fixed top, but removable center pillar so that the body may be completely open at the sides. Greater use of stainless-steel and chromium-plated metal trim is in evidence, these materials being found inside, as well as outside.

Modern-art motifs, which have been used in the interior for several years, are beginning to find application to the exterior treatment; this is observable in the numerous bright-metal effects and in the use of simple contours depending on light and shade for decoration and omitting the stereotyped moldings. In the formal cars this influence is not much felt. These have adhered

Roadster with disappearing top, by Locke, on Lincoln chassis. The top folds into a recess behind the seat, the deck panel being lifted to receive it. Finished in black, with gray stripe. The doors, as well as the seats, are plaited with Eagle-Ottawa gray veal-skin leather

A sport roadster by Le Baron on Chrysler "Imperial" c h a s s i s. The slanted V-type windshield is unusual for an open job. A sloping door line gives a smart appearance and facilitates en-

trance. Seats are trimmed with Calflyke leather in narrow European plaits. A roll running completely around the doors and cowl gives the appearance of an airplane cockpit

closely to the classic treatment depending on detailed betterments, rather than striking changes. As practically all town cars now have the all-weather front, considerable attention has been given to preserving the roof contour and to the neat fitting and stowing of the driver's canopy. In several instances, detachable "limousine roof" sections are provided so that, during the period of inclement weather, these cars present the appearance of an enclosed limousine; an emergency driver's canopy is also supplied to take care of sudden storms. Another town car presents a modification of the rolled reveal for the windows and at least one limousine will have chromium-plated moldings, in consonance with the application of such moldings to formal cars abroad.

Some Interior Changes

Interiors of the town cars remain conservative for the most part, but numerous novelties are embodied in owner-driven and sport models. Some of these represent only the individual designer's preference, but may lead to a general adoption. In the sport cars, the rear

seats are now often placed ahead of the axle, and foot wells are becoming more numerous. Occasionally a combination of leather and fabric is used for the seats. In one instance, the main squab is of fabric and the leg and head rolls are of leather. In another—and this a formal car—the down-filled cushions are faced with broadcloth on one side and with soft imported goat skins on the reverse side, thus giving the option of leather or cloth seats in all seasons. Front seats are almost invariably adjustable, and this feature is being applied occasionally to the rear seat. This year, there is to be noted a greater variety of woods—sometimes tinted to accentuate or harmonize with the color scheme. Plaited door trim or other modification of the generally plain treatment will be seen in several sport cars. Door treatment of the formal cars is generally limited to geometric stitching or beading under a plain garnish rail or a wide belt panel, simply inlaid, but elaborate cabinetwork and some marquetry are being used by two or three builders. Companion cases are sometimes built into armrests or recessed into the rear quarters. Ash

This sport convertible coupe on Rolls-Royce chassis was designed by Brewster for the "younger generation." It is suggestive of speed and dash. The wide door is occasioned by the peculiar shape of the window,

complementing at the rear the angle of the windshield. A single deck seat is provided in the rounded boat-type rear. The New York job is being brought through in the interesting gunmetal finish

This convertible roadster by LeBaron, Inc., on Packard chassis has a new type of close-folding top. It partially disappears in a recess behind the driving seat and gives an exceptionally low, clean line. The slanting door conforming to the inclination of the windshield gives easy entrance. There is a deck seat, and a folding trunk rack at the rear

Convertible Coupes and Sedans at the Chicago Salon

This convertible coupe by Brunn on Franklin chassis with large trunk at rear is suggestive of the European fashions. The effect is further emphasized by the belt treatment with the special recessed panel on the door. Ti'bury Tan is used for the body color; moldings are in Dixie Brown, with two fine lines of Mustard Yellow striping. Interior wood trim is of natural-finished zebra wood and the specially designed bronze hardware was executed by Sterling. Seats and walls are trimmed with Lackawanna top-grain leather

LeBaron convertible victoria on the Pierce-Arrow A chassis. This seats five passengers forward of the rear axle and is finished in two shades of maroon, with vermilion striping. The slanting windshield and the metal trunk of unusual capacity conforming to the body lines give the car a smart appearance

A "sportsman's coupe," of distinctly modern trend, is mounted by Locke on Marmon chassis. It is finished in Valentine's Morocco Maroon, with elbow rail in Burmah Rose. The fabric top is Aerial Teal and an imported English maroon leather is used for the interior. The pillar between the door and quarter lights folds down over the latter, leaving the body side entirely open when the quarter light is lowered

A convertible 4-passenger sedan by Le-Baron on Packard chassis. This converts to a phaeton of genuine open-car smartness, the swept quarter panels and close-folding top retaining the streamlining of the forward portion of the car. All four seats are of the bucket type and are trimmed with veal-finished steer hide of a russet-tan shade, done in tufts and plaits

Locke presents this dashing modernistic design for a convertible sedan on Chrysler chassis. It is without moldings and depends on its contours and high lights for its appeal, suggesting the newer trend in custom bodies. The painting is equally spirited, being in Ditzler's Henna, with the chassis and under side of the fenders in du Pont Primrose Yellow; these colors are repeated on the cabinet in the front seatback. Seats have combination leather-and-fabric trim

receptacles on both sides of the cars, and a wireless lighter on the master's side, are now general.

The following summary has been made up from advance data received concerning the various exhibits:

BRUNN & CO.

On Franklin chassis, Brunn will exhibit a "sportsman's cabriolet"; this is a convertible coupe seating four passengers comfortably within the enclosure, all on individual seats; the rear seats fold up to allow increased carrying space for baggage, although there is a capacious Berg-Winship trunk at the rear, in accordance with the current fashion. The car is finished in Tilbury Tan, with moldings in Dixie Brown, striped with two fine lines of Mustard Yellow; a recessed panel in the

An interesting 4-passenger coupe by Brunn on Pierce-Arrow chassis. It is finished entirely in black, with gray striping, the top material being a special imported gray leather of fabric grain. All passengers ride forward of the rear axle, a large trunk of special trim being mounted at the rear. Seats and lower body panels are trimmed with gray leather, but an imported French gray cloth is used above the belt

door-belt molding is painted in the body color. The interior is trimmed with a Lackawanna leather on both seats and walls. Garnish rails are in natural finish zebra-wood and the hardware is of special Brunn design executed in bronze by Sterling.

On Lincoln chassis, Brunn shows an all-weather brougham and a "semi-collapsible cabriolet." The latter is entirely finished in Valentine's Royal Agate Green; the top leather and that for the driving seat is Thistle Green. The rear compartment is upholstered in a Wiese Palmetto Green broadcloth. The nickel-plated hardware is the special Lincoln design. The other town car is of the severely formal type, finished in two shades of Pilot Blue, with the Radel top leather of the same color. The driving compartment is trimmed with Eagle-Ottawa top-grain leather and the passenger compartment in a De Luxe broadcloth.

On Pierce-Arrow chassis, Brunn exhibits an all-weather "town landaulet" and a 7-passenger limousine. The latter is finished in Mulberry Maroon and black with carmine striping. This body is noteworthy for its headroom, being 50 in. from floor to center bow. The front compartment is trimmed in Eagle-Ottawa morocco-grain black leather; the rear is done in a French bedford cord specially imported by the body builder. The garnish moldings are of mahogany and the bronze-finish hardware of modern design was executed by Sterling. The all-weather landaulet has a V-type slanting windshield and is noteworthy for maintaining perfectly the roof contour at the junction of the driver's canopy and the permanent roof; when not in use, the canopy is concealed in a neat paneled compartment over the division window. An attractive feature of this job is the swept rear, with embossed center line, which was introduced by Brunn at a previous Salon. This body is finished in Thorne and Dixie Brown, and the top leather is a specially imported beige-colored French leather with "finger-print" grain. The passenger compartment is trimmed with a light-tan Wiese hairline broadcloth. The hardware is of special Brunn design in Sterling bronze.

On Stutz chassis, Brunn is showing a "sport cabriolet"—an all-weather-front, semi-collapsible model—finished in blue and striped with a lighter blue. The front compartment is trimmed in black leather and the passenger compartment in a powder-blue De Luxe broadcloth. The hardware is of special design in butler finish and the wood trim is of India satinwood.

Cunningham will exhibit their cars as usual with their own coachwork, of which no details have been received.

DERHAM

In the Derham stand one of the interesting bodies will be a Duesenberg phaeton in an extremely low and sporting design. The windshield is installed at a rakish angle which is repeated in a special tonneau windshield operated by a regulator through a short stationary cowl. The body is finished in Primrose Yellow with fenders, moldings and top bows in Verdancia Green; the latter color is also used for the striping over and under the molding and on the bonnet louvers. The trimming leather is a Lackawanna morocco-grain finished in Verdancia Green, and the top is a Haartz fabric bound with the same leather. A large trunk at the rear completes the sporting effect. The treatment of the tonneau interior is unusual, having a green rubber-tile floor bound with chrome-plated moldings. Chrome-plated fitments and belt panels are also used in this interior.

On Franklin chassis Derham will have a special 4-passenger coupe of "coach design." This has a coupe-pillar effect and paint treatment segregating the passenger section from the rest of the car. An ovaled quarter window and specially rounded back also add to the distinctive appearance of the car. The trunk at the rear carries out the contour of the back. The coupe pillar and lower panels of the "coach" section are finished in Washington Blue, the window reveals being in Orville Blue. The bonnet, cowl, moldings and upperworks are in Briarcliff Beige, as is also the roof leather. Passengers are all carried on individual seats, the rear seats folding to provide increased luggage space when desired. Seats are trimmed in Colonial-grain leather and the rest of the interior is in a Wiese blue-and-gold "heathertone" broadcloth.

Derham has two other jobs that depart from the conventional. One is a "semi-convertible" sedan on Packard chassis and the other a convertible phaeton of the Hibbard & Darrin type on Lincoln chassis. The Packard sedan differs from the usual collapsible sedan, which it resembles in appearance, by having a stationary roof which is almost as low as the conventional roadster. It is close coupled, but by means of a depressed floor the rear seat is located forward of the axle. The center pillar has a double hinge permitting it to be folded into a compartment in the tonneau, and the door windows, in chromium-plated frames, are lowered by regulators; this gives an unusually low and light car completely open at the sides and having the appearance of a phaeton. It is finished in two shades of brown and has a Haartz fabric top of corresponding shade. The seats are trimmed with Devon-grain leather, the wall and head lining being a Wiese doeskin. A metal trunk at the rear is finished in the body color. The Lincoln convertible phaeton is painted in Dustproof Gray and has moldings of Lorelei Green; the top is a fine-weave Burbank and the seats are trimmed in Eagle-Ottawa top-grain leather.

DIETRICH, INC.

Dietrich, Inc., has developed an interesting 4-passenger "club sedan" which gives to the Packard a new allure, without departing from the conventional so far as to repel conservative buyers. It has the new sloping visorless front, Campbell clear-vision corner posts, a coach sill, doors hung by only two combination hinges attached to a T-iron center pillar, door bottoms curved to harmonize with the curved sill and contrasting pleasantly with the angular lines of the Packard radiator and bonnet.

The other Dietrich exhibit will be a convertible sedan on the new Pierce-Arrow "A" chassis; it follows closely the convertible model that this firm has specialized in for several years.

RAYMOND H. DIETRICH

Raymond H. Dietrich has designed for Franklin two bodies of new and refreshing lines, with respect to contour and molding treatment. They have the new sloping, visorless front with rounded header, and a well rounded roof and back. The sedan has a swept rear harmonizing with the fender line, while the coupe has a specially designed trunk supplementing the contour of the body. Besides the unusual contours, the molding treatment departs from the conventional by omitting the customary through molding widened at the belt. Instead, the bonnet molding is swept up the windshield

The interior is trimmed with a Wiese tan doeskin and a harmonizing glove-finish leather.

FISHER-FLEETWOOD

Fisher Body Corporation, and the Fleetwood division thereof, will both exhibit exclusively on chassis of Cadillac production. Fisher will have bodies mounted on Cadillac and La Salle chassis and Fleetwood will show eight of its creations on the Cadillac V-8, V-12 and V-16. Details of these bodies are not yet released.

JUDKINS

Two bodies on Lincoln chassis, a 5-passenger berline on Duesenberg and a 7-passenger enclosed limousine on Pierce-Arrow chassis will constitute the exhibit of the J. B. Judkins Co. The Lincoln bodies will be a 2-passenger coupe and a 5/6-passenger berline intended for either owner or chauffeur driving. In both jobs a single-angle front pillar and sloping windshield assures clear vision and freedom from back reflections; the front pillar is so located as to give an unusual amount of entrance room. The berline is finished in two shades of green and the interior is entirely trimmed with a Wiese bedford cord of Forest Green shade. The sixth passenger in this body is accommodated on the single auxiliary seat on the left side, facing the curb. The Lincoln coupe is finished in Ravenswood Brown and trimmed with a Wiese broadcloth of harmonizing shade. There is package space back of the adjustable driving seat and a commodious luggage space in the tail access to which is by a counterweighted deck lid or by the small golf-club door on the curb side.

The Duesenberg berline by Judkins is of the sedan-berline type, the channels for the division glass being concealed by flaps so as to give the appearance of a sedan when the owner is driving. Though a compact body intended for five passengers, there are two opera-type auxiliary seats recessed into the division. The body is finished in two shades of blue, and has a harmonizing interior with cabinetwork of bluish tint and an

Derham has developed this "semi-convertible" sedan, with disappearing center pillar, for Packard chassis. The center pillar folds into a compartment in the tonneau and with the chromium-framed windows lowered, the passengers have all the air of a phaeton with California top. This gives a light, low car with complete weather protection. The rear seat is forward of the axle, permitting a large trunk at the rear

pillar, continues unbroken over the windows, down to the belt at the rear quarter and then encircles the back of the body. Replacing the customary widened belt is a simple half-round molding on the door, just above the door handle; on the sedan this molding extends across the center pillar, and on both jobs the molding ends a few inches short of joining the other molding at either the front or rear quarter. This sedan was built by Walker and is displayed in the Walker stand. The Franklin sedan exhibited by Raymond H. Dietrich is known as the "Tandem" sedan. It is a 4-door sport body with V-type sloping windshield and an angular rear, showing some characteristics of the old Brewster broughams. The front-door pillars follow the slope of the windshield, but are swept rearwood at the bottom.

unusual combination of fabric and leather upholstery matching the body color. The front- and rear-seat cushions and backs are down-filled, reversible cushions with one face of morocco goat skins and the other of a Wiese Cadet Blue broadcloth, thus affording the owner a constant option of leather or cloth seats. The bluish frieze on the doors is continued under the quarter windows where companion cases are provided. The same fine-grained wood of bluish tint is used for the division cabinet, where a refreshment compartment is fitted between the panels concealing the auxiliary seats.

The Pierce-Arrow 7-passenger enclosed limousine by Judkins is finished in Sybarite Maroon on the lower body panels and window reveals, the remainder of the car being in black. The rear and auxiliary seats are trimmed in a henna "heathertone" Channel bedford cord and for the walls and headlining, a Wiese henna broadcloth. The driving seat and the front compartment below the belt are trimmed with Eagle-Ottawa Tiffany-grain leather; above the belt the henna broadcloth is again used.

LA GRANDE

La Grande's victoria coupe on the Cord front-drive chassis will have an effective color scheme, with the lower body panels and window reveals in a light brown, the remainder of the body being in Capucine, dark; this combination is set off by flame-colored striping. The flame color is also used for the chassis. Seats are trimmed with a maroon broadcloth, a fawn cloth being

giving an unobtrusive but new effect. The passenger compartment is trimmed with a Wiese powder-blue doeskin and seats five passengers, two of whom are on side- and back-facing auxiliary seats.

LOCKE

The Locke exhibit will comprise four bodies noteworthy for their individuality and departure from stereotyped models. One of these will be a landaulet on Duesenberg chassis with an unusual molding treatment, introducing a chrome-plated molding on formal cars, in accordance with the European vogue; this is not a through molding, but is used only on the doors and is so placed that it appears to join the curved door handles and create an unusual design. On the sta-

La Grande's victoria coupe for Cord front-drive chassis. The wide door conforms to the slant of the windshield pillar and provides easy entrance. The body is finished in two tones of Capucine, with the chassis and striping flame red. The interior is done in a 2-color combination, maroon broadcloth being used for the seats, the side walls and head lining being of fawn broadcloth

used on the walls. A coupe on Duesenberg chassis will be upholstered with a Wiese fawn shadow-striped broadcloth and lined with a plain broadcloth of the same color.

LE BARON

The Le Baron exhibit will be noteworthy for its examples of convertible bodies of quite different aspects, as well as its formal coachwork. It will also have two interesting open cars on Chrysler chassis, a sport roadster and a sport phaeton, both of which will have slanting V-type windshields—rather unusual for open cars—slanting front-door line facilitating access to the driving seat and low-folding tops that do not break the streamline flow. They are trimmed with Calflyke leather in the European manner, with narrow plaits and a roll running completely around the top of the doors and cowl in aeroplane-cockpit style; the phaeton has tonneau-cowling built into the general streamline of the body and a smart folding secondary windshield.

Two "convertible roadsters" by Le Baron on Packard and Lincoln chassis have lighter superstructures than the usual convertible coupes, and the tops, when folded, are recessed or lie close to the body with the normal appearance of a roadster, and do not "cut off" the rumble passengers as on some convertible coupes.

The Le Baron convertible victoria on Pierce-Arrow chassis seats five passengers inside, forward of the axle, and has a large trunk at the rear conforming to the body lines. The convertible 4-passenger sedan on 145½-in. Packard chassis has the body panels swept at the rear quarters to permit the top to fold on a line with the elbow rail, thus giving the normal appearance of a phaeton when used as an open car. Le Baron will exhibit a cabriolet-type town car, with V-type windshield and all-weather front, on Lincoln chassis and possibly another town car on a Chrysler. The Lincoln town car is distinctly formal in appearance; the molding treatment is simple, the bonnet molding tapering on the cowl to a medium width belt and being swept at the rear quarter to a narrow encircling molding at the back. A distinguishing feature is the "rolled" window reveals

tionary part of the roof there is a removable chromium-plated baggage rack; other chromium-plated items include the window channels, the cowl band, wire wheels, head lamps, etc. The body is finished in Valentine's Brewster Green, dark, a lighter shade being used for the upperworks and for the other body moldings. The front door line follows the inclination of the sloping V-type windshield, but is swept backward as it approaches the base molding. In addition to the customary canopy over the driving compartment there is provided a solid detachable roof section permitting the body to be dissembled as an enclosed limousine—the head fittings for the landaulet section are not exposed. The door friezes and division cabinet of natural Circassian walnut are by the Hayden Co., a new entrant into this field though well known for its fine furniture and other cabinetwork.

One of the advanced jobs on the Locke stand is the convertible sedan on Chrysler chassis. This is done in the modern manner relying entirely on the light and shade of the contours and omitting the stereotyped molding treatment. The body, fenders and splashers are painted in Ditzler's Henna; the chassis and underside of the fenders are in du Pont's Primrose Yellow. The top material is a double-coated Burbank. The interior is trimmed with a combination of fabric and leather; a coral-tan-and-gray-mixture De Luxe broadcloth is used for the seat cushions and backs and for the plaited centers of the door panels; the seats and backs have leg and head rolls of Eagle-Ottawa veal-finish light-brown leather, which is also used as a roll border for the door panels. The cabinet of the front seatback receives the center pillars, when not in use, and also has space for two thermos bottles. The cabinet is painted in the body color and the doors have imitation canework in Primrose Yellow.

On Marmon chassis Locke will show a "sportman's coupe," a 5-passenger convertible with quarter light. It is finished in Valentine's Morocco Maroon trimmed with Burmah Rose. The top is of Aerial Teal and the large trunk over the fuel tank is covered with the same material. Wheels are chromium plated. The interior is trimmed with an imported English maroon leather. The other Locke exhibit will be a Lincoln roadster, with disappearing top which is concealed under a hinged deck panel. This is similar to the model shown last year. It is finished in black, with a light-gray stripe. The interior is trimmed with Eagle-Ottawa veal-skin leather done in the plaited style; the door panels are also plaited to harmonize with the seat trimming.

No details were received of the Murphy exhibits though it is understood that these will be mounted on Cord and Duesenberg chassis.

PACKARD

Besides the bodies exhibited on Packard chassis by various custom coachbuilders, the Packard company will exhibit three bodies from its own custom department. Details of the finish and trim are not determined at this writing but the body types will include a convertible victoria, a sedan with sloping, visorless front and swept tail, and a landaulet with quarter window and transformable front.

ROLLS-ROYCE AND BREWSTER

Rolls-Royce has scheduled four cars, with coachwork by Brewster, for its Chicago exhibit: A Newmarket, a 4-passenger convertible sedan, will be finished in the handsome gunmetal lacquer introduced by Brewster in a previous Salon; the wheel disks will be in this finish with raised circular moldings in carmine; the belt line will be marked by a narrow molding of the same color, and carmine Velveau leather will be used for the upholstering. The Huntington, a 7-passenger enclosed limousine, will be finished in Oxford Blue with black trim. The passenger compartment will have tan "heathertone" upholstery, a harmonizing rug and lap-robe, damascened bronze hardware with tan inlay and Karolith knobs matching the mahogany of the marquetry panels. The St. Andrew, a 7-passenger town car

superstructure and Katonah Brown striping. The top leather will be of turtle grain and the driving seat will have morocco grain; the passenger compartment is trimmed with a De Luxe broadcloth. The other town car is on a Duesenberg chassis and has a straight V-type windshield. The interior trimming is similar to the Packard, but will have elaborate cabinetwork of walnut marquetry. Opera-type auxiliary seats are recessed into the division. The body is finished in Normandy Blue and black, with ivory striping.

WALKER

The Walker exhibits will be mounted on Franklin chassis. Details have been received for three bodies: A sport sedan and a town car designed by Raymond H. Dietrich and a Walker-designed and -built sedan. The last is arranged for five passengers and upholstered with a Wiese patterned broadcloth, the walls being of a plain matching broadcloth in sage color. The sport sedan has a sloping windshield, rounded header and swept tail; the moldings on this job are similar to those of the Dietrich coupe, but the base molding which extends over the rear fenders is widened across the tail which has a special door to receive luggage; the interior is trimmed with a Wiese sand-finish broadcloth, piped with leather harmonizing with the exterior colors. The town car is a glass-quarter brougham with facing-forward auxiliary seats and is trimmed with a silver-gray Wiese doeskin.

No information has been received concerning the Waterhouse exhibit, but it is understood that this will include a 4-passenger convertible coupe on the long-wheelbase Chrysler chassis.

WEYMANN

Weymann will exhibit both the new metal-paneled and standard fabric-paneled bodies. The metal-paneled job will be mounted on the 142-in. Duesenberg chassis. The main body panels will be painted black, but will

A sport sedan, produced in Packard's own custom-body department. It embodies the modern trend of sloping front with rounded header and a fully designed rear, permitting space for luggage in addition to a folding trunk rack

with all-weather front, is finished in two tones of brown with cream striping; the interior will be similar to that of the Huntington, but the upholstery is a brown broadcloth and the cabinetwork is of walnut with scroll inlay of a lighter wood. The other Rolls exhibit will be—if completed in time—a sporting convertible coupe with sloping windshield and complementary angle for the back edge of the door window and top; it will have a rounded boat-type rear with rumble seat for one; this job will be finished in Cairo Gray and Mojave Green; the fabric top will match the body color and the seats will be in Mojave Green Velveau leather.

ROLLSTON

Two cabriolet-type town cars will comprise the Rollston exhibit. One, with sloping windshield, will be mounted on the Packard 845 chassis and will be finished in Mountain Brown, dark, with black moldings and

have the fashionable chrome-plated belt and coupe-pillar moldings. The roof and rear quarters are covered with natural-color pigskin which is also used for covering the trunk at the rear. The seats are trimmed with Italian goat hides of a soft green shade and the headlining is a Wiese sea-green broadcloth. The door friezes and the panel under the windshield are in burl walnut and two cabinets of the same wood are recessed in the front seatbacks. On a Stutz chassis there will be a fabric-paneled 5-passenger sedan, known as the Versailles. The top and quarters are of Burbank but the other body panels are of pebble-grain fabric leather of light-green shade. The interior is trimmed with a Wiese slate-gray basketweave broadcloth. On a Marmon 136-in. chassis Weymann will mount another fabric-paneled body, the Longchamp design. This is paneled with fabric "enameled" with Ditzler's Town Car Blue, light. The belt moldings will be black, with carmine striping. The interior is trimmed with a soft-toned De Luxe broadcloth.

One of the interesting Willoughby exhibits will be the "limousine town car" on Pierce-Arrow chassis; this has the removable "limousine deck" introduced last year by Willoughby giving the car the exact appearance of

Willoughby. A standard-type limousine, and a square-cornered paneled brougham with coupe pillars will be shown on Lincoln chassis. The former is finished in two shades of Bolivian Calcite Gray, and will have a gray roof leather; the passenger compartment is trimmed in a Laidlaw gray bedford cord.

The Willoughby-Duesenberg limousine is finished in two new brown shades, and has a small raised oval

Chauffeur-Driven Cars by Brunn, Judkins and Willoughby

Brunn all-weather "town landaulet" on Pierce-Arrow chassis. This has the V-type slanting windshield, neat fitting "tendelet" and swept rear, characteristic of a body style introduced by Brunn at a previous Salon. It is finished in two shades of brown and the top is a beige-colored French leather having a special "finger-print" grain. The passenger seats are trimmed with a light-tan Wiese broadcloth with hairline stripe

Willoughby "limousine town car" for Pierce-Arrow chassis. A special, solid deck section is provided for the driving compartment during stormy weather; its perfect fit makes the car indistinguishable from an enclosed limousine. The customary emergency canopy is carried for the driving compartment, when the car is operated as a glass-quarter brougham. A special molding treatment marks the lower body

A berline by Judkins for Lincoln chassis. This body has narrow corner pillars and is finished in two shades of green. It is arranged for either owner or chauffeur driving, the upper portion of the division not being apparent when the glass is lowered. Both the driving and rear seat are trimmed with a Wiese bedford cord in Forest Green shade

This Willoughby-Duesenberg limousine is finished in two new brown shades. It has a wide belt, with special raised oval surrounding the base of the door handles. The driving seat is trimmed in brown leather, and the rear compartment in a Wiese doeskin. The rear seat is adjustable both as to cushion and back. Wood trim is of a special antique finish

an enclosed limousine during inclement weather, but providing town-car appearance for good-weather driving; in addition to the removable-deck section, a regular driver's canopy is supplied for emergency use. The body is finished in three shades of Vineyard Green and has the unusual molding treatment lately employed by

panel in the darker color which forms a setting for the door handles. The front compartment is trimmed with brown leather and the passenger compartment in a Wiese buff doeskin. Wood trim is of antique finish. A special feature of this body is the rear seat which is adjustable, both as to cushion and back.

Opening of 26th *Automobile Salon* New York Nov. 30

NEW exhibitors and new exhibits will be seen at the 26th Annual Automobile Salon, which opens in the Hotel Commodore on Sunday evening, Nov. 30. The New York Salon will thus have its own points of interest and will not be merely a repetition of the Chicago show. There will be three new exhibitors: Isotta-Fraschini and Minerva, with Italian and Belgian coachwork, and Merrimac Body Co., whose exhibit will be mounted on du Pont chassis. In addition, some of the body builders will show jobs not previously released, notable among which will be bodies on the new Lincoln chassis. The latter has a more powerful V-type, 8-cylinder engine, wider tread, lower frame, free-wheeling features, head and cowl lamps of new shape and an altered radiator shell having an embossed center section, or point, on the front face at the top.

The hours for the New York Salon have been slightly changed, the morning opening having been retarded to 11 o'clock; the week-day hours of the Salon are thus

with a Wiese doeskin. The exterior is finished in Raven Black with chrome striping. The other three exhibits will comprise: An enclosed limousine, finished in dark green; a 5-passenger enclosed drive for owner or chauffeur driving, finished in coach maroon and striped in vermilion, and a 7-passenger phaeton, finished in gray with striping in argent.

DIETRICH, INC.

Dietrich, Inc., will have in its New York exhibit a new 7-passenger convertible berline on Duesenberg chassis. The sloping windshield is V-shaped, but a straight division glass is used. The car is finished in two shades of Autumn Russet Brown and the top fabric is a light tan shade to harmonize with the paint and upholstery schemes. The seats will be trimmed with a figured broadcloth, but vealskin leather will be used for the door panels and side walls. The cabinetwork will include friezes on the division, doors and rear quarter.

Convertible Victoria with Semi-Disappearing Top

The vogue for semi-disappearing tops for convertible coupes has been extended to this 5-passenger victoria built by the Waterhouse Co. on 145-in. Packard chassis. Although the envelope shows, this top when folded does not actually project above the body

The finish of the Salon job differs from the 2-color effect shown. The body is painted entirely in black, with ivory striping on the moldings; the top is a light-gray Burbank

from 11 a. m. to 11 p. m. According to the latest list, the chassis to be exhibited at New York will include the following: Cadillac, Chrysler Imperial, Cord, Cunningham, Duesenberg, du Pont, Franklin, Isotta-Fraschini, La Salle, Lincoln, Marmon, Minerva, Packard, Pierce-Arrow, Rolls-Royce and Stutz. Coachwork exhibits will be made by Brewster, Brunn, Derham, Dietrich, Inc., Raymond H. Dietrich, Fisher, Fleetwood, Judkins, La Grande, Le Baron, Locke, Merrimac, Murphy, Rollston, Walker, Waterhouse and Willoughby. The following information has been received of exhibits that were not shown at Chicago:

CUNNINGHAM

All four cars in the Cunningham New York exhibit will differ from those at Chicago. One of the most interesting will be a cabriolet with interior cabinetwork of crotch mahogany, with simple gold inlay. The companion cases will be of similar materials and have glass covers. The hardware will be in platinum finish, with genuine horn mountings. Interior trimming is done

Being mounted on the 153½-in. chassis, the auxiliary seats are forward facing. Folding armrests are provided in the backs of both the front and rear seats.

JUDKINS

Two of the Judkins exhibits in New York will be on the new Lincoln chassis. One is a 2-passenger coupe, and the other a 5/6-passenger berline intended for either owner or chauffeur driving. Both have sloping windshields, narrow corner pillars and "undercut" doors providing easy entrance to the driving seat. The coupe is finished in Ravenswood Brown and is trimmed with a Wiese matching broadcloth; exceptionally large luggage space is provided in the swept tail. The berline has a "V" front and is finished in two shades of green; both compartments are trimmed with a Wiese bedford cord of Forest Green shade.

MARMON

Though the new Marmon Sixteen will not be formally announced until the National Automobile Show, it is being given a pre-showing in the Chicago and New

York Salons. This car has a wheelbase of 145 in. The all-aluminum engine is stated to be capable of 200 hp. and has the highest power-weight ratio of any car to date. The "sixteen" is shown in the Le Baron stand, the body having been built after designs by a New York artist, Walter Dorwin Teague.

ISOTTA-FRASCHINI

The Isotta-Fraschini stand will show four cars, with bodies by Castagna. One will be a close-coupled 4-passenger "sport touring" with a single door on each side; the belt rail on the driver's side is lowered to afford more arm space for the driver; running boards are pontoon shape and a luggage compartment is pro-

a red-and-gray combination; the interior is trimmed with Devon-grain leather. The other new model for the New York Salon will be a sport berline on Packard chassis. This has the light appearance of a convertible body. The rear seat is well forward of the axle and there is a large trunk at the rear. The top and quarters are of turtle-grain leather; body and chassis are finished in black, with ivory striping. Seats are trimmed with a Wiese tan bedford cord and the headlining is a matching broadcloth.

WATERHOUSE

The Waterhouse Co. will have two new exhibits in the New York Salon. One will be a 5-passenger con-

Willoughby Limousine on the New Lincoln Chassis

This 7-passenger limousine by the Willoughby Co. is mounted on the new Lincoln 145-in. chassis. It has a sloping windshield,

special corner-pillar construction and an interesting color treatment for the saddle and belt panel

vided in the tail; the car is finished in two tones of light blue, with black striping. A cabriolet, seating four passengers, is finished in Tuscan red and has a Burbank top. A 6-passenger landaulet, with all-weather front, is finished in dark blue with red striping and has a black leather top. Another landaulet is finished entirely in black, but has silver striping. The interiors of these town cars will be trimmed with plain fabrics, tan or beige, generally with a light tone for the headlining and a darker shade for the seats and doors; where the same color is used throughout, the seats will be trimmed with a fabric having hairline striping.

MINERVA

The Minerva exhibit will comprise four cars, which at this writing are in transit from Belgium. The bodies were all designed by Paul Ostruk and executed by Belgian carrossiers. They will present some interesting features in molding treatment and in the use of a patented sliding roof for the driving compartment of the town cars. If the cars arrive without damage, the exhibit will comprise: A cabriolet-type town car on the small 8-cylinder Minerva chassis; this body was built by the Carrosserie Van den Plas and has bright metal moldings and the Ostruk patented sliding roof already referred to; the interior is done in Louis XVI style with painted woodwork and brocade trimming. A larger cabriolet-type town car, constructed by Van den Plas, also has the Ostruk patented sliding roof; it seats 7 passengers and has forward-facing auxiliary seats. A glass-quarter brougham, with all-weather front, built by Van den Plas, has the sliding roof for the driving compartment and a new roof sweep at the rear. A 7-passenger enclosed limousine, constructed by D'Ieteren Frères, presents an interesting molding treatment.

ROLLSTON

On the Rollston stand in New York there will be two new jobs. One is a 4-passenger convertible coupe, on Duesenberg chassis, swept at the rear quarters to permit the top to fold level with the body rail; it is finished in Desert Sand, with Pyramid Gray moldings striped with

vertible victoria, with disappearing top, on 145-in. Packard chassis. It will be finished entirely in black, with ivory striping on the molding. The top is of Burbank and the seats are trimmed with Velveau tan leather in diamond tufts. A Visolite cigar lighter and two ash receptacles are provided in the rear, and two reading lights are set in the corners of the wide rear bow. In addition to a folding trunk rack, there is a large aluminum trunk of special design. The other new Waterhouse exhibit will be a convertible coupe, with disappearing top and rumble seat. It is mounted on Pierce-Arrow chassis and is finished in two shades of gray, with black moldings and wheels; gold striping is used on both moldings and wheels and there is a small green recessed door panel above the molding. The top is of light-gray Burbank and the seats are trimmed with gray Colonial-grain leather. This car has unusually wide main doors and a small door on the right side to give easy access to the rumble.

WILLOUGHBY

In its New York exhibit, the Willoughby Co. will have two bodies on the new Lincoln chassis: A French brougham similar to that exhibited last year, but with a slightly slanting windshield, and inlaid division and door friezes instead of the needlework panels previously used. The other body will be a 7-passenger enclosed limousine with sloping front and corner pillars of special construction, also with a distinctive belt and saddle-panel color treatment, which is shown in an accompanying engraving.

The Willoughby-Duesenberg enclosed-drive limousine will be similar to its Chicago exhibit, but in a different color scheme, Boatswain Blue and black. The rear seat of this body is adjustable, the one operation changing both the position of the cushion bench and the angle of the back. The walnut friezes are done in a style different than that usually employed.

The general trends in body features are outlined in an accompanying article on the Chicago Salon by George J. Mercer. Most of his comments will apply to the cars at the Commodore.

Trends at the Chicago Automobile Salon

By George J. Mercer*

MUCH of the general information relative to the Chicago exhibition was forecast in the November issue of Autobody, in which were presented the names of the exhibitors and numerous views showing the trend of exterior design. My impressions, gathered at the exhibition itself, will consequently be devoted to a review of general trends and will be accompanied chiefly by illustrations of interiors, though a few exteriors not available last month will also be included.

This year's Salon was interesting both for its technical and for its business aspects. It was not "flat", but decidedly up and doing. Only in rare instances, were the exhibitors tied to the conventions of standardized production, yet there were few extremes in design. The trend of the work is always along predicated feature lines. However, there were a few outstanding departures that might be mentioned here. In one of

A Weymann sedan on Duesenberg served to introduce the new flexible construction employing metal panels. The extreme in the trend toward sloping fronts to minimize air resistance was represented in the Brewster 4-passenger sport body on Rolls-Royce chassis. Because of its novelty, this attracted much attention; the design especially in the forward half of the car was well developed, as will be noted in an accompanying illustration, but the extreme angle of the rear of the door presents difficulty in hinging it satisfactorily and when it was opened, the car did not impress one so favorably.

The illustrations here given, and those published in November, will afford readers a general grasp of design features. Briefly, the tendency is to amplify beginnings made at previous Salons: First is the sloping front, minus the exterior visor or sunshade. Elimination of obstruction to wind pressure is further ex-

Dignity and formality distinguish this panel brougham, by Brunn, on the 153½-in. Duesenberg chassis. The entire car is finished in black, with ivory striping. There is a construction of special interest back of the driver's seat where a small cowled compartment is provided for stowing the canopy and other units for enclosing the driver. This construction also provides extra knee room for the forward-facing auxiliary seats, a sliding division glass being used

the Murphy bodies, the builder provided increased entrance room by letting the doors extend into the roof quarters; this is in response to the demand that bodies be high enough for average persons to enter without undue stooping; the idea is advantageous if the problem of keeping water from entering around the roof cut has been solved.

A Brunn town car on Duesenberg chassis had the canopy, and other units for enclosing the driver, stowed in a small covered compartment back of the driving seat where these units are quickly accessible to the driver; another advantage of this arrangement was that it permitted a large amount of knee room for auxiliary-seat passengers, a sliding division glass being used.

Another interesting construction feature was the Campbell concealed hinge employed on the Franklin "Tandem" sedan, designed by Raymond H. Dietrich and built by Walker. This new hinge enabled the designer to provide a truly flush-sided job and still retain a narrow pillar. A sketch shows the opposed-cone principle upon which this hinge operates, but lack of space at this time prevents a full description. Because of its importance and novelty, a detailed article and illustration will be presented in an early issue of Autobody.

pressed in the minimizing of the size of the upper structure of enclosed bodies; the front is inclined toward the rear and the rear part toward the front, not so much in the manner of the tumble-home effect that was used a few years ago, but with a slanting line giving the angular effect. Another noteworthy tendency is the use of "undercut" doors; by that is meant the sloping forward of the front line of the door toward the bottom, following the slope of the windshield. This gives added room for entrance to the front seat, but it necessitates hinging the front doors at the rear. The base lines of the bodies are more and more losing that straight-line effect from front to rear, and instead, are being given the sweep or compass line that was used in carriages; this is accomplished by overhanging the chassis and bringing the body line close to the running board. The curved line at the base of the body is often supplemented by a similar line obtained by sweeping the running board into the front fender. Another feature is the extension of the body at the rear to cover the chassis ends and sometimes to make use of the rear for a luggage or spare-wheel compartment. When this is not done large trunks generally cover the rear end of the frame. Rear-seat passengers are thus placed forward of the axle in most of these

* Consulting body engineer, 7310 Woodward Ave., Detroit.

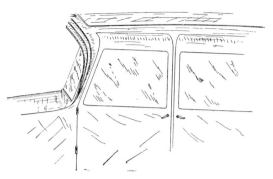

Murphy body with doors extending into side-roof panel, thus providing increased entrance room. Note also the visor formed by steps down from the roof

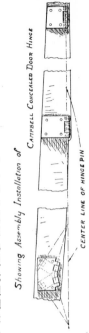

Campbell concealed door hinge on the Franklin "Tandem" sedan

custom bodies. The use of wells to obtain more legroom in low and close-coupled bodies can now be said to be common practice. Phaetons tend to be close coupled and to have secondary cowls and windshields operated by regulators.

Interior trimming embraced all the standard methods, with a tendency to conform more generally to the plain design, either with a single back and cushion, or divided in the center. This method is general with the open bodies. Cushions and backs are made both in tailored

shape to fit the form and also with the soft effect into which the occupant makes his own indentation. Personally I thought the tailored or shaped back was preferable. Broadcloths—occasionally with hairline stripes, but rarely figured—were the predominant fabric. Bedford cords were considerably used, but this year were chiefly in one color. Leather was used a little more than customary perhaps because of the softer textures now provided and the large number of convertible bodies, although nearly half of the convertibles were trimmed with bedford cord. No car was observed trimmed in mohair. Interior woodwork was freely used, though generally confined to panels on the divisions and doors; occasionally the panels were extended under the rear-quarter windows and had smoking or companion cases swept into them. A few cars had cabinet-work over the entire division. In two instances radio-receiving sets were installed.

Super-Sport Body by Brewster on Rolls-Royce Chassis

Interior views of the 4-passenger sport car built by Brewster on Rolls-Royce chassis. This car illustrates the extreme in the present tendency toward eliminating wind resistance. It is finished in Sea Fog Gray, with white striping. The spare tire is carried in the tail, which is swept to harmonize with the sport-type fenders

Group of 2-and 4-Door Bodies Shown at Chicago

The Duesenberg "Beverly," built by Murphy, suggests a convertible sport car, but it has a fixed head and is in reality a berline. It is finished in three shades of green and has an unconventional interior that is characteristic of this builder

A "coach-type" victoria by Derham on Franklin chassis. This is one of an interesting group of Franklin bodies, four of which are shown on this page. The large trunk at the rear was specially designed to harmonize with the body contour

A victoria coupe designed by Raymond H. Dietrich and executed by Walker on the Franklin series 15 chassis. It has the modish sloping front and rounded front header, the curved motif being repeated at the back and on the special trunk

The Franklin "Tandem" sedan, designed by Raymond H. Dietrich and built by Walker Body Co., was noteworthy not only for its square back and undercut door, but also for the narrow pillars and flush side. The use of the new Campbell concealed hinge permitted a center pillar of minimum width; a sketch on p. 170 shows the hinge installation

Sport sedan, designed by Raymond H. Dietrich and constructed by Walker, on Franklin chassis. This bears a close relation to the coupe shown above, but instead of the large swept trunk, this body has a swept rear that can be used for luggage; access is by a small door at the back

Some Interiors at the Automobile Salon

Two views of the passenger compartment of the Brunn-Duesenberg town car. The long chassis permits forward-facing auxiliary seats, but extra knee room is provided by using the space under a compartment at the back of the driver's seat

The Newport sedan by Dietrich, Inc., on Packard chassis is trimmed in plain style with a Wiese fine-wale bedford cord of light-tan color. The swept door friezes are repeated on the front seatback where a smoking case is swept into it

Interior of the Le Baron-Chrysler town car. This is trimmed in "bolster" style and loose bolsters are used for the armrests. A mohair rug, as well as mohair hassocks are provided for the floor

The Fleetwood enclosed limousine, on Cadillac V-16 chassis, is trimmed with a Wiese Palmetto Green broadcloth in plain style with a French seam at the edge of the cushion, and two welts, about 4 in. apart, on the front face

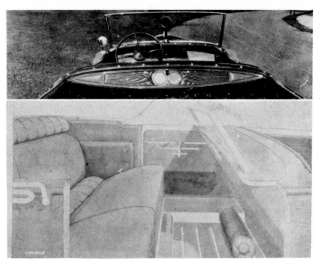

Note the individual seating of the convertible sedan by LeBaron on Packard chassis. The trimming is soft veal-grain steer hide in russet-tan color; diamond tufting is used on the back and biscuit tufts on the cushions; the door panels have a vertical welt running down to the horizontal panel about 6 in. above the bottom. Bellows-type pockets with soft rolled flaps are provided on the front seatback; there is also a tonneau light in the center and a cord "robe rail" covered with leather

Above is the carved-walnut "secondary instrument panel" on Fleetwood's Cadillac V-16 phaeton; in the center is mounted a clock and extra speedometer. The secondary windshield is operated by a regulator

Below: Design for the tonneau of the Derham-Duesenberg phaeton. The depressed floor is covered with a green rubber tile bound with chromium-plated moldings, which are also used for decorating the door panel. The secondary cowl is stationary, but the windshield is controlled by regulator

Colors at the Chicago Salon

By Howard Ketcham*

THE annual Automobile Salon, always important as foreshadowing color trends, displayed this year certain distinctive and in some ways outstanding developments in this line. Although the trend of colors was, in the main, somber, nevertheless there was apparent a definite leaning toward pastel hues.

Use of Pastel Hues

This was apparent in the offerings of certain manufacturers. Packard, for instance, showed a "cabriolet sedan limousine" with upper works, molding and wire wheels in Riverhead Green, the remainder of the car being in Bonaventure Green, a lighter value than Riverhead. A Packard-Dietrich sport

* Director of Duco Color Advisory Service and editor of the "Automobile Color Index."

sedan in Oakhart, a rich warm tan, was also an interesting example of the new color trend. Duesenberg made effective use of Courier Cream as the all-over color on a Murphy roadster, and Neenah, a blue-grey value, on a Murphy convertible berline. The trend was also shown by Cadillac with Caramel, a pastel brown, on the upper structure of a 2-passenger convertible coupe, the lower body being finished in Rose-Rust Straw with a cream-color stripe, and wire wheels in the color of the upper. Another outstanding Cadillac entry, a 5-passenger phaeton, was finished with molding and fenders in Fennimore Green and the lower body in Laurel Green. Pierce-Arrow showed a Dietrich convertible sedan with molding and fenders in golden Yedaz Tan and body in Cracker Buff. Lincoln displayed a coupe by Judkins, finished in soft, rich Ravenswood Brown and striped with Rosewood, a pale pink.

Soft, flexible goat hides were used for trimming these fixed-head bodies at the Chicago Salon. At the left is the Weymann metal-paneled sport sedan on Duesenberg chassis; it has individual front seats, with special compartments in the backs thereof; the narrow French plaits of the seats are repeated on the door panels; the headlining is a Wiese basketweave broadcloth. At the right, the Judkins-Duesenberg berline is arranged to give the owner the option at all times of leather or cloth seats, one face being trimmed with goat hides and the other with a Wiese Cadet Gray broadcloth; wide, flat plaits were used on the seats and backs, as well as in the central panel of the doors, which have friezes of tinted wood harmonizing with the color scheme

Reflections of Recent Salons

AS some of the newer manifestations on the custom cars at recent exhibitions will eventually find their way into production work, it is well for production builders not to dismiss too hastily the improvements developed in the custom field. Not all of these features, of course, are suited to production cars but some, which at first appear too expensive, may in time filter through and get on the production lines. The vogue of the radiator screen may be cited as an example, and it may revive the "fashion-industry" talk of which we heard so much a few years ago. At least, it illustrates the fact that any development in the custom-car field may prove important to the production-car builder—and to the sales manager. When one observes a gadget so useless—in this country—as a radiator stone screen, coming out of the European custom field and being applied to some of the low-priced American cars, one realizes how much more sensible it is for the inventor or designer to develop something

CONVERTIBLES WITH DISAPPEARING TOPS

One cannot predict fashion changes with any assurance, but an engineering development of the recent American Salons that seems certain to make a permanent impress is the disappearing or semi-disappearing tops for the smaller convertibles. This is not a new idea but it has now been applied in a simple manner and the convertibles have an attractive appearance in both the open and closed positions. These new convertible roadsters, coupes and victorias have a definite appeal both to the eye and to comfort—especially for the motorist's emergency passengers or guests, who during the last few years have been riding out in the open rumble and often behind a folded top that was so high as to preclude easy conversation with those riding inside. Such conditions have been abandoned by the custom builders and we anticipate that sales resistance will be found by production builders who let this lesson slip by un-noticed.

Murphy interiors always present interesting variations from the conventional

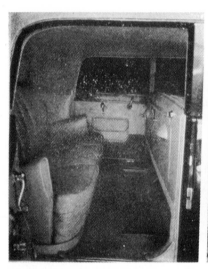  

At the left is the rear compartment of a Murphy convertible berline on Duesenberg chassis. The top has zipper fasteners which permit neat fitting and quick opening. The division is recessed, as is also the floor, and triangular hassocks provide a comfortable angle for the rear passengers' feet; an unusual feature is the two hooded lights on the division. The view at the right is the rear seat of a 4-passenger stationary berline, by Murphy, on Duesenberg chassis. Cases are recessed in the rear quarters and the reading and ceiling lights have a modernistic framing; the door trim is in a similar spirit. The division, shown in the central view, has special cabinets at each side and clock, speedometer, etc., in the center. One of the cabinets at the side contains the loud speaker of a remote-control radio set. Besides the railing on the cabinet, ash receivers are inset in the top. In the recess under the division, hassocks of circular section are provided and the brackets into which they fit give two adjustments for distance

with sales appeal than to invent a device that merely increases the comfort or usefulness of the car to the motorist.

RADIATOR SCREENS AND WHEEL DISKS

The principal service of the radiator screen is as a decorative feature, and though more of them were to be seen in our recent Salons than heretofore, it is worthy of note that some of our custom builders were still chary about adopting this European equipment. Its value as a style feature is largely dependent on its exclusiveness. The extent of its adoption on production cars will determine its fate as a custom feature. Another European device, even more popular than the radiator screen, is the *flasques* or wheel disks for covering wire wheels. These have been sparingly used on American custom cars, though intrinsically more valuable as a design feature than the radiator screen.

When convertible coupes first "crashed the production gate," it was of course a problem to build any sort of a convertible within the price limits. Such body types have now been in regular production for several years and have a neat, trim appearance as long as the top is up. When the top is folded, two glaring deficiencies are observable. The lined top usually folds so high that it separates the rumble passengers from those on the driving seat almost as effectively as a division excludes a chauffeur from the master compartment. Also, when the top is lowered, it leaves an ungainly vertical corner post and windshield, often with an inclined visor projecting forward without a complementary element in the design, and thus gives the suggestion of a tree denuded, by hurricane or fire, of its leaves and of all its branches but one. The present custom jobs with slanting windshields and semi-disappearing tops have a sleek appearance giving genuine open-car effect, when so operated, and indicate that production models will soon have to eliminate their straight fronts and high-folding tops.

Among the custom convertibles, the victoria seating all passengers inside made a new appeal by adding the disappearing top, so that this body type can also give open-car sleekness. A depressed floor provides sufficient legroom for a close-coupled seating arrangement forward of the rear axle. The space between the chassis members at the rear is usually filled by a large trunk designed to conform to the roof contour. If the rear seat is not in use, small luggage or golf bags may be carried there without the necessity of opening a deck lid or the trunk. Wells for the disappearing and semi-disappearing tops were generally without a metal

the car. It may spell the disappearance of the uncoated fabric top which often detracts from the appearance of convertibles, when carelessly cleaned.

In England, the sunshine roof still maintains its popularity. The latest versions, however, permit not only the opening of the roof but also the lowering of the landaulet back which gives a nearer approximation to the standard convertible and may ameliorate the drafts to which rear-seat passengers have been subjected. Modifications of the sunshine roof also permit (1) opening from the front (part or all the way), (2) opening from the rear (part or all the way) or (3) opening from both front and rear. On a town car, Hooper & Co. used their patented arrangement with a pivoted arm at each side; when the arms are swung

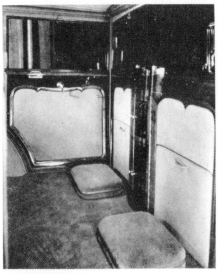

A special curtain was used to conceal the auxiliary seats in a Brunn-Duesenberg brougham. The curtain is mounted on a spring roller and when the auxiliary seats are not in use, snap fasteners on the tabs secure the curtain to sockets in the floor. When released from the sockets, the curtain rolls up automatically. Note the special hassocks on the sheepskin rug and the Wedgewood medallion in the zebrano door frieze. Unusual legroom is provided for the auxiliary-seat passengers, the recess under the division extending under the special canopy compartment behind the driver

The interior of a Rollston-Duesenberg town car, at the left, was noteworthy for its handsome cabinetwork in two shades of walnut, and for its exquisite workmanship throughout. Opera-type seats fold flush with the division

At the right is the unusual door trim of a Willoughby limousine on Duesenberg chassis. The division frieze is similar to that on the door but is noteworthy for the use of separate robe rails for each side. The forward-facing auxiliary seats, with special arm on the outside, fold into the division and are concealed by hanging curtains. The rear seat is adjustable both as to cushion and back

lid, the opening being covered by the fabric top boot or a fabric flap attached to the body by snap or button fasteners. The outline of this boot was "designed" into the contour of the body, thereby retaining the smart effect. Convertible sedans and berlines also showed betterments of details. One neat-fitting berline top had zipper fasteners instead of the more usual snap fasteners. The problem of a really washable top fabric was solved by one builder who used a new coated fabric having a fabric grain printed thereon. This material can be easily cleaned, is waterproof and is said to be capable of withstanding any flexing that would be given the top during the life of

over, the upper and inner head fabrics are rolled on spring rollers; the roof rails are covered by hinged flaps which are loosened for the conversion but which preserve the appearance of a fixed head at other times. On the Continent, the sunshine roof has apparently declined in favor and the standard head fittings are generally used for convertibles.

At the Paris Salon, the developments were chiefly variations in details rather than in body-type changes. Noteworthy, however, was the expanded use of the Vizcaya frameless body introduced a year ago. This consists of six units, for a 2-door body, each section having the edges flanged at right angles so that they

A Belgian and an American interior. The conservative interior at the right is that of a Lincoln semi-collapsible cabriolet by Brunn. This was trimmed in the plain style with a Wiese sage-green broadcloth and is noteworthy for its simple elegance and workmanship. The more decorative interior at the left is a Minerva town car, by the Carrosserie Van den Plas. An Ostruk patented sliding roof for the driving compartment is concealed in a pocket in the roof of the master compartment. This interior is novel in many respects, the upholstery fabric being a fawn broadcloth with pressed pattern. The rear seat with folding, center armrest is trimmed in the plain style, but the decorative treatment of the doors and division, and of the cabinets recessed in the rear quarters, reflects the shell motif of the lighting fixtures. The cabinetwork was in walnut, inlaid with a fine line of ivory. A housing was provided for the curtain over the division window

may be joined by bolts through a rubber gasket. The seats are bolted directly to the chassis. In refinishing the car, it is expected that the shell will be taken apart and new gaskets inserted between the sections. Much attention was given by French designers to belt treatments and to the design of running boards and fenders. The coach sill was much used but visors and cowl bands were rare. A number of bodies had metal roofs which make a neater appearance for the present low cars, the roofs of which are more observed than in the past; insulation against drumming must, of course, be provided for this type of roof. Coachwork for the small cars received much attention at Paris, and this was also a noticeable feature of the Olympia show.

Large trunks, designed to harmonize with the body contour, were mounted on most of the popular 4-passenger 2-door bodies at Paris, though occasionally large luggage boots resembling trunks in outline and decoration were provided. The development of luggage boots and swept rears was particularly in evidence at the British show, several of the prize-winning bodies having such rears.

At the American Salons, luggage boots were rare but all rears received designing attention and were generally praiseworthy. For close-coupled jobs, however, trunks of special design were usually provided. Approximately 80 per cent of our custom cars omitted the outside visor.

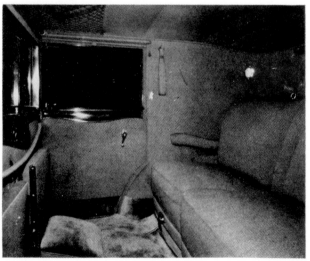

Interior of the Willoughby-Lincoln panel brougham. This is trimmed with a Wiese olive-drab doeskin, in the plain style, with self-beading. The door and division friezes are of inlaid walnut. The treatment of the fabric panel of the doors is in harmony with the swept pattern of the frieze. The emergency seats fold flush with the division and between them is a small package compartment, the lid of which is spring hinged at the bottom. To accord with tradition, a carriage-type armsling is provided

A Fleetwood town car trimmed in plain style with a Wiese tan doeskin; each rear seat is adjustable both as to cushion and back. The door and division friezes have a center of amboyna and a French-walnut border, with an outline inlay of rosewood; a companion case is swept into the division frieze. The same door and division treatment was used in Fleetwood's French brougham on Cadillac chassis but the seat was trimmed in the tufted style with diamond points, and the entire rear cushion was adjustable

Review of the National Automobile Show

THE National Automobile Shows were well attended this year which indicated a maintenance of interest on the part of the public and the certainty of a good demand for cars when business takes an upward trend and the conservation of cash resources is no longer uppermost in the public's mind. Sales of cars were fair and in some instances good, and really interested prospects were reported to be about as numerous as in preceding years.

With respect to bodies, the production cars with few exceptions followed closely the previous trends, but there were marked differences in details when compared with those of two years ago or even with those at the last show. Features of the Salon cars were repeated in some of the high-grade standard cars. Numerous custom models on the medium- and high-priced stands also served to give interest and tone to the exhibition as a whole.

Because of the business conditions, most manufacturers confined their changes to details instead of completely re-designing their bodies, but several makers notably Auburn and Reo, had the courage to re-design their lines and consequently attracted much attention. Intense interest was also displayed in the two stands offering the American versions of small European cars;

have the rear apron swept to conform to the fender lines. When trunks are provided, they are designed so as to repeat or harmonize with the roof contour. Most cars still have a deep chassis valance below the body, but some of the higher priced models using the "coach" sill have the body sides carried below the chassis level, though not to the running boards as is frequently done on European cars. A number of cars are wider and lower, the body sills being fastened level with the chassis, by brackets, thus providing lower appearing bodies without sacrifice of headroom.

High-grade cars continue to use the composite body, but in the medium- and low-priced groups, there is a liberal use of all-steel construction. The composite bodies have more metal bracing than heretofore and some have the wood-to-wood contacts held apart by metal braces, with felt or other gaskets between. Continuous strips of padding between body sills and chassis are being replaced by blocks of felt, or of rubber and interbedded fabric. Many composite bodies have all-steel front units and several have center pillars on which both doors are hinged. When properly engineered, this construction stiffens the body and gives better vision for the rear-seat passengers. Driver vision is better cared for this year by the increased use of narrow

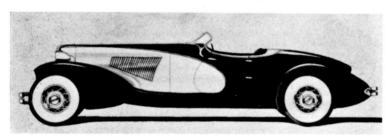

One of the striking bodies at the National Show was the Cord sport roadster, with disappearing top, finished in a special shade of yellow and red. The parabolic design of the fenders was repeated on the chassis valances and on the door fittings. This effect was also carried out in the painting of the body. The tail was of the skiff type, but aprons were provided at the rear to conceal the chassis mechanism

although the American Austin and American Mathis stands were on the second floor at the Grand Central Palace, the crowds around the exhibits were generally so great that it was necessary to wait for an opportunity to examine these cars. Stripped chassis were also popular foci. An important group of cars adopted either "free wheeling" or the silent "synchro-mesh" transmission. More cars used double-drop frames, and a number stiffened their chassis notably.

Exterior Changes

The exterior aspect of the cars has been modified by the adoption of a more slanting windshield on several makes and a lessened use of the hooded visor, but production cars as a group still retain the sharp-angled hooded metal visor and the practically vertical windshield. However, a great number than heretofore used the inside adjustable visors. Frontal appearance of the cars has been altered by the generous adoption of chromium-plated radiator screens and by the introduction of V-type and inclined radiator shells on several makes of cars. Bonnet louvers have now been generally supplanted by door-type ventilators for the engine compartment of medium- and high-priced cars, but most of the low-, and a few high-priced, lines retain the old-type louvers which are generally disposed in a single vertical grouping. At the rear practically all cars now have an embossed apron over the fuel tank; many have a definitely developed rear design. The new coupe and roadster designs of several makes

metal corner posts. Running boards are about the same as heretofore and have not received much designing attention, except on the luxury cars.

More Convertibles; Fewer Open Cars

Body types among the closed models were about the same as heretofore, but there was an important increase in the number of convertible cars exhibited and a decrease in the number of open types. At the 1930 show there were 36 open cars, against only 15 this year. In 1930 only four convertibles were shown; this year there were 25, embracing convertible roadsters, coupes and sedans, as well as the new convertible structures with disappearing and semi-disappearing tops which have been described in connection with the Salon reviews and in previous articles.

Painting

Approximately 50 per cent of the cars at the National Show were finished in a single color. The greatest change in painting was in the increased number of cars using contrasting colors and the corresponding decline in chromatic-sequence combinations. Black cars again outnumbered those in any other single color, and green was next in popularity, thus conforming closely to last year's exhibition. The decline in the use of blue was noteworthy, this color falling below both the maroons and the browns. (Two years ago, blue was the predominant color.) Gray enjoyed a moderate popularity. Yellow and cream were sparingly used and for the first time in several years aluminum was not represented at all.

There were comparatively few bright-colored cars even among the convertibles and open models. A noteworthy exception was the Cord sport roadster, with disappearing top and "parabolic" fenders. This was finished in special shades of yellow and red, the latter color being used for most of the car. As will be noted from an accompanying illustration, the painting was planned to suggest an effect of speed and to emphasize the "parabolic" fender design by the use of a similar yellow area on the body side. The body rail was also in yellow and this color was extended aft, in pennant form, over the compartment covering the disappearing-top well. Although the general vogue of a few years ago for contrasting window reveals was absent, several bodies that were otherwise finished in a single color did have a touch of contrasting color on the window reveals.

Striping Generally Double

Striping of moldings was generally double though on one or two groups of cars a triple stripe was employed. The double striping was usually in the center of the molding on the bonnet, but often split at the front corner, one line following the molding across the cowl, or up the corner pillar, and the other extending aft near the bottom of the belt molding. When the belt

20 per cent were trimmed in the plain style, as against practically 40 per cent at the recent exhibition. In 1929, mohair plush was the principal upholstery fabric; this year flat-woven fabrics were used in approximately 70 per cent of the closed cars. The convertible jobs were trimmed chiefly in leather, but there were a number of bedford cords and one flat-woven mohair in this group. Broadlace has nearly disappeared from the 1931 cars, although it was used on some small armslings or hand loops which appear to be supplanting the standard toggles. Some of these loops were covered with a cross-woven fabric. Small fabric loops were employed on one line of cars as door pulls.

Interior Hardware in Modern Style

Interior fitments continue to be in the modern style on most of the cars, though such designs have made little progress among the high-priced cars. Ash receivers were generally provided on both sides of rear seats and in a few instances on the right side of the front compartment. No accommodation was made, however, for the driver, who perhaps smokes more frequently than other occupants. His attention is presumed to be centered on the controls and instruments. This makes it all the more difficult for him to have his smoke. Some designer will eventually provide a pocket in the left corner of the instrument panel, equipped with a lighter and the other necessities. In many instances,

Design for a phaeton by the Walter M. Murphy Co., on the new Lincoln chassis. This body will be exhibited this month at the California Salons. One of the features is a low top made possible by a special hinging arrangement for the secondary cowl. The glasses which serve as wind deflectors lower into the front door in the same manner as an ordinary door window, the slot being automatically covered by a spring flap. The car is finished in two shades of green and striped with argent

striping was double, the stripes were seldom in the center, one being placed near the top and the other near the bottom edge. Striping of the windows as a group was done on a fair proportion of the bodies and about an equal number had individual striping of the windows; for the latter purpose single striping was used far more than double striping, but in treating the windows as a group double striping was nearly as popular as the single; one car used triple striping to frame the windows as a group.

Interiors

Interiors were trimmed chiefly in buttoned plaits and in the plain-stretched style, the latter being more used in this year's cars than at any previous National Show. Plain plaits were employed on less than 25 per cent of the cars. About half of the seats done in the plain-stretched style were piped with leather, and a few with the seat fabric or with lace-covered piping. Plaits varied in width from 2½ to 9 in., but most of them were from 4½ to 6 in. wide; on one group of cars, diamond points were employed.

This year, flat-woven fabrics forged far ahead of pile fabrics which were represented on less than 30 per cent of the closed cars. Broadcloth was the most popular fabric, with bedford cords second and mohair plush third. In fabrics and in trimming styles, the upholstering of cars has experienced practically a reversal in the last two years. In 1929 there was only a "sprinkling of plain-stretched jobs"; last year about

ash trays were installed flush in rear quarters, armrests or doors. In the higher grade cars, cases were often placed in recesses in the rear quarters; occasionally when in the armrests, they were provided with flaps covered with the seat fabric. One interesting disposition of a cigar lighter was in the end of a circular armrest where it appeared to be a knob or rosette. Interior woodwork was generally in walnut and most of the higher priced cars had the door friezes of this wood, sometimes plain, but more frequently with a line of inlay. On the medium- and low-priced cars, the garnish rail was often combined with a swept frieze, generally done in walnut-finished metal, and sometimes striped to imitate inlay. Comparatively few cars had a simple garnish rail, though several high-grade cars were in this category.

Taxicabs Represented Only by Checker

The only taxicab exhibited at the New York Show was that of Checker. Its recent design is ornate in style and not so acceptable to the body builder's eye as their effective Model K of a year or two ago, but taxicab designers must appeal to their public which evidently approves ornate designs. This seems confirmed by some taxicabs recently put on the streets of New York which have the bonnets covered with chromium-plated gadgets simulating ventilators or ship funnels, but which have no functional purpose. A study of taxicab exteriors is therefore useless to the average body designer. Interior arrangements of the new Checker, however, present several changes of interest.

II

The Salons & Shows of Europe

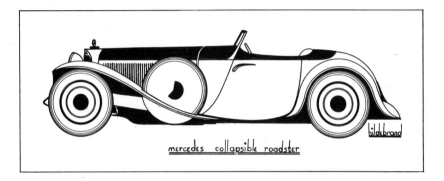

Mercedes model "S" roadster, designed by George Hildebrand in 1930
with the sporting flavor very much in vogue at the European salons
and Concours d'Elégance.

Le Concours d'Elégance de Paris

FOLLOWING the success of the Riviera *concours d'élégance*, entries for the Paris elegance contest proved so large that a preliminary elimination contest was staged, this year, prior to the final which was held as usual at the Parc des Princes. As these elegance contests have proved a sort of forerunner of the body styles to be exhibited at the Salon in October, we present below some excerpts from the review which appeared in the June issue of *l'Equipement Automobile*:

Some tendencies were clearly defined. Metal paneling and especially the use of air-drying enamels are coming more and more to the fore. Notwithstanding that decks of leather or of leather cloth remain practically without criticism, the use of leather cloth for sheathing shows a marked decline. The products having a real success are the "reptile leathers" which are used for interior garniture and even for tire covers—a mode which will probably last not more than one season; these leathers are offered in a great variety. On the contrary interior trim in Nacrolaque, and all sorts of garniture with

In 4-seaters, a vehicle that made a great impression was that of S. E. Apdel Hamid Shawarby Bey; this body was built by Million-Guiet on a Boulogne-type Hispano-Suiza. Gallé again did himself proud in the superb car of Madame Tindel, on a Panhard-Levassor chassis, in the class *sport fermées, plus de 2 places*. Grummer, who was successful with all his entries, secured a first and second prize in this category.

Belvallette and Million-Guiet were well rewarded for their fine productions in the closed-car classes, the former carrying off a *grand prix* with a superb sedan and the latter a *grand prix* with a *conduite intérieure avec separation*.

Space is lacking to deal with each production in detail but besides the big winners, Lavocat & Marsaud, Gallé, Million-Guiet, Belvallette and Grummer, the creations of Hibbard & Darrin, Janssen, Gillotte, Bourack & de Costier, Guettault and of the Carrosserie Nouvelle Henri Levy were practically perfect from all points of view. Levy specialized in closed bodies sheathed entirely in metal and painted with Duco. It might be remarked that the finish of these bodies was practically as brilliant as that of the former varnish types. Kremiansky, Binder, Duvivier, Figoni, Alin-Liautard, Currus, Brun and

"Grand Prix" Sport Bodies by Lavocat & Marsaud

→

Lavocat & Marsaud also won a grand prix with this sport torpédo, built on Bugatti chassis, for Mlle. Pierrette Faroux. This differs from

a somewhat similar model, illustrated below, in having the spare wheels carried behind the trunk. Steps are used in place of a running board

A grand prix was awarded this 2-seater sport body built by Lavocat & Marsaud, on Bugatti chassis, for Madame Galangau. This body is extremely sporting in character, the fenders joining with practically no running board and the step plate being exceedingly high

This "torpédo à 4 places" for Mlle. A. Rolland on a Peugeot chassis gave Lacovat & Marsaud a clean sweep of the "grands prix" in the "sport découvertes" categories. Note the decorative effect which has been given to the chassis valances, and the radiator screens on all three bodies

this product, seem destined for a more permanent success. A fashion which dates from the last Salon, but which may decline if it becomes too popular, is the use of light-colored impermeable cloths for tops.

In body models, devotion to the sedan, abandonment of the classic torpedo, a slight gain on the part of the sporting torpedo and a stationary position for the other body styles marked this contest. There seems to be a tendency in "roadsters" toward the use of the pointed rear. In painting, the light tints were dominant on all of the bodies that were at all suggestive of the sport type.

In the sport torpedos, Lavocat & Marsaud took the lion's share with three *grands prix* in the three different categories of 2-, 3- and 4-seaters. Perhaps in the 2-seater the jury wished to honor the sporting *allure* of the car of Madame Galangau, and in the 3-seater the harmony of line, for in the first the body lacked finish and in the second, comfort.

Henri Labourdette obtained important prizes and maintained the high standing of these excellent firms. (Some American cars were exhibited and among the *palmarès* were those mounting bodies by Brunn, Dietrich and Fisher; the exhibitor of a Lincoln coupe-roadster, with body by Dietrich, won a *grand prix*.—EDITOR.) The list of the awards follows:

Torpédos ordinaires, 4 places et au-dessus

1. Automobiles La Salle, Carrosserie Fisher.
2. Carrosserie Bourack & de Costier (Barron-Viale).
3. Voisin, Carrosserie Gallé (Gradis).
4. Delahaye, Carrosserie Gallé (Bacque).

Sport découvertes, 2 places

Grand Prix. Bugatti, Carrosserie Lavocat & Marsaud (Madame Galangau).
Carrosserie Fisher (Automobiles La Salle).

Some Striking Examples at the Paris Salon

(Courtesy of Motor Body Building)

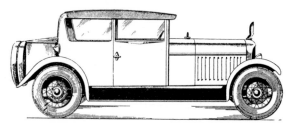

Voisin 2-door "sun saloon," shown at right with detachable roof covering removed

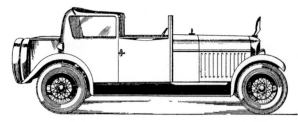

The Voisin 2-door "sun saloon," at left, opened for fair-weather driving

Sport coupe exhibited by Chenard-Walcker, of Gennevilliers (Seine). These models, with pointed tail and extremely low overall height are designated as "Tanks"

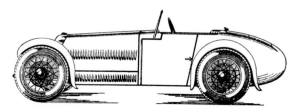

A sporting 2-passenger roadster of unusual design exhibited by Automobiles B. N. C., of Levallois-Perret (Seine). Note the extended bonnet and lower treatment

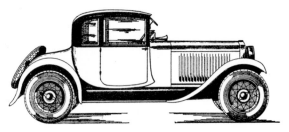

"Chariot coupe" by the Carrozzeria Sala, of Milan on Isotta-Fraschini chassis

A cabriolet with all-weather front exhibited by Georges Kellner et Fils on Hispano-Suiza chassis

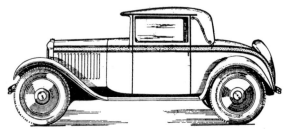

A Citroen coupe with snakeskin belt, built by Guillaume Busson, of Levallois-Perret, on the new "six" chassis

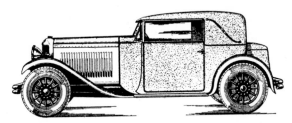

A 2-door fabric job exhibited by Etablissements Ballot, exemplifying the valanceless vogue

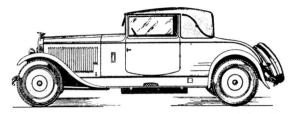

"Demountable" coupe of flexible metal construction, designed and built by Etablissements Bellvalette

The Bellvalette coupe showing detachable units removed; these are held in place by spiral-spring fasteners

Types of Coachwork at the Olympia Exhibition

(Courtesy of Motor Body Building)

Aero-type 2/4-passenger roadster on Bentley chassis by Barker & Co. (Coachbuilders), Ltd., of London

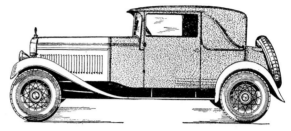

Fabric covered 4-passenger coupe on Delage chassis by Rippon Bros., Ltd., of Huddersfield

Flexible fabric-covered saloon exhibited by Vanden Plas (England) 1923, Ltd., The Hyde, Hendon, N. W.

Weymann saloon on Bentley chassis by J. Gurney Nutting & Co., Ltd. This is sheathed with the new "tôle souple"

"Faux-cabriolet" exhibited by Thrupp & Maberly, Ltd., of London, on Bentley chassis

"Coupe de Ville" on Rolls-Royce Phantom chassis, exhibited by Mann, Egerton & Co., Ltd., of Norwich

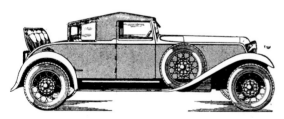

Unique design of a 6-seater "coupe runabout" exhibited by Renault, Ltd., Westfield Road, Acton, W. 3

Sportsman's coupe with convertible roof on Rover chassis. This is a Weymann-type body

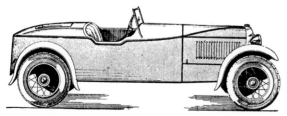

Valanceless 2-passenger roadster by Grose, Ltd., of Northampton, on Alvis F. W. D. chassis

Sporting "cabriolet saloon" on Hispano-Suiza chassis by Hooper & Co. (Coachbuilders), Ltd., of London

Million-Guiet Bodies at the Paris Salon

"Cabriolet berline" with all-weather front on the Reinastella chassis, the new Renault 8-cylinder model. This may be used as a completely closed berline, half open or as a completely open car. It is finished in two shades of rose beige. The top fabric is beige and a broadcloth of the same shade is used in the passenger compartment; the driving seat is trimmed with pigskin

"Conduite intérieure" on Mercedes chassis. It is finished in light green-gray, with black moldings, wings and upperworks. The polished-aluminum disks of the wheels have a circular molding painted black. Toolboxes are set in the running boards, with flush tops. The interior woodwork is in old walnut

A 4-passenger sport coupe-cabriolet on Marmon chassis. The body is finished in two tones of blue and the top, wheel covers and trunk are covered with white canvas piped with blue. Exposed metalwork, including the edges of the fenders, is chromium plated. The rear cross seat is extremely low and is stuffed with down; M. G. folding seats are used in front.

Hispano - Suiza faux-cabriolet with all-weather front. It is finished in granite, deep, the moldings and wings being in black. The body color is repeated on the circular molding of the polished-aluminum wheel disks

Another view of the Hispano-Suiza faux-cabriolet, arranged for fair-weather driving. The light-colored fabric top was a feature much used at the last Paris Salon. Some of these were white, but a light beige was used in this instance, the passenger compartment being trimmed in a darker shade of the same color. The two auxiliary seats are center facing

This body by the Carrosserie Weymann on the Bugatti Royale chassis won the grand prix d'honneur de "l'Auto" at the recent Concours d'Élégance in Paris. It is finished in yellow and black, and has at the rear a large pigskin trunk. Although it has a flexible frame, the body is not of the usual Weymann construction, having special light steel panels below the belt; the entire exterior of the doors is also sheathed with metal. The interior is trimmed with a light-gray fabric and the woodwork is of amaranth-colored palissander

Le Concours d'Élégance à Paris

THE eighth Concours d'Élégance at Paris under the auspices of *l'Auto,* had a number of new features this year which added to the interest of the coachbuilders and of the public. For the latter there was the special *Trophée d'Élégance Féminine Automobile* which was awarded for the combined chic of owner and automobile. To the body builders there was the new *Coupe de l'Originalité* which was offered by *La Carrosserie* in addition to its usual *Coupe de La Carrosserie.* Categories were reduced this year from 17 to 11, but the increased number of entrants necessitated elimination trials on the three days preceding the final awards. Among the *palmarés* will be found the names of practically all the well-known carrossiers, except a few who did not compete because of being members of the jury. This consisted of: Messrs. Charles Faroux, Jean Henri-Labourdette, Gaston Grummer and Jacques Kellner, representing the industry, and Messrs. Ravigneaux, Petit, Gerster, Da Costa, Vasseur, Fraisse, Gaudin, René-Charles Faroux, d'Estrez and Mathières, representing for the most part sporting artists and writers of the daily and technical press. We are indebted to *l'Auto-Carrosserie* for the accompanying list of awards and for the following general comments on this year's contest:

The workmanship this year was generally impeccable, at least more carefully done than in preceding years. It gave, however, an impression of monotony perceptible to all, and this is certainly dangerous. The builders seem to have copied to a great extent series models, and a buyer might readily hesitate between the tailored and the series product, but this probably represents only a pause before a greater effort, which will be apparent at the approaching Salon. There was a general tendency to return to metal sheathing; it is not necessary to point out the use of metal on the Weymann-Bugatti which was in a class absolutely special. It was more particularly from the point of decoration that the note of too great similarity appeared. It is of course necessary to accede to the public demand just now concentrated on the Hibbard & Darrin style of molding, but we felicitate those rare designers who carried their efforts toward research for profiles that might slowly lead to an evolution of the taste of the buyer. With reference to colors, the mode has not sanctified any particular shade. One again found beige, gray beige, gray green, a little of red, yellow and cream and a great group of blacks for most of the town cars, always brightened however, by a bright molding, and a top or false top of dust color or black,

The coupe de l'originalité, a new award this year, was won by the Carosserie G. Busson with this creation on a Citroën Six chassis for Mme. A. Gérard. This prize was offered by "La Carrosserie" as a stimulus to original work

for which metal, fabric or leather was used. There were fewer open cars again, but more transformables and cabriolets, and transformable fronts for *coupé-limousines* and similar town cars.

Interiors were more carefully done than ever. Reptile skin has disappeared and in its place were found haircloth and other special fabrics by Rodier. The reps and velours were generally supplanted in favor of lighter fabrics. Accessories, both interior and exterior, were in greater number; practically all the cars had disks for the wheels and stone guards for the radiators. Chromium has replaced nickel almost completely, but the designer should be on his guard not to place too much of this brilliant finish on the vehicles.

The jury selected for the *grand prix d'honneur* the Weymann *carrosserie* on the Bugatti chassis. While this was beautiful in line and color, it was of an extremely special character and price. (One talked of 500,000 francs for this car!) The body, contrary to what one might have expected, was covered with metal

Grand Prix des Voitures Fermées: Weymann (Bugatti; Weymann)

Grand Prix des Voitures Transformables: Mme. la princesse Médiha-Djellal (Hispano; Proux)

TROPHEE D'ELEGANCE FEMININE

Trophée d'Élégance Féminine Automobile; Mme. Proux-Gallé (Panhard & Levassor; Proux)

Premiers Prix ex aequo:

1. Mme. Dancausse (Hispano; Ottin)
2. Mlle. Maud Loty (Packard; Gallé)
3. Mme. Martinoff (Voisin; Proux)
4. Mlle. Blanche Montel (Oakland; Muhlbacher)
5. Mlle. Elvire Popesco (Delage; Delage)
6. Mme. Huergo (Minerva; Proux)

OUVERTES
Torpédos

1. M. Nègre (Bugatti; Lavocat & Marsaud)
2. M. Lecomte (Ballot; Felber)
3. Mlle. G. Bayonne (Bugatti; Lavocat & Marsaud)

Door trim and cabinetwork of the Ottin all-weather cabriolet on Hispano-Suiza chassis for Mme. Dancausse; this won highest honors in the cabriolet class and also a first prize ex aequo for its owner in the "Feminine Elegance" contest. The view at the right shows the trimming of Mlle. Montel's Oakland cabriolet-coupe by Muhlbacher; the fabric is a special "tissu Rodier" with silver-gray background and polychrome "striations giving a soft rainbow effect"; the door friezes are of walnut and lemonwood

to the belt, but still used a flexible frame of three principal units. It was lacquered in yellow and black with a superb effect. The bonnet panels had unusually large louvers striped with yellow on the edges. The wide doors were entirely covered with metal like the lower part of the body. The rear of the car was terminated by a large trunk, harmonizing with the body lines and covered with pigskin. The interior was trimmed with a special gray-beige fabric, the cabinetwork being of amaranth-colored palissander. Special mention should also be given to Maurice Proux, a comparatively young carrossier, though not an absolute newcomer, but whose success was particularly noteworthy both by reason of the quality and finish of his productions and by the great number which won recognition in this contest. The list of prizewinners follows:

AWARDS OF THE 8TH CONCOURS D'ELEGANCE

Grand Prix d'Honneur de "l'Auto": Weymann (Bugatti; Weymann)

Coupe de "La Carrosserie": Weymann

Coupe de l'Originalité: Mme. Antoinette Gérard (Citroën; Busson)

Grand Prix des Voitures Ouvertes: *Toubiana* (Hispano; Million-Guiet)

4. M. Robert Sénéchal (Bugatti; Lacovat & Marsaud)
5. M. F. Moullé (Ballot; Figoni)

FERMÉES
Coupés-Limousines et Limousines

1. Carrosserie Belvallette (Panhard; Belvallette)
2. M. Novodrowski (Ballot; Saoutchik)

Coupés et Faux-Cabriolets

1. Mme. J. Potherat (Renault; Guettault frères)
2. Mme. Assumpcao (Packard; Gallé)
3. Mlle. Rahna (Bugatti; Proux)
4. Mme. Margarita Lacaille (Hotchkiss; Gallé)
5. Mlle. Marthe Chenal (Panhard; Gallé)
6. Mme. Marcel Mayer (Voisin; Gallé)
7. M. Wormser (Hispano; Saoutchik)
8. Établissements Grümmer (Lorraine; Grümmer)
9. X. (Talbot; Belvallette)
10. Miss Martin (Rosengart; Rosengart)

Conduites Intérieures, Deux Portes

1. Mme. Proux-Gallé (Panhard; Proux)
2. M. J. Thouzelier (Panhard; Proux)
3. Mlle. R. Latour (Voisin; Proux)
4. Automobiles Bugatti (Bugatti; Bugatti)

American Cars at the Paris Salon

Custom Bodies by Some of America's Best Builders will be Seen This Year at the International Exhibition

THIS YEAR America is putting its best foot forward at the Paris Salon, as will be noted in some of the illustrations presented herewith. For a number of years the American car manufacturers were satisfied to exhibit their stock cars in competition with European cars mounted with bodies by the best European builders. During the last few years, however, a change has been taking place and several of the high-grade American cars have been shown in Europe with custom-built bodies. Latterly some of these bodies have been by American builders. More than 30 makes of American cars will be represented at the leading European shows and this year there will be a representative showing of custom bodies by some of America's best builders.

and interior decoration, and should compare favorably with the creations of foreign builders, although they may not be so elaborately treated as some of the Continental bodies.

LeBaron Brougham on Lincoln Chassis

LeBaron has prepared on Lincoln chassis a graceful town car of pleasing silhouette and without moldings, depending on the simple combination of well-rounded panel surfaces with the modernistic touch given by the etched metal plate on the master door and the use of colorful bindings with the otherwise plain interior of blue-gray pastel shade. The narrow etched chromium plate on the door enlivens the solid French blue in which the entire car is painted. The front compart-

Panel brougham by Le Baron on Lincoln chassis. This is without moldings and depends on its well rounded panel surfaces and excellent composition for its appeal. An etched chromium-plated panel is placed at the point where attention should focus in a town car, on the door panel, and affords the only relief from deliberate plainness. Contrast is provided by the judicious use of the plate against the solid French blue in which the car is painted. The front compartment is trimmed in a matching blue leather in plain style. The passenger compartment is trimmed with French broadcloth of a blue-gray shade. Trimming is featured by special rolls and bindings. Ash trays of glazed pottery and hassocks and carpets of crushed plush are all toned to match the car lining. The garnish rails are in Ceylon satinwood of light tone

Among American cars that will be seen at the Paris Salon for the first time will be the new Cord, the Marquette, the Roosevelt and the Viking. Standard cars that were scheduled to be shown at this exhibition, in addition to those already referred to, are: Auburn, Buick, Cadillac, Chevrolet, Chrysler, Dodge, Duesenberg, Durant, Erskine, Essex, Ford, Franklin, Gardner, Graham-Paige, Hudson, Hupmobile, La Salle, Lincoln, Marmon, Moon, Nash, Oldsmobile, Oakland, Packard, Pierce-Arrow, Reo, Studebaker, Stearns-Knight, Whippet and Willys-Knight. Only Ford and Studebaker have drawn places in the central display area, but there is little doubt that most visitors will take the trouble to hunt up and inspect all of the American exhibits.

For the moment, we are concerned only with the custom cars of which advance illustrations have been released in time for this issue. These cars have been styled to suit the best American taste, both in exterior

ment is trimmed with a plain-paneled leather, dyed to match the body color. The passenger compartment is lined with a French broadcloth dyed a pastel shade of blue-gray. The characteristic formal tone of plain severity for the town-car interior is relieved by the unusual trimming and bindings on the seats. Hassocks and carpets of crushed plush, ash trays of glazed pottery, toned to match the car lining, and other appropriate fittings give this interior a distinguished and conservative modern atmosphere.

Brunn's Semi-Collapsible Cabriolet

Another interesting body on Lincoln chassis is illustrated on the succeeding page. This is a Brunn semi-collapsible cabriolet with a V-windshield, beige leather top and a boat-like stern or deck. The angular effect of the windshield is carried out by the contour of the roof and by the embossed center line of the back panel. This panel is carried well over the fuel tank and makes a clean-cut rear. The design also offers a space for stowing packages or luggage, access to the compartment being gained by lifting out the back squabs of the rear seat. The body is unusually low, sills being set outside the chassis so that the floor is about 2½ in. lower than on standard bodies. The front is, of course, transformable, the canopy and side arms being stowed in a compartment above the division glass. As will be noted in one of the views, this car is provided with a

hogany. A single folding seat with lazy-back and armrest is attached to the partition. Telephone, buzzer and cigar lighter are positioned conveniently in a side armrest; the center armrest is of the hinged type.

FLEETWOOD FEATURES COACH SILL

Fleetwood prepared three bodies for Cadillac's Paris exhibit. One of these is illustrated on page 129. This is designated as an "inside-drive imperial cabriolet",

A Brunn semi-collapsible cabriolet with all-weather front on Lincoln chassis. This body is set particularly low, the body sills being supported outside the chassis, the floor being thereby lowered approximately 2½ in. The treatment of the rear panel is particularly intersting with its embossed center line and special base molding. The rear forms a luggage compartment, access being through the rear seatback. The car has a slanting V-windshield and this angular effect is carried out by the roof contour and also by the embossing of the center line of the back panel. The top is a beige-colored landau leather. Non-shatterable glass is used throughout and it will be noted in the view below that a radiator screen is provided, in accordance with the European practice. The interior views show the exceeding simplicity of the trimming and the interesting treatment of the door panels. The upholstery material is a French chamois-colored broadcloth.

chromium-plated radiator screen, in accordance with European practice. Other exterior hardware is also chromium plated, and non-shatterable glass is used throughout. The windshields have crank-type controls mounted at the top center. The interior is trimmed with a chamois-colored French broadcloth and is done in the plain-stretched style. A simple panel treatment is used on the doors, the bronze hardware for which is of special Brunn design executed by the Sterling Bronze Co. The wood trim is of natural-color ma-

although it is not convertible. The main body panels are finished in deep maroon and tan and the top is of a fabric-grained tan leather.

It has the fashionable coach sill which, combined with the long bonnet and cowl and the slanting front pillar, give an effect of fleetness and power that is characteristic of these cars. A Neutralite visor is used and all windows are of non-shatterable glass. The division window lowers completely; the channels therefor are concealed in the pillars and roof so as to give

Among the Fleetwood bodies in the Cadillac stand will be this "inside-drive imperial cabriolet," finished in deep maroon and tan. The top leather is also in tan and has the modish fabric grain. The long bonnet and cowl, the slanting line of the windshield and front-corner pillar and the coach sill give this car a suggestion of both fleetness and power. The interior is extremely simple and both compartments are trimmed with a Wiese tan doeskin piped with matching leather. This body is in reality a 7-passenger berline, with opera-type seating for the emergency passengers

a sedan effect if the car be driven by the owner. To make it adaptable for owner driving at any time, both compartments are trimmed with a Wiese tan doeskin, piped with matching leather, the entire interior being in character extremely simple. The other Fleetwood bodies, mounted on 140-in. Cadillac chassis, will be an all-weather phaeton and a 7-passenger berline, this body differing from the one illustrated by being slightly longer, having quarter windows and a metal back and full auxiliary seat equipment. The job illustrated is equipped only with opera-type seating for emergency passengers.

Hibbard & Darrin's All-Metal Body

Hibbard & Darrin, the well-known American designers and builders in Paris, will present on 153½-in. Duesenberg chassis an "imperial cabriolet" in their new all-metal construction using duralumin and other aluminum alloys, together with a small amount of steel, the aim being to make a lighter and stronger body and yet one that is adaptable to small-series production, which most custom builders are nowadays compelled to undertake. Another feature of the construction is its freedom from climatic difficulties. This car has the narrow corner pillars and slanting windshield which are now practically universal on custom work. The slanting

door windows lower, without gap, in "Southern-Darrin" channels. The body exhibited is finished in beige, with chocolate trimming. Other examples of this construction will be seen in Hibbard & Darrin's own exhibit.

Waterhouse-Packard Convertible Coupe

On a Packard custom chassis of 145½-in. wheelbase, the Waterhouse Co. has mounted an exceedingly good-looking convertible coupe of 4/5-passenger capacity, all passengers being housed within the enclosure. The car is effectively finished in aluminum and black, the latter being used for the chassis, moldings, saddle panels and upperworks. The top is a light-gray Burbank. A large trunk at the rear is covered with aluminum of the same gage as the body and conforms to the general lines of the design; chromium-plated deck irons protect the surface when the top is lowered; a trunk rack, of cast aluminum, is also specially designed. The visor is covered with the same Burbank as the top and is adjustable by means of slip quadrants and wingnuts.

The overall height of this Packard coupe is only 66 in., ample head and leg room for rear passengers being provided by sinking the floor between the chassis members. The front seats are both adjustable and have folding backs. This style of body, with all passengers

This sporting design for Duesenberg chassis was made by Hibbard & Darrin, of Paris. A cablegram from this firm of American designers and builders states that they will exhibit a "Duesenberg imperial cabriolet using their new all-metal construction, embodying chiefly duralumin and other aluminum alloys." The car will be painted in beige with chocolate trimming and have a beige-colored top

housed inside, calls for unusually wide doors; these are 41 in. wide and are consequently hung on extra-heavy hinges and have diagonal steel bracing. The door latches are operated by two controls, a lever for the rear-seat passengers and a recessed, rotary, remote control for the front passengers. All the interior hardware was especially designed by the Waterhouse Co. Fitments include a Visolite cigar lighter which is installed on the right side of the rear seat. At each end of the instrument board a small cabinet is provided for gloves or parcels. The interior is trimmed with gray

trimmed. The top does not differ essentially from those for similar bodies but was designed to fold compactly as will be seen in one of the accompanying illustrations; there are two reading lights installed in the rear bow and nickel-silver plates reinforce the corners; ball-end wing studs on the windshield pillars insure a solid junction when the top is up. The windshield pillars are of manganese bronze and are covered with sheet aluminum which is a continuation of the aluminum forming the cowl; this construction eliminates the chance of the paint breaking at the joint.

A convertible coupe on 145½-in. Packard chassis by the Waterhouse Co. This comparatively new firm of American builders is achieving a notable success in designing for high-grade cars. This fleet-looking body is only 66 in. in overall height, carries 5 passengers all under cover and has at the rear a commodious trunk, finished to conform to the color and contour of the body. Unusually wide doors are required for this style of body; they have diagonal steel bracing in the frame and are hung on especially heavy hinges; the door latch is operated by two controls, a lever control accessible to rear-seat passengers, and a recessed remote control for front-seat passengers. Both front seats are adjustable and have folding backs. A recessed floor provides ample legroom for the rear-seat passengers. Two reading lights are installed in the rear bow, the corners of which are reinforced with nickel-silver plates. The top is trimmed with light-gray Burbank and the interior with a gray leather. Below the belt the body is painted with aluminum, the belt and saddle panels being black; black is also used on the wire wheels, with a pencil stripe of Fire Opal

Colonial-grain leather and has a carpet of the same color. Recessed flap pockets are positioned in each side convenient to the rear-seat passengers. A shield, outlined below a wide belt, decorates the door panels. Aft of the door pillars, there are leather protection flaps on the belt rail where the top is not permanently fastened. The outside frame of the back window is also covered with leather, and the top envelope is similarly

Safety Glass will be used in 4,500,000 cars by the end of this year, according to the estimates of the Triplex Safety Glass Co. of North America. The great majority of these cars will have been turned out during 1929 because the movement toward safety glass has only gathered its full momentum this year. Non-shatterable glass was introduced to the automobile industry by the Triplex company about three years ago.

Further Impressions of the European Shows

By John W. J. Ackermans *

ONE of the first items to attract my attention at the Paris Automobile Salon was the new radiator design of several French makes which resembled somewhat the later Chrysler molding-type design. I noted several fabric bodies that used *tôle souple* throughout; one striking job had a black body, red roof and bright-metal belt molding, edged with red fabric beading on each side. Weymann's body, "La Royale," on Bugatti chassis, which won the grand prize at the Concours d'Élégance, attracted large crowds. The most remarkable part of this car was its large rear trunk made of deer pelt with the hair left in natural condition; large corners made of pigskin, wide leather straps with bright buckles, rings and escutcheon with initials made this trunk the cynosure of all eyes.

Painting Extremely Varied

Polished-metal moldings and others painted in aluminum were much in evidence. Painting embraced all colors and hues of the rainbow; red roofs, green roofs,

bodies had cabinets built into the upper rear quarters with electric lights and mirrors in the back. In one coupe, mirrors about 10 x 16 in., with small draperies, were installed in the rear quarters. Toilet cases were often put in flush with the upholstery and in a few instances ash trays were installed in the door friezes.

Many of the cabriolets, and even the faux cabriolets, used half-doors and chromium-plated frames for the glass; flaps, however, seemed much in vogue again and were generally well made. Barker-type fronts were used on practically all the cabriolets and town cars. A body by Driguet had silver moldings, radiator and top joints and the inside door friezes were decorated with paintings of a whippet race. Another job had birds painted on the door friezes.

Town Car With Convertible Roof

An interesting town car, by Hooper & Co., had a new "sunshine" roof for the rear compartment, the headlining and top leather being taken up by automatic

A coupe-cabriolet built by Carrozzeria Touring, of Milan, on Alfa-Romeo chassis Note the use of the coach sill, and the special headjoints

A "transformable surbaissée" body by Gaston Grummer, on the Renault Reinastella chassis, illustrating this carrossier's new patented "E. V. B." low construction. This also illustrates the tendency toward the use of steps, body sides carried down below the floor, and disks for the wheels

black bodies or mauve ones, any kind one desired could be found. Striping was used on about half of the cars and generally there was a stripe on each side of the molding, but some times on the molding itself. A body by Gallé had finish moldings and door friezes painted green, with silver striping. Another by Hibbard & Darrin had the finish moldings painted, but in a dark green, with light-green striping.

A sedan-landaulet was shown to advertise a make of genuine leather with reptile graining. The roof and folding rear sections were covered with this leather and the driver's compartment was entirely upholstered with it; the rear compartment had a combination of this leather and cloth to match. Among other novelties, a coupe had a rear window hinged to open outward and a sedan had the back squab of the rear seat hinged at the top to give access to a built-in trunk. Several high-class

rollers; the conversion could be quickly made. Another feature of this body was a large concealed sliding ash tray in the end of the center armrest. Toilet cases with electric lights and mirrors were set flush in the quarters. The individual rear-seat cushions could be moved forward about 10 in. by turning a crank positioned in the rear quarters. Upholstery in this car was unusual, the material consisting of woven silk and leather strands. Pillows of brown fur were placed on the rear seats. The whole job was a fine example of the coachbuilder's art.

Copper Moldings

Fernandez showed a faux cabriolet with polished-copper belt molding, extending around the body; on the doors it was about 3 in. wide. Reveals in the door and other bright-metal parts such as windshields, etc., were in contrasting chromium plating. Saoutchik showed a large coupe with concealed top of striking

---

* Body engineer and designer, 6520 Sterling St., Detroit.

design and appearance. Bright-metal instrument and lockboards were used. The upholstering was of special black woven leather, consisting of strips about ⅛-in. wide; vertical red strands were injected at intervals of about 2½ in. The body was finished in black and had aluminum-painted moldings with the characteristic Saoutchik cowl molding sweeping down to the lower corner of the bonnet. These moldings were also used by a number of other builders and the rear edges of the bonnets in many instances had a curved or coupe pillar design.

Kellner showed a collapsible coupe with a large seat in the tail; protection for the rumble-seat passengers was provided by a *tendelet* stowed, when not required, in the upper rear of the top and covered by a flap; there were supporting rods which were fitted between the top and an extension panel normally concealed behind the seat back in the deck lid but capable of being raised, when needed, by a mechanism similar to a windowlift. This looked like the best solution yet offered for enclosing a deck seat. There were doors on each side for easy access.

Panel Material of Cork

A new panel material made of cork by the Gilco process was shown on a body (partly in the white) by M. & C. Snutsel. It was applied over the wood frame and permits a large lower back panel with decided corners and turnunder to be made in one piece; painting was applied directly on the cork.

Van den Plas, S. A., showed a smart 4-door inside-drive job, with leather rear quarters and roof, on Minerva chassis. The whole car was painted Almond Green and had a bright-metal belt molding running to the radiator and another at the base of the body. Below

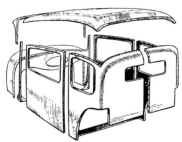

An all-metal coupe body, without framing, made by the Carrosserie Marbeuf of 32 rue Marbeuf, Paris. It is composed of eight units made of sheet aluminum, the edges being turned in to form a flange; a strip of rubber is placed between each unit before joining and in order further to reduce noise, a large section is cut out of the roof unit and replaced by a soft panel. The doors are hung on a continuous hinge, the body being wider at the bottom than at the roof rail. This coupe was mounted on a Hispano-Suiza chassis fitted with bumpers on the sides. (Reproduced by courtesy of "The Autocar")

the belt, this body was trimmed with cream cloth, but above the belt, both compartments were finished in birdseye maple and had moldings of lemonwood. The radiator ornament was a large Indian head made of special crystal by Lalique. The job was a credit to its makers and worthy of its owner, the crown prince of Kapurthala.

Great Variety In Upholstery

It might be mentioned that in the matter of upholstery, there was a great variety, with many new designs and hardly two jobs with similar trimming. Some had metallic effects which enhanced the beauty of the whole interior. Others had lace or other designs stitched on the seats and back cushions.

Having recently visited the "world's fair" at Barcelona, I might add a few words about this remarkable exposition and the part that the automotive industry is taking. The American and English sections are very small, with nothing of interest in bodies except the "Golden Arrow," for which special admittance has to be paid. Germany and Italy are fairly represented with standard makes and one fine Mercedes collapsible coupe. French cars have the best showing at this exposition. Henri-Labourdette is the only carrossier represented, showing a roadster with polished-metal rear. A few Belgian cars are shown, but honors in the Belgian pavilion go to the well-known body builders, Van den Plas, S. A., and D'Ieteren Frères, of Brussels, both of whom had beautiful jobs, the most interesting of the

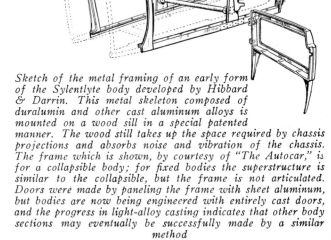

Sketch of the metal framing of an early form of the Sylentlyte body developed by Hibbard & Darrin. This metal skeleton composed of duralumin and other cast aluminum alloys is mounted on a wood sill in a special patented manner. The wood still takes up the space required by chassis projections and absorbs noise and vibration of the chassis. The frame which is shown, by courtesy of "The Autocar," is for a collapsible body; for fixed bodies the superstructure is similar to the collapsible, but the frame is not articulated. Doors were made by paneling the frame with sheet aluminum, but bodies are now being engineered with entirely cast doors, and the progress in light-alloy casting indicates that other body sections may eventually be successfully made by a similar method

entire exhibition. Several remarkable old coaches were shown, the golden coach of Carlos IV, and an extremely old golden coach without springs, hanging on four large straps and having rear wheels 6 ft. high. Both of these antiques were wonderful examples of the art of the old coachbuilders.

Coachwork at Olympia

The striking thing at Olympia, in contrast with the Paris show, was the popularity of fabric bodies which were to be found both on high-grade and low-priced chassis. Leather upholstery was much in vogue here and red leather seemed to predominate; examples were also shown of the woven leather upholstering similar to that seen on some of the exhibits at Paris. Tapestry trimming was observed on a number of seats and backs. Many bodies were built down to the running boards and large trunks were carried in the rear or were built into the rear of the bodies and extended down over the chassis. Center armrests in several bodies did not go to the top of the back cushion, but stopped about 5 in. below the top; the recess, when the armrest was down, had a concealed flap of the upholstery fabric, thus avoiding the awkward-looking opening and giving the back a normal appearance.

Auxiliary seats in several bodies, in which cabinetwork was provided on the partition, were attached to a board; this mounting permitted them to be easily concealed and required no cutting of the carpet. Gray, "pickled" sycamore was used to a great extent in cabinetwork.

Molding and Belt Treatments at the Paris Salon

PARIS CORRESPONDENCE

THE general lines of the cars at the last Paris Salon remained about the same as previously, but there were numerous innovations to be noted in details which gave the cars a certain stamp of originality. The belt molding swept across the front, which a year ago was in general use, was found much less frequently at this Salon. It has today passed to the domain of the production body; all the Paris taxis are now provided with this molding treatment which extends the entire length of the body to the radiator and at the windshield

tions worthy of note; the access to the rumble was by means of two side doors, as in an ordinary phaeton. The back of the rumble seat was of a comfortable type and had a special movable panel with window; this panel could be raised by a windowlift mechanism and supported a canopy held by two bars which fastened under a flap at the rear of the top so as to provide a comfortable and efficient protection for the rumble passengers who are ordinarily exposed to the weather. When the canopy is not required, it is rolled up with

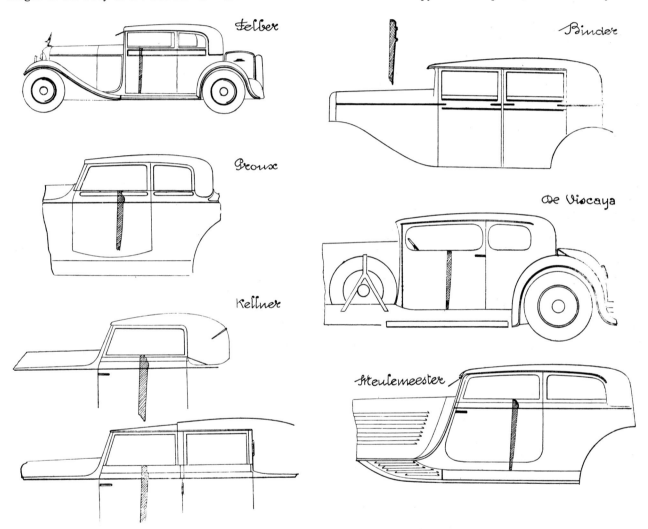

Belt and molding treatments used by various French carrossiers

pillar is swept into a transverse molding, making a U on the cowl, open toward the front. Hence, it is not astonishing that numerous carrossiers have searched for something else to give their models a distinctive character.

The accompanying illustrations show different designs of moldings observed at the Salon on bodies by well-known carrossiers. Kellner ornamented his belts with a band of medium size, surmounted by a wide rolled-in frieze or panel. This frieze is sometimes relieved at the top by a light listel, as in a small sport "cabriolet" which he exhibited on Renault chassis.

This Renault "cabriolet" offered some other innova-

the bars and stowed in a leather bag. Thus nothing on the outside betrays its presence or detracts from the general appearance of the car.

On the Rolls-Royce stand an inside-drive body by Binder presented an essentially new treatment of interrupted moldings, as shown in one of the illustrations. These moldings in an attractive jade green enlivened the mass of black with which the vehicle was painted. Similar beadings were to be noted on the interior woodwork.

In an admirable sport torpedo with disappearing top, on Mercedes chassis, Saoutchik used a belt molding that, instead of prolonging itself on the bonnet, de-

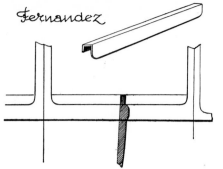

Fernandez used a polished-aluminum garnish rail to enliven his bodies which otherwise had a paucity of decoration

scended in line with the pronounced slope of the windshield and formed an accentuated coupe-pillar molding which added to the sporting lines of the vehicle. The interior likewise presented a distinctive feature, being trimmed in black and red woven leather reproducing the exterior colors of the car. It gave an impression of being trimmed in a rich rattan, in the manner of certain rustic seats.

On an extremely sporting 2-door body, Meulemeester used a similar molding that prolonged itself all the length of the lower portion of the bonnet; at the top of

Instead of the usual belts, Million-Guiet employed these metal friezes, in contrasting colors, on the doors

the windshield pillar, the molding was swept into and continued by the drip molding. The peak of the roof was practically suppressed in favor of a glass visor, with the controls hidden by a narrow strip of sheet metal soldered to the top of the roof, its curve harmonizing with that of the windshield pillar. This strip of sheet metal also served to prevent infiltration of water between the roof and the windshield. One also noticed that the bonnet was prolonged to within 5 or 6

cm. of the base of the windshield, giving a line that harmonized with the entire design and providing easier access to the motive units. A narrow sober beading at the belt was surmounted by a rounded frieze which reflected a high light along the length of the body, and emphasized the elegance of the whole composition.

A similar rounded front with roof flowing directly into the windshield, without a peak or visor, was found on sundry models of Weymann and Grummer. The models of Macquet & Galvier also displayed a coupe pillar, but having this difference that it was not a question of a molding but of bringing down the body itself in cast aluminum in the form of a coupe pillar.

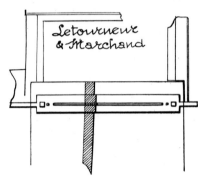

A wide door-belt panel of stainless steel and a molding of the same material was used by Letourneur & Marchand

The bodies of Proux, a young carrossier whose reputation is no longer in question, had an interesting belt treatment, a typical example being shown in one of the sketches. The belt treatment of Ottin, of Lyons, presented a series of superimposed surfaces, reminding one of the conceptions of some of the modern decorators and providing a pleasing combination with the other lines of his bodies. Billeter & Cartier, also of Lyons, used a belt similar to that of Proux, but sufficiently different to give it a certain individuality. Each window was underlined by a double molding and frieze, or panel.

A certain number of carrossiers replaced the belt moldings with polished-metal plaques. The most original conception in this respect was certainly that offered in a convertible body by Henri-Labourdette, of which the rear is shown in one of the accompanying sketches. The belt up to the level of the windshield was marked by a triple redan of alternate bands of steel and brass; this began narrow at the windshield and tapered aft to the end of the body. On the rear deck, the median line was also marked by a triple metallic band, the central one of brass being concave, while the outside bands were fixed by exposed rivets which were also used on the side redan. On several 2-door models by

Belt treatments of Billeter & Cartier, of Muhlbacher and of Ottin

Letourneur & Marchand, the door belt was marked by a wide plate of stainless steel. A molding of the same metal continued from the center line of this frieze forward to the radiator and around the back of the body.

Million-Guiet also presented at this Salon some novel belt designs which allow numerous variations. Instead of the usual belt molding, there were metal friezes on

Division cabinetwork by Kellner and Saoutchik

the door panels as shown in a separate sketch. These were marked by contrasting colors, recalling the compositions of Dunant, famous specialist in modern furniture and decoration. The front and rear of these bodies were without any molding or other decorative treatment at the belt line.

De Viscaya, a young carrossier, exhibited a number of closed bodies without moldings of any sort. This produced an original effect which is worth noting. The construction was also novel. The panels of the doors, quarters, backs and the roof panels are independent elements. The inside seats are mounted independently of the body and have underneath them tool compartments that are easily accessible. The panels or units of the body are easily demountable by unscrewing wing nuts. All the interior trimming is mounted on panels. At the rear of the body is placed a large steel trunk, the cover of which simulates the end of the body. This trunk is susceptible of two utilizations, one as a receptacle for baggage which permits the placing of a number of small bags one above the other, or if desired, two supplementary seats may be installed. For this use are furnished removable cushions and a back squab, secured by straps. Wells are provided to permit the feet of the occupants to stretch out. In addition to bumpers at front and rear, the car is provided with lateral bumpers on the edges of the running board, without increasing the width of the vehicle.

To sum up, the Paris Salon brought no revolution in exterior lines, but manifested on the contrary quite definitely the care that the carrossier has taken to free himself from the swept molding which has become a veritable obsession in the last few seasons. This molding has today become the ornament of the production vehicle, indeed even of taxicabs. The luxury vehicles are signalized on the other hand by great diversity of

View showing tendelet in position to protect deck-seat passengers of the Kellner - Renault convertible coupe

The large trunk at the rear of de Viscaya's bodies provides space for a number of suitcases or trays, but may also be used for emergency passengers by inserting seat cushions and back which are held in place by straps

Triple metallic bands used on Henri-Labourdette's convertible coupe on Hispano - Suiza chassis

An entirely different treatment was adopted by Felber for all of their vehicles. An example of this treatment is illustrated in a sketch of a 2-door body, with large trunk, on Voisin chassis. Under the windows there was a large rectangular frieze, slightly concave. The lower line was prolonged, but without continuity, by a molding to the radiator and an accentuated coupe-pillar molding. The rear of the body was encircled by a single molding on a level with the lower edge of the frieze, but not joined to it. All of the bodies were noteworthy for their excellent proportions.

On the bodies by Fernandez, one noted a special reveal of aluminum under the windows. This massive note of silver color sufficed to enliven the somewhat somber note of these bodies which were without other decoration, except a narrow beading on the edge of the rear-quarter windows. A somewhat similar use was made of polished metal by Currus & Vog.

treatment of the belts and moldings. A certain tendency manifests itself in the vehicles of the luxury class in favor of the complete suppression of all exterior decoration.

In interior treatment, the carrossiers exercised greater freedom in providing the maximum of comfort and of accessories, conferring at the same time a feeling of distinction and giving the interior a personal character. Therefore, the interiors defy generalization, except possibly the two characteristics of comfort and convenience already mentioned. Two sketches show divisions by Kellner and by Saoutchik. In trimming the rear seats of the luxury cars, the general practice was to provide fauteuils with large armrests and a central hinged armrest, folding into the back. A new feature of the wood trim of the seats was the irregular framing and carving. This framing descended a few centimeters on the backs of the front seats.

At the Brussels Automobile Salon

A handsome "faux cabriolet" built on Stutz chassis by Établissements Généraux, of Brussels. It is finished in sand gray, with black moldings, and "chrome souci" roof and rear quarters. Note the sweep of the sill, fender and running board

A convertible sedan, with *exceptional vision*, built by Gyselynck & Selliez on Minerva chassis. This model, designated as the "Centenaire," offers little obstruction to vision either at the corner or at the center pillars; the latter are less than 2 in. wide

A well-proportioned 5-passenger sport sedan, built on the 32-hp. Minerva chassis, by the S. A. Anciens Établissements D'Ieteren Frères. It is finished in two shades of gray

An interesting coupe cabriolet by Carrosserie Van den Plas, S.A., on Minerva chassis. Note the deeply crowned fenders, the coach sill and the *special treatment* of the door belt panel

A "faux cabriolet," on the 32-hp. Minerva chassis, by Antoine Van den Plas et Fils, 61 Ave. de l'Armée, Brussels. A carriage step is used instead of a running board, and the front line of the door is swept to harmonize with the curve of the coach sill. Note the large trunk at the rear

At the Monte Carlo Elegance Contest

This "Jockey Club cabriolet," with "Plein-Ciel" convertible roof, was mounted on Hispano-Suiza chassis by the Carrosserie Henri-Labourdette, of Paris. The exterior is entirely in black except for the encircling molding and other exposed metalwork. Note the rather large kick plates, and the ample trunk with its chain anchorage. The interior was trimmed in a special "gray-white" fabric

This interesting sport cabriolet on Renault chassis was designed and built by the Carrosserie Kellner, of Paris, and is a refinement of an earlier design by this firm. Note the special treatment of the cowl and belt rails

A pleasing "conduite intérieure" for six passengers on Hispano-Suiza chassis. This body was also mounted by the Carrosserie Henri-Labourdette. A nickeled molding encircles the body and the bright metalwork is continued up the slanting windshield pillar. An unusual feature is the fact that the entire body is covered with black leather, the interior being trimmed with a handsome fawn-colored leather

Some Bodies at Recent French Concours d'Élégance

An interesting body by Million-Guiet on Hispano-Suiza chassis. This is of extra-light construction, after J. de V. patents, in which flanged edges of aluminum panels are bolted together without the use of pillars

With this "torpédo," Mlle. Suzanne Albaran won the Trophée d'Élégance Féminine Automobile. Also the Grand Prix at Touquet. It was built by Million-Guiet on the Reinastella chassis of Renault

Mme. Dieudonne Costes was one of the prizewinners in the Concours d'Élégance Féminine Automobile with this "faux cabriolet" by Gallé on Hispano-Suiza chassis

A "conduite intérieure" with unusual window treatment by the Carrosserie Gallé on Delage chassis

Bodies by Castagna at the Milan Auto Show

A phaeton-sedan by the Carrozzeria Castagna, of Milan, on Duesenberg chassis

Another body for Duesenberg chassis by Castagna. This is designated as the "imperial landaulet-limousine"

An attractive sedan, built by Castagna, on the 8-cylinder Lancia Dilambda chassis. Note the etched belt moulding, the small parking lights on front fenders and rear-quarter pillars, and the unusually capacious trunk at the rear

Prize-Winning Bodies in Recent French Contests

This "faux cabriolet" by Gaston Grummer, on Bugatti chassis, won the grand prix d'honneur for all categories and the Coupe de "La Carrosserie" at the recent Concours d'Élégance de "l'Auto," and first prize for Mlle. Kira Sklarova in the Trophée d'Élégance Féminine Automobile

The transformable of Mme. d'Aygues-Vives, which won second prize at the Concours de "l'Auto." The body is by Gaston Grummer, and is mounted on Renault chassis. A body of similar design, but not transformable was awarded the grand prix d'honneur at Vichy and at le Touquet

First prize in the category of "Voitures Transformables" was awarded to Mlle. Yvette Laurant for this convertible coupe on Minerva chassis by Gaston Grummer

The "grand prix d'originalite" was won by this car on Chenard-Walcker chassis, with body by Carrosserie S. P. C. A.

A similar design with a "faux cabriolet" body by the Société Parisienne de Carrosserie Automobile

Design Trends *at the Paris Salon*

By Amos E. Northup*

NO individual or race is born with a particular taste for anything. Taste is developed by our environment, by what we daily see and, often, it is affected by other peoples' opinion. European taste has therefore developed different characteristics than ours, but the predominance that the American automobile industry has attained in the world is not only changing manufacturing practices and construction, but is also changing the taste of other people to our designs. It seems to me that the Paris Salon was of more interest to the American visitor than in previous years, due to the fact that their standards of beauty in automobile design resembled ours more than they had in any previous European show.

There were, however, standard practices that differ distinctly from ours and numerous individual designs,

on the ground where it belongs. They are more in harmony with aerodynamic lines, and they hide the front end of the running gear which, at its best, is no ornamentation to the front view.

Several all-metal roofs could also be seen at the Salon this year. There is no doubt that metal makes an extremely beautiful roof, and it is an item of importance now that cars are being made so low that the large area of the roof becomes prominent in the appearance of the car. A construction must eventually be devised that will permit the use of steel here.

As in years past, radiator screens were exceedingly popular at the Salon, though not so popular as they will be at our shows in 1931. Ornaments of this class are usually introduced to the public under the excuse of some utilitarian purpose; that was the case

Fig. 1. The strikingly original design for the new 12-cylinder Voisin. A continuous hinge is possible for the wide doors, because of the vertical body sides. Note the absence of moldings and the special handle for the door. The novel rear, combining a deck effect with that of a large trunk, is complemented by an equally unusual front with special fender braces, "circumscribing" louvers near the front of the bonnet, cowl panels hinged at the center line to permit access to tool box and instrument board, and a windshield slanting forward instead of the customary, backward inclination

Fig. 3. A convertible coupe by Million-Guiet on Hispano chassis. It is finished in a salmon rose, and illustrates some of the newer tendencies in its inclined door lines; flat-folding top, completely designed rear harmonizing with the sweep of the fender; deep side valances of fenders and the use of side bumpers

departing from the general and pertaining only to the car exhibited. The spare tire or wheels are carried, as a rule, in the rear whether the car is equipped with a rear trunk or not. An extra wheel or tire, when mounted on the side, hides the bonnet treatment and destroys the continuity of lines. There is no selection as to the position of a wheel at the side. It must be placed behind, or in, the front fender and this, European designers think, is too close to the front wheel to create a good balance in the composition of the side view.

Another standard practice is to bring the front end or nose of the front fender much lower toward the ground than is usually done by our designers. American and European ideals in this respect seem to be entirely different. Here we have been making wing-like fenders—in fact, front fenders that would seem to lift the car up in the air as it moves along. In Europe front fenders are so designed as to help keep the car

with the screens in France, but here we have frankly adopted them for their ornamental value. I have wondered if the same thing may happen with the popular European wire-wheel cover. Many were the cars equipped with screens, but more were equipped with wheel covers. No usefulness is claimed for them, unless it be that the outside of the wheels may be kept cleaner. This will be, at any rate, no more than an excuse. The reason for its popular adoption is that you can produce a massive looking wheel, in chromium finish, in which the size of the hub cap, its shape and cross section of the cover are entirely up to the taste or ability of the designer, without interfering at all with the construction of the wheel.

It is evident that European designers pay more attention to running boards than we do here. As a matter of fact, it could be said that there is not a marked style or standard in the treatment and shape of the running board, but instead, there is great variety of design, good taste and much individuality.

NOTE—Excerpts from an address before the Body Division, Detroit Section, of the Society of Automotive Engineers, at the Book-Cadillac Hotel, Dec. 8, 1930.
* Chief designer, Murray Corporation of America, Detroit, Mich.

Interesting Bodies at the Brussels Salon

An unusual design for a convertible roadster, on 6-cylinder Delage chassis, by Antoine van den Plas et Fils, of Brussels. The triangular motif is carried out in the front design, as well as in the side elevation. The car was painted in **Carnation Red**, with

the large triangle of the side elevation in black. The small triangle in the middle of the door was in red. Note the tool boxes in the fender valances. The red-and-black color scheme was repeated in the upholstery. The design is copyrighted

A sport "torpédo transformable" on the 40-h.p. Minerva chassis by the Anciens Établissements D'Ieteren Frères, of Brussels. The sporting effect is also noteworthy when the top is folded

Another view of the convertible phaeton by D'Ieteren Frères, with the top down. The car is finished in yellow and black, and was trimmed with a soft, yellow leather with black piping. The cabinetwork is in curly ash, with silver inlay

A 4-passenger "conduite intérieure" on Voisin chassis by Vesters & Neirinck of Brussels. This car, finished entirely in black, is distinguished by its great simplicity and its sober, rounded lines which give an impression of elegance and speed. The rear seats are of the fauteuil type trimmed with a brown fabric and the cabinetwork is of French-polished mahogany, inlaid with silver

A 4-passenger coupe cabriolet on the small Minerva chassis by the Carrosserie Van den Plas. This design uses the popular coach sill and, at the rear, a large trunk harmonizing with the body contour

III

Selected American Coachwork

American coachbuilders featured rumble seats with right-hand side door entry in many sport roadsters and coupes. This convertible coupe was designed by Hildebrand in 1931 on the Duesenberg model "J" 153½-inch wheelbase chassis.

A special body by Fleetwood for a prominent motor-car official. This 5-passenger "inside-drive cabriolet, with collapsible rear quarters" is mounted on a Cadillac chassis having a 152-in. wheelbase. The sporting effect of the body is enhanced by the mailcoach sill and the light leather top which has a Burbank grain. The car is finished in maroon and Paris gray, the latter being used for the splashers, fenders, moldings, top leather and trunk which is covered with the same Burbank-grained leather as the top, and harmonizes pleasingly with the contour of the top. The wire wheels are chromium plated. Other features of the exterior are the Neutralite glass visor giving true traffic-light colors, the narrow front-corner pillars, the automatic ventilator in the roof and the elimination of the necessity of any finish molding over the roof joint. The interior is also interesting by reason of the use of maroon Aero leather on the seats and doors and a dark maroon snake-wood on the door and division friezes

Recent Bodies by *American Custom Builders*

SOME recent special bodies by American builders indicate that our custom designers are realizing that the conventional features of American production cars must be avoided. The accompanying views illustrate what these designers can do when not restricted by executive orders not to depart too far from the family resemblance. Individual clients are apt to give custom designers a greater freedom than is enjoyed by the designers of the car manufacturers who must consider the acceptance of the new designs by the general public. The views presented depart from standard lines sufficiently to make these cars attractive and distinctive, without approaching the freakish.

FLEETWOOD'S INTERESTING BERLINE-LANDAULET

The design at the top of this page is for a 5-passenger berline landaulet of sporting lines recently completed by Fleetwood for an important motor-car executive. Prominent features of the exterior are the mailcoach sill and the use of a light Burbank-grained leather for the top.

This leather was introduced at the last Paris Salon by Kellner to overcome the difficulty experienced in cleaning the light canvas tops so much in vogue in Europe. These leather tops can be satisfactorily cleaned and avoid the annoyance heretofore experienced with the light-colored canvas. The trunk at the rear is also covered with the Coupienne fabric-grained leather, and its silhouette harmonizes with the upper rear of the body. The sloping windshield eliminates light reflections and narrow corner pillars provide exceptional vision for the driver who is protected from sun dazzle by the Neutralite glass visor which also permits him to observe traffic signals in their true colors. A special construction eliminates the usual finish molding across the top at the rear standing pillars and assists in maintaining a pleasing roof line. Harnagell rack-and-pinion window regulators are used on the front-door windows and there is an automatic ventilator in the roof.

The sporting effect of the body, which is mounted on Cadillac chassis, is enhanced by the long wheelbase,

Seven-passenger berline built by the Willoughby Co. on Duesenberg chassis for Nelson B. Nelson, of New York. It is finished in black and Chartreuse green. Instead of the usual windshield the front glass is set stationary; ample ventilation is provided by large top and side cowl ventilators. Seats are trimmed with a Wiese Channel bedford cord of greenish cast; auxiliary seats are extra wide, seating three in emergency

152 in. The car is finished in maroon and Paris gray, the latter color being used for the splashers, fenders, moldings, window framing and top leather. The exposed metalwork, including the wire wheels, is chromium-plated. The maroon-and-gray color scheme is carried out in the interior with an Aero maroon leather on the seats and doors. The cloth lining of the wall and ceiling is a Wiese taupe doeskin. The division glass drops completely, giving a sedan effect when desired; there is no exposed channel or beading at the top where the division glass fits into the roof, the headlining of the two compartments practically meeting, concealing the channel, but permitting the glass to pass through the slit into the channel. The interior wood trim is of snakewood which has a dark maroon cast. This is used as a frieze on the doors and on the division in which there is a swept case containing a clock, notebook, mirror and pin cushion. A Cuno wireless electric lighter is also provided, and concealed ash trays are located in the door panels.

Willoughby Berline on Duesenberg Chassis

The 7-passenger berline designed by the Willoughby Co. on Duesenberg chassis for Nelson B. Nelson, of New York, is an extremely commodious but low car. It has several unusual features, most noteworthy of which is the stationary plate glass in the front of the car instead of the usual windshield. In stormy weather drivers must depend upon the wiper and cannot swing the windshield out far enough to secure ventilation without getting most of the storm; in consequence the front glass has been set stationary and ample ventilation provided by top and side cowl ventilators. Greater driver visibility is obtained by using narrow heat-treated, aluminum-alloy pillars and by omitting the conventional ledge molding on top of the cowl under the windshield; the glass in this job sets flush with the rear of the cowl panel. A Neutralite glass visor is set in narrow chrome-plated frames. The belt panel is deeply crowned and a raised oval extends across the center pillar into the door panels, surrounding the location of the door handles. The body is finished in black and Chartreuse green. The seats are trimmed with a Wiese

Channel bedford cord of greenish cast and the lining is a harmonizing doeskin. The auxiliary seats are extra wide, seating three in emergency.

Judkins Bodies on Lincoln Chassis

The two upper cars in the Judkins group shown on the opposite page are noteworthy for departure from current practice. The all-weather town car shown at the top of this group has a decided sweep in its lower panels and a "tumble-home" belt; in addition the marked concavity of the cowl at the front-corner pillar gives a lengthened effect to the forward portion of the car. The interior is done in an extremely simple manner, with plain-stretched upholstery and down cushions on the rear seat. The one auxiliary seat, with right armrest facing the curb door, is concealed flush in the partition when not in use and this disposition is effected without preventing the slanting partition window from lowering out of sight. This car was recently delivered to a Chicago customer.

The unusual "coupe-phaeton" for five passengers was built by Mr. Judkins for his personal use. It is especially interesting because of the entire absence of moldings and the deep sweep of the top, which incidentally results in the rear-seat occupants riding very much in the open; when the top is down it is really flush with the door line—an effect seldom achieved, though often promised. The entire body is painted in Burmah Rose, with the chassis in a rich maroon; there is of course no striping. The seats are trimmed in a Wiese 2-tone henna-brown Channel bedford cord. The remainder of the interior is trimmed with a harmonizing Colonial-grain leather; the top is of Burbank. The floor of the rear compartment is depressed below the chassis level, giving the occupants ample leg and head room and permitting an exceedingly low car. Easy access to the rear seat is provided by the wide door and the fact that both right and left front seats have movable backs, but it is not actually necessary for the front passengers to move to permit this access. At the rear is an unusually commodious trunk designed to conform to the body lines.

← *Interior of the Judkins all-weather town car, trimmed in plain style, with a Wiese rose-drab doeskin. The slanting partition window drops completely but permits the auxiliary seat to fold into the partition of this close-coupled body*

→ *Interior of the Judkins all-weather landaulet. This is trimmed with a Wiese castor-drab doeskin. The wide auxiliary seats can carry three passengers and fold into the partition, the opening being completely closed by the extension plates around the bottom of the seats*

An all-weather town car built by the Waterhouse Co., of Webster, Mass., on a lengthened Rolls-Royce chassis for H. C. Orndorff, of Providence, R. I. The long sweep of the fenders suggests the power and dignity of the chassis. The difficult cowling problem on the Rolls has been cleverly solved in this design. Belt treatment is in accordance with the current vogue. The opera light on the front face of the partition panel has the owner's crest etched in red glass. The ventilating panel in the rear quarter is hinged at the front

Town Car by Waterhouse on Rolls-Royce Chassis

A Car of Pleasing Proportions, with Unusual Features Many of Which were Specified by the Owner

THIS interesting town car was recently completed by the Waterhouse Co., custom-body builders, of Webster, Mass., and delivered to H. C. Orndorff, of Providence, R. I. Its pleasing proportions are in keeping with the dignity of the Rolls-Royce chassis and the difficult cowling problem has been happily solved. Molding treatment is in the current mode, and the front and rear of the car have received some designing attention as will be noted in the views below. The front valance is readily removable by unscrewing a wing nut on each side; these two wing nuts, with dowels at the back of the valance, hold it securely in place. The trunk at the rear was specially designed to have its lines conform with those of the back molding. The car is mounted on a lengthened Phantom chassis and has a wheelbase of 160 in. which gave an opportunity for a roomy body and the seating of the passengers forward of the rear axle. The fenders have the characteristic Rolls-Royce section, but they have been lengthened and changed at the running board, which is of walnut, with strips of rubber let into it, and bound on three sides with a nickeled brass molding.

BODY PANELS EXTEND BELOW CHASSIS

The cowl and body panels are carried down to the running board, but the bottoms of the doors are only a few inches below the chassis level. Under the rear doors are removable panels which provide access to the rear springs. For the all-weather front, there is a special roof section which is attached by ball-end wing nuts; thick sponge rubber in the solid top presses against an oval molding in the front of the partition and makes a waterproof junction, without the necessity of a finish molding. In addition to the solid top,

Front and rear view of the Waterhouse town car on Rolls-Royce chassis

Another view of the Orndorff town car with driving compartment enclosed for inclement weather. This body was designed and mounted by the Waterhouse Co. on a 160-in. Rolls-Royce chassis. A roof section for the driving compartment carries out perfectly the line of the roof; however, for sudden emergencies, a special canopy is carried under the seat. The body panels are carried down to the running board and the doors a few inches below the level of the chassis. Access to the rear springs is provided by a removable panel under the rear doors

there is a standard canopy top which is carried in the car, in case of sudden rain, while it is operated as a town car. In the center of the division header is an opera light with the owner's crest etched in the red glass. The front doors have removable headers which when in place give them the same appearance as the rear doors. Heavy bus hinges are used on all the doors. The small leather-covered panel in the rear quarter is a ventilating panel; it is hinged along the front edge and the operating mechanism, except the handle, is concealed on the inside.

The car is finished in two shades of dark blue, the body being in Bennington Blue and the small door panels above the belt in Ridge Blue. The top leather matches the darker shade. The front compartment is trimmed in a similar dark-blue leather. Recessed remote controls operate the latches, and three-quarter-turn quick-action regulators control the windows of the front doors.

UNUSUAL INTERIOR EQUIPMENT

Interior equipment is chiefly the selection of the owner, an observant motorist of long experience, whose specifications represent what he felt was necessary—for him—in the perfect car. The rear doors and the division are equipped with walnut shutters, in addition to the usual glass. The shutters are operated by crank regulators similar to those for the glass. The positioning of these fittings form the motif for the decora-

Interior view of the Orndorff town car by Waterhouse. The fauteuils in the rear are trimmed with a Schumacher imported cut velvet in dark blue and tan and have loose down seat and back cushions, and a silk fringe at the bottom. In addition to the regular carpet, there is an Oriental rug that exactly fits the rear compartment. Stuffed saddle bags serve as footrests in place of the usual hassocks. In the view at the left will be noted the back window, which is controlled by a Rawlings regulator, and the partly open ventilator panel in the rear quarter. A blue broadlace is used across the door and partition, instead of the more common wood frieze. Two removable emergency seats are provided which are anchored in the partition by tapered male and female joints. When not needed, they are replaced by large flap pockets which have a stiff back and an attaching lug that fits into the seat socket of the partition. One seat and one pocket are shown in position. The driving compartment is interesting for the treatment of the door panels, the recessed remote-control handles for the door and the large cranks of the quick-acting, three-quarter-turn windowlifts

tion of the door panels. A toggle door pull is provided and broadlace harmonizing with the seat upholstery is used across the doors and partition in place of the usual wood friezes. Instead of the customary toggle, an assist handle covered with leather is provided on the door-hinge pillar. A cord hat or parcel rack is attached to the ceiling and an electric fan is mounted on the division header. The three switches just aft of the ventilating panel control the fan, domelight and corner reading lights. Lamps set in the

Another interior of the Waterhouse town car showing the special slip covers for summer use, and the interesting door trim and placement of regulator handles for window and shutter

pillars illumine the entrance automatically when either front or rear doors are open.

On the right side, not showing in the photograph is the transmitter of the chauffeur's phone, concealed under the side lining, but having the usual group of embroidered holes over the transmitter. The loud speaker is of the flush type and is mounted in the left-hand front door at the chauffeur's shoulder, connections being run through spring contacts in the door pillar. This positions the loud speaker much nearer than when mounted on the instrument board and less conspicuously than when in the front of the partition.

The reading lights in corners of the rear compartment are of the sconce type with the socket projecting at the bottom of an ornamental plate which includes a concave reflector. Fairly powerful translucent bulbs are used; the protecting shield is made of the same material as the rear curtains and bound with blue velvet. If a particularly bright reading light is desired, the shields can be turned to one side, and with the division shutter up, no annoyance is experienced from the lights of approaching cars. The back window is fitted with a Rawlings lift so as to provide adequate ventilation in hot weather.

The passengers are seated slightly forward of the axle, in fauteuils trimmed with a Schumacher imported cut velvet in dark blue and tan. Loose down cushions are provided for both the seats and the backs of these chairs. The lining is a De Luxe broadcloth which is also used for the auxiliary seats and for the flap pockets that are installed on the partition when the auxiliary seats are not carried. The special set of slip covers, made at the time the car was built, is shown in one of the accompanying views which also illustrates the interesting door panel. Although there is the usual carpet on the floor of this compartment, above it has been placed an Oriental rug that just fits the space. This Oriental touch is supplemented by the use of stuffed saddle bags for footrests.

REMOVABLE AUXILIARY SEATS

The auxiliary seats represent a departure that has often been urged with respect to these units. They are entirely removable and when not in use are replaced by large flap pockets that fit tightly against the partition and cover the socket fittings of the auxiliary seats. The castings for the auxiliary seats were special and comprise V-type male and female fittings, affording a wedge-tight fit. The flap pockets have a stiff back to which are attached wooden male fittings that go into the same sockets as the auxiliary seats. Although this body presents an array of unusual features, all are of a practical character and meet needs that the owner had encountered in the course of a long experience in town and country driving.

"Riviera" Town Brougham by Brewster on Rolls-Royce Chassis

"Derby" Speedster Phaeton by Brewster on Rolls-Royce Chassis

Rolls-Royce Town Car with "Drawing-Room" Interior

This "Salamanca de Ville" on the Rolls Phantom chassis illustrates the tendency, at recent Salons, to introduce the atmosphere of the drawing room into the motoring home. Most of the paneling in view of the passengers is hand-carved walnut, done in the style of Louis Seize; the division paneling was similar to that on the doors; a wide walnut molding was used around the roof rails and a smaller carved molding in the ceiling panel which was lined with a plain tan broadcloth. The seat fabric, the pattern of which is exaggerated by the photograph, was an imported novelty by Wiese, in two tones of golden brown. Note the signal button in the end of the carved-walnut armrest, the superimposed squab, and the smoking and toilet cases set into the walnut-paneled recess in the rear quarter. The hardware had gold-bronze or old-ivory finish, but the domelight rosette was of carved walnut. Instead of the usual door pulls, a groove was carved in the garnish rail

Weymann Bodies on High-Grade American Chassis

Design for a 4-passenger sport sedan built by the Weymann American Body Co. on Duesenberg 142 1/2-in. chassis. The main body panels are sheathed with smooth Zapon Liss of cream color. The upper panels are covered with light green, seal-grain Zapon. The seats are trimmed with Italian goat skins and the door friezes are of burl walnut. This car was purchased by Thomas J. Lewis, of New York

Versailles 4-passenger Weymann sedan mounted on Stutz 134 1/2-in. chassis. The roof and quarters are covered in gray Zapon, the lower body being in black with chronium-plated wheels and other exterior metalwork. This body was in the Stutz exhibit at Saratoga and was also sold to a New York customer

The Monte Carlo model built by Weymann-American on 145-in. Stutz chassis. The exterior is sheathed in light and dark brown, pebble-grain Zapon. The interior is trimmed with Italian goat skins and there is a large storage compartment in the tail. This was one of the Stutz exhibits at Saratoga

A 4-passenger Deauville on the Packard 6-40 chassis. The roof and quarters are gray Burbank, the remainder of the car being sheathed in black seal-grain Zapon. The rear quarter is collapsible and the wide doors give ready access to the rear seats; the front seats are individually adjustable. A tan Morocco leather is used for the seats and broadcloth for the headlining

A 4-pasenger 2-door sedan on 143-in. Pierce-Arrow chassis. The exterior is sheathed throughout with gray seal-grain Zapon, the chassis being finished in light green. The interior is trimmed with a Wiese green-tinted heather mixture, and burl walnut is used for the door friezes. All of the designs on this page have the rear seats positioned forward of the rear axle

New Standard Models Now in Production

The new Chrysler cars again exhibit the most outstanding changes in design. The narrow radiator shell which distinguished the Chrysler line last year is retained. A striking feature of this year's design is the treatment of the bonnet louvers. This gay and sprightly design appears to particularly good advantage on the open cars of the "77" series, the phaeton of which is shown above; on the roadster the concave through molding encircles the body aft of the deck seat instead of continuing down to the chassis. The view at the right shows the "77" Royal sedan. The drip molding accentuates the framing of the windows as a group, and an unusual feature of the super structure is the mounting of the parking lights high on the front pillars. The interior hardware and door friezes have modern-art motifs. Although no emblem appears on the radiator, the series number is mounted on a small horizontal name plate at the center of the lamp bar

Hupp Motor Car Corporation's new six in the $1,000 price field bears a family resemblance to its Century Eight, but with sufficient changes of detail to make the models easily distinguishable. A characteristic change is the slight turn-in or off-setting of the lower panels at the belt.. The phaeton is the most costly of the four body types mounted on the Six and differs markedly from the closed models. The door lines are unusual for a production car; the front door supplements the line of the upper cowl treatment but the rear door is more conventional. The view at the right shows the sedan which lists at $1,060. Interior hardware is designed with angular motifs and emphasizes the tendency toward modern art in interiors

Gardner introduces a new molding treatment on its series 140 "brougham." This close-coupled, landau-type sedan has the popular concave front, the molding of the front pillars sweeping into the belt molding which in turn is swept to the center of the cowl. The molding at the rear-door window is similarly blended into the belt molding which is swept at the rear quarter to its narrowest dimension as it approaches the rear corner and then swells to pleasing proportions in passing across the back of the body

The new Model 612 sedan of the Graham-Paige Motors Corporation. This series is mounted on 115-in. wheelbase and now resembles the company's higher-priced cars and exteriorly presents little change. One of the marked improvements in the interior is the adoption of rubber-covered floorboards in the driving compartment. These are produced by a patented process in which the rubber is molded on the boards and extends over the edges so as to form an air-tight joint. The lever openings are kept practically air tight by overlapping rubber flanges

Bodies by Fleetwood for the New Cadillac

This 4-passenger sedan has the modish coach sill and slanting windshield which characterize the latest constructions of the custom-body builders. The top is a light-colored, fabric-grained leather and the dummy head joints are painted to match the leather, instead of being nickel or chromium plated

A square-cornered brougham with metal upper panel and canework below; the latter is carried forward to emphasize the sweep of a coupe-pillar molding that flows into the base molding. The front is transformable into a closed compartment, in accordance with modern practice, and a V-windshield is used

Fleetwood's "transformable limousine brougham" on 140-in. wheelbase. This has the fashionable coach sill and a new cover at the rear for the chassis members

An unusual phaeton recently built by Alexander Wolfington's Son, Inc., of Philadelphia, on 153½-in. Duesenberg chassis for a New York client. The "wave" effect of the upper moldings and fore-door rail is carried out in both the lower molding and the chassis valance. The color scheme, selected by the client, was beige and two shades of brown, the darker color being used for the moldings and the lighter brown for belt panels, fenders and chassis. The wire wheels and other exposed metalwork are chromium plated. No black is used on this job; even the instrument panel is finished in brown to conserve the color scheme and to match the leather trim of the interior

Wolfington Re-Enters Field of Private Coachwork

THIS unusual 4-passenger phaeton on 153½-in. Duesenberg chassis signalizes the re-entry of Wolfington, of Philadelphia, into the field of high-grade custom bodywork for private cars after a lapse of about five years, during which this firm devoted the major part of its production to de luxe motorcoaches, with only an occasional special body for private clients. Fifty-three years of experience in high-grade coachwork enabled this organization to change from one line to the other, and to revert in one step to private-car bodies of exclusive design and equipment.

Accompanying illustrations present a phaeton of unique design, built by Wolfington to carry out the owner's ideas for a roomy and comfortable car for four passengers. The color scheme is in the fashionable brown field, the body panels being in beige while two

shades of brown are used for the moldings and for the belt panels, mudguards and chassis. The moldings are in the darker brown shade and are striped with a brown-tinted white, all colors having been specially mixed by the Beckwith-Chandler Co. to conform to the ideas of the client. Even the instrument panel was brought through by Duesenberg in brown and a matching shade was used in dyeing the pigskin for the interior trim.

The unique belt-and-molding treatment is supplemented by embossing the chassis valances with corresponding sweeps. The moldings are unusual in having a rectangular cross section instead of the half-round or half-oval section ordinarily employed. The double moldings on the cowl and bonnet panels sweep to the center of the bonnet and end in a chromium-plated casting of arrowhead shape. The base molding follows the

Interior of the Wolfington-Duesenberg phaeton was trimmed in brown pigskin to conform to the general color scheme of this strictly 4-passenger car. The seat construction is interesting, comprising a Trenton lace-web spring of 2½-in. thickness above which is an adjustable air cushion of about three inches and a 2½-in. layer of down; the cushions measure 24 in. from the back. A removable center armrest of sponge rubber is provided for each cross seat. The door trim is unusual, having a series of peripheral overstuffed plaits and large shirred pockets on the rear doors and locked flap pockets, for tools, on the front doors; the oak frieze at the top of the doors has a leather "inlay," and at the bottom is a 4-in. strip of carpet. A radio set is concealed in the tonneau cabinet at the center of which is a crank for raising the tonneau windshield. Hassocks of triangular section replace the customary footrail

sweep of the front fender and then the wave effect of the upper molding treatment. The center body panel is capped by a casting with a diamond-shaped relief, on which is placed the owner's crest, and marks the beginning of a double molding and belt extending aft across the rear doors and around the back of the body.

The upholstering of the interior is done in a brown pigskin, harmonizing with the general color scheme. The seat construction is interesting; a special slope was specified for the backs, and the cushions are built up on a Trenton lace-web spring of 2½-in. thickness upon which is an adjustable air cushion of 3 in., superposed by a 2½-in. layer of down. The air in the cushion is adjustable, enabling the passenger or driver to sit at the height desired. Cushions are of exceptional dimensions measuring 24 in. from the back. The front seat is adjustable longitudinally 4 in.; the removable center armrest and the low door line enable the driver to assume a restful position. The rear seat, with its side armrests, has an armchair effect and was built entirely outside the car and then bolted in place. The central

which are trimmed with chromium-plated strips. The top, side curtains and top boot are of Burbank and are bound with the brown pigskin. The top boot is loose fitted so that it may be easily put on. Between the decking and lining of the top, the radio aerial is interwoven in such a manner as to permit folding without damage. The oak trunk at the rear has two compartments which are accessible, by key, from the near side. The spare-wheel carrier is of metal but is covered with brown pigskin and is fitted with two Yale locks.

Brown Leads Automobile Color Index

Black, which was the leading color at the Automobile Salons and even at the National Automobile Shows, is relegated to fourth place in the January Automobile Color Index recently issued by the Duco Color Advisory Service. Brown has for the first time gained leadership over all other automobile color families. It gained steadily during 1929 and at the beginning of the year

A closer view of the unusual belt-and-molding treatment of the Wolfington-Duesenberg 4-passenger phaeton. The wave effect of the moldings is accentuated by the brownish-white striping and by the embossing of the chassis valance. Moldings have a rectangular cross section instead of the usual half-round or half-oval section. The owner's crest instead of being placed on the door is framed by the striping in the belt of the central panel. The "secondary cowl" is stationary and two grab handles are fitted to assist the rear-seat occupants to arise. The chromium-trimmed oak box set in the running board contains the battery, tools being carried in front-door pockets and in the 2-compartment oak "trunk" at the rear. The metal spare-wheel carrier is covered with the brown pigskin. The Burbank top is piped with pigskin and conceals the antenna of the radio set

armrests for both seats have a deep padding of sponge rubber. Hassocks of triangular section supplant the customary footrail, and fit partly under the tonneau cabinet. Carpets have a deep pile and are bound with pigskin.

The door trim is another interesting feature of this car, being done with the brown pigskin in a series of peripheral plaits around a central pocket; on the rear doors a shirred leather pocket is used, while on the front doors the pockets are of the bottom-hinged flap type and are provided with locks to permit the storing of frequently used tools. Door friezes are 4 in. deep and are of light oak with an "inlay" of the brown pigskin. At the bottom of the doors are 4-in. scuff strips of carpet. The tonneau cabinet, also of the light oak, conceals a radio-receiving set when it is not in use. In the center of the cabinet is mounted a crank handle for raising the secondary windshield.

The "secondary cowl" is stationary, and is fitted with grab handles to assist the rear-seat occupants in rising. To conform to the brown color scheme, oak is used for the running boards, the battery box and trunk, all of

has an index record of 168 as against 122 for blue, 121 for green, 79 for black, 58 for maroon and 47 for gray. Green and maroon both exhibit a rising tendency. The dominance of brown in the dress industries of America and France is perhaps responsible for its present ascendancy in the automotive industry. Brown and green are expected to be the outstanding colors in the automotive world this spring. Soft mellow browns with considerable yellow in their make-up are continuing to prove of interest, as well as some of the lighter neutral shades. Gray and blue have shown marked declines since the middle of 1929. Black on the other hand showed a steady rise from June, reaching its high point on the index in December; it now exhibits an abrupt fall, possibly due to the work on spring schedules.

Bryan Specialty Co., manufacturer of school buses, moving vans and other commercial bodies, at Bryan, Ohio, has taken a contract to build 300 or more stake bodies to be fitted to Willys-Knight and Whippet chassis. From previously published reports, it has been erroneously assumed that these were panel bodies.

Glass-quarter brougham built by Brunn & Co., on Pierce-Arrow chassis, as a ceremonial car for the Shah of Persia. It is a one-passenger car, no other person riding with the Shah on such occasions. The car is finished in white and gold, and replicas of the Persian crown on the headlamps and doors are the only points of notable ornamentation. The simplicity and beauty of the design, and the perfect artisanship make it an impressive vehicle, notwithstanding this modicum of decoration. The finish of the car is a white of unusual brilliance and purity, heightened by the yellow of the gold-plated metalwork. The designers are to be congratulated particularly for their remarkably successful treatment of the front and rear design of the car, of which unfortunately no views are available

Royal Brougham, *by Brunn*, on Pierce-Arrow Chassis *for Shah of Persia*

A HANDSOME, but simple, ceremonial carriage of modern type is now en route to Persia, having been shipped from New York late in April. The glass-quarter brougham, with open front, shown in the accompanying illustration, is destined for Teheran and will be used on ceremonial occasions by Riza Khan, Shah of Persia. It was designed and built by Brunn & Co., custom-body builders of Buffalo, and was mounted on the Pierce-Arrow "A" chassis. The car is finished e n t i r e l y in white, and trimmed judiciously w i t h gold. All the e x p o s e d metalwork is gold plated, including the replicas of the Persian crown on the headlamps and doors, which constitute practically the only p o i n t s of ornamentation. The impressive simplicity and dignity of the car are derived from its fine proportioning, its beauty of line, a n d restrained decorative treatment.

The modicum of ornamentation for this new vehicle will perhaps be a matter of wonderment for many Westerners who are accustomed to visualize all Eastern objects as decorated with elaborate tracery. But a new Persia is dawning, and Riza Khan is a modern and

Interior of the Shah of Persia's ceremonial brougham is marked by simplicity. The color scheme is champagne and gold. Decoration on seat is Shah's family emblem.

energetic monarch. Having grasped the vacillating helm of state, he is now directing his country into an era of modernization and progress, through the development of Persia's dormant resources and by providing better transportation facilities. Railroads have been extended and about 4,000 mi. of highways are opening country that until recently was only traversed by camel caravans. Telephones and telegraph service, including wireless, are already a part of the life of Persia. Hence, a modern state carriage from the most modern country of manufacture is merely a corollary of the progress that is gradually transforming Persia into a 20th Century country.

The Shah's new car is noteworthy not only for the dignity apparent in the side view, but also for the attention that has been given to the design of the front and rear, of which unfortunately no photographs are available at this writing. This is one of the few cars that have achieved an attractive frontal appearance. The radiator has been raised and narrowed at the top and the rounded effect of the windshield is in harmony with the attractive but simple design of the division front.

An interesting sport roadster, with disappearing top, built on a Miller Special chassis, for a Santa Barbara sportsman by the J. Gerard Kirchhoff Body Works, of Pasadena, Calif. This is a front-drive car with 8-cylinder V-type engine, equipped with a supercharger, and is capable of a speed of 135 mi. per hr. No steel was used in the bodywork, all body braces, fender supports and similar strength members being made of duralumin, the panels and fenders being of aluminum. The front fender, with its brackets, weighs only a little over 11 lb. The disappearing top and deck are unusual, as will be noted in the views shown below

A Disappearing-Top Roadster for *Front-Drive* Chassis

THIS interesting 2-passenger roadster was built to order for a wealthy Santa Barbara sportsman by the J. Gerard Kirchhoff Body Works, of Pasadena, Calif. It is mounted on a front-drive chassis personally engineered by Harry A. Miller, the well-known builder of racing cars. The car is powered with an 8-cylinder, V-type engine equipped with supercharger and capable of developing 325 hp., sufficient to drive the car at a speed of 135 mi. per hr. Because of the high speed of which this car is capable, the body, bonnet and fenders were of special design and construction. Throughout the whole construction, weight was cut without sacrificing strength. The fenders are of aluminum; one front fender weighs only a little more than 11 lb. All body braces are of duralumin, instead of the customary steel. The car is finished in Ditzler's Ivory Jet Black, set off by polished metal. There is a chromium-plated molding running from radiator to rear, and the entire chassis is plated. Fender braces are of polished duralumin.

Wind resistance has been cut to a minimum, streamlining having been applied to the radiator shell, bonnet louvers and general outline of the car body. There are no outside door handles and even the bonnet is unlocked and raised by special removable handles. The disappearing top is of novel construction; there is no overhang at the windshield, the top ending in a metal nose that holds it securely to the windshield and eliminates eddy resistance at this point. With the top erected, the height of the car is only 4 ft. 10 in. overall. When it is not desired to use the top, it is stowed in the tail, the entire rear deck being raised as shown in the view below. When the deck is down, there is no trace of a top nor of a break in the deck. The latter is locked securely at three points by one handle. To operate this handle, however, it is necessary to pull the seatback forward. The seatback cannot be restored to its position without locking the rear deck. Hence the car cannot be driven when the deck is not in proper position. This and several other features of the body are being covered by patents. The seat is trimmed in a special plaited style, with Eagle-Ottawa black seal-grain leather. The extra cap shown on the radiator is for water to cool the supercharger which operates at a speed of 36,000 revolutions per minute.

The disappearing-top speedster built by the J. Gerard Kirchhoff Body Works, of Pasadena, Calif., on Miller Special chassis. The disappearing top and rear deck are of novel construction, specially designed to withstand the high speed of which this car is capable. The top has a metal header which is securely attached to the windshield without overhang. No running boards or steps are provided and the overall height of the car is only 4 ft. 10 in. Note the special attachments of the deck and the streamline design of the bonnet louver. The entire chassis is plated, a chromium-plated molding runs from radiator to rear and the faces of the door pillar are of polished stainless steel. The car is finished in Ditzler's Ivory Jet Black. The extra radiator cap is for water to cool the supercharger

Special Bodies by Fleetwood

A special 7-passenger "Imperial Cabriolet" (4-window ber'ine) on the Cadillac V-16 chassis. There is no striping on the body, the finish being of such character as to bring out the features. The main body panels are in a deep maroon; saddle and belt panels of polished aluminum; the moldings and superstructure in light tan; and the rear quarters and top in leather of the same color, fabric-grained to imitate Burbank. The visor is of amber celluloid

Interior of the passenger compartment of the special Fleetwood body, on Cadillac V-16 chassis, shown at the top of the opposite page. The seats, side squabs and door panels are trimmed with a special henna-maroon, tan-figured broadcloth, supplied by William Wiese & Co. The door panel is plain trimmed, but seats and side squabs are in a tufted style; in the armrests there are pockets with flaps, covered with the seat fabric. The lining fabric is a plain henna-maroon broadcloth. This is also used in the front compartment above the belt; the driving seat and lower panels are trimmed with Radel Aeroleather of a deep maroon color. The swept division frieze has a center of amboyna, with rosewood beading and edges of French walnut to match the garnish moldings; there is a swept smoking case in the center. In the panel, above the division window, a "vanity clock" in an inlaid case is installed. The swept door friezes are of amboyna and rosewood to correspond with the other wood trim

A 7-passenger "Imperial" (6-window berline) built for a private client on a Pierce-Arrow chassis. It has a wheelbase of 143⅝ in. and about 1½ in. more of headroom than is customary. The interior is trimmed in the plain-stretched style with a Wiese greenish broadcloth of lizard-skin pattern. The wood trim is of French walnut, without inlay

IV

Selected European Coachwork

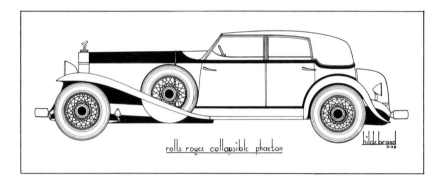

rolls royce collapsible phaeton

European coachbuilders favored unusual saddle panel treatment and taut roof structures, as shown on this Rolls-Royce Phantom II with body designed by George Hildebrand in 1930.

One of the Prize-Winning Bodies of the Carrosserie Grummer

The Carrosserie Gaston Grummer, which was successful with all its entries, won one of its first prizes with this Zapon-covered 4-passenger "sport fermées," which was mounted on Panhard - Levassor chassis. The beige-colored fabric covering is carried down on the sides to the bottom of the chassis and a step is used instead of a running board. The chassis is in red. The interior is trimmed with genuine snakeskin (Karung, Alpina). The interior wood trim is done in lemonwood which is inset with Chinese-shark leather

Sliding and Folding Seats as Used in Great Britain

By H. J. Butler*

I N Great Britain, nearly every saloon has some form of adjustable front seats; there is consequently a steady and even increasing demand for fittings on which to mount these seats. Adjustable front seats are required for two purposes: (1) To provide a variable driving position; (2) to facilitate entry. The latter requirement is easily the more important, especially when the saloon is a 2-door model, so that a gangway is required to the rear seats. With the 4-door body a sliding seat allows the gangway in front of it to be temporarily increased; this is much restricted when the seat is in its normal position, because of the prevailing custom of keeping the screen as close to the steering wheel as possible. A close-up screen not only gives a better outlook for the driver, but it gives scope for the maximum length of scuttle panel, a feature preferred by most owner drivers.

For the 2-door saloon the front seats are usually of the bucket type, with the driver's seat made to slide and the passenger's either to tip forward, or to slide. When this seat tips it does so from the front edge of the seatboard, but if it slides then the back merely folds forward.

*46 Hart Grove, Ealing Common, W. 5. England.

The sliding front seat used for saloons, various types of coupes and open cars, is mounted on a pair of runners. Each runner is of flattened "J" section having an opening just wide enough to take another runner of similar section which is inserted in the opposite direction and fastened to the floor. In this way the amount of open runner exposed for the entry of dirt is reduced to a minimum. The seat is adjusted by means of a spring plunger fastened to the front of the seat. The plunger engages with a plate screwed to the floor and provided with holes spaced at close intervals.

The plunger may also be mounted on the outer side of the seat, in which case the holes for adjustment are drilled in the corresponding floor runner of the seat slide and no middle adjustment plate is required. If interlocking runners are not employed, brackets are screwed under the seat and drilled for the passage of a pair of rods that are mounted on end bearings providing the necessary clearance from the floor. The spring-plunger adjustment is much the same as for the interlocking runners.

Adjusting Mechanisms Used by Austin Motors, Ltd., for Bucket and Cross Seats

Two types of adjustment for cross seats of the "Clifton" tourer. The method of operation will be readily

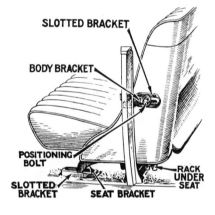

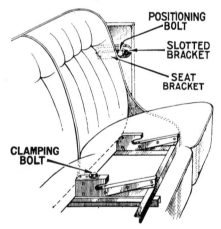

understood by an examination of the sketches. The view at the left shows the later development

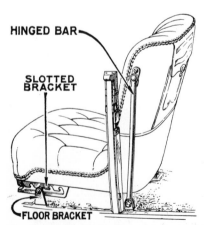

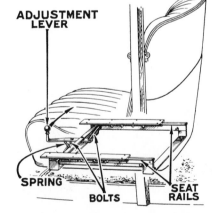

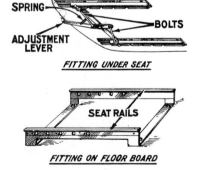

Austin adjustable bucket seat for tourers and metal-sheathed saloons. The special rack on the bottom of the seat engages, on each side, a horizontal pin supported by small floor brackets. Five positions give the driver a 6-in. adjustment

Adjustable seat developed for the Austin fabric-covered saloons. The rails are raised above the floor and slightly inclined. They are drilled in five places and give a maximum adjustment of 8 in. Adjustment is effected by the knob at the front and the lever arrangement shown in the upper right-hand view

Group of Auxiliary Seats Used by Arthur Mulliner, Ltd., of Northampton

Occasional seats which permit emergency passengers to face either forward or backward. The backrests can be turned over and the opposite side of the seat can be sat upon, the division itself then forming the backrest. The seats are trimmed both sides and fold flush into the division

An occasional seat on which the emergency passenger faces to the center. This is used in a body with restricted leg-room for the rear occupants. The backrest folds down and the seat fitments operate in slotted runs permitting the seat to fold flush into the division

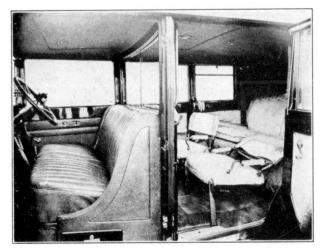

Forward-facing seats with armrests. The type at the left has a double-folding backrest which can be let down to form a leg rest for the rear-seat occupant. The seats have polished-wood bottoms to match the remainder of the division into which they fold flush. At the right is a forward-facing seat with extra high armrests and a padded back. The bottom of the seat is trimmed to harmonize with the remainder of the interior

From One of Germany's Best Body Shops

An interesting 4-passenger cabriolet observed recently by a correspondent at Lugano. This body was built by Joseph Neuss, of Berlin-Halensee, on Packard chassis. With the top up, as shown, the car looks especially smart. Note the interesting line of the body side which is carried below the top of the chassis. Fenders are deeply crowned and the running board, fitted with a scraper grille, is heavily rounded. Two spare wheels are carried aft of a large trunk at the rear. Unusual features are the bonnet treatment and the circular ventilator in the side of the cowl

Two Bodies by Papler, of Cologne

A berline by the Papler Karosseriewerk G. m. b. H., on Maybach chassis. The doors do not extend above the belt. Windows are in nickel frames and operate against special rubber moldings, shown in the sectional view below. This special rubber molding may be readily renewed by the driver or owner. The construction gives passengers greatly improved vision. This berline is finished in ultra-marine blue and dark Bordeaux red, with white striping on the belt. Note the continuous-window-reveal effect. The running-board facing is carried up on the rear fender, with beading around the edge. Zeiss direction signals are mounted at both front corners. The passenger compartment is trimmed with a dark blue cloth, in combination with a blue-gray fabric for the ceiling and sides

Papler enclosed cabriolet completely opened. It may also be operated as a standard cabriolet with open front. Note the sectional view of the renewable rubber moldings against which the nickel-framed windows operate

A 6-window "Pullman-cabriolet" by the Papler Karosseriewerk G. m. b. H., on Cadillac chassis. This has a patented head fitting which will be noted above in the folded position. The upper portion of the door-hinge pillar folds into a compartment dissembled in the division. All windows are nickel framed and their tightness is secured by special rubber moldings which may be readily renewed when worn. The windows are stated to be absolutely noiseless in every position

Group of Bodies by D'Ieteren Freres

A 4-passenger "transformable torpédo" on Minerva chassis. One of the exhibits of the Anciens Établissements D'Ieteren Frères, S. A., at the Brussels Salon. The lengthened bonnet, extending in one panel to the windshield, gives the car an air of unusual power and permits ready access to the wiring and tubing; a shutter controls the ventilation of the louvers aft of the dash

This cabriolet-type town car, with all-weather front, on Cadillac chassis, attracted much attention at the Brussels Salon by reason of its excellent proportions and simplicity of design. The doors were carried down to the running board with a marked turnunder, and the absence of belt molding is noteworthy. The car was finished in two shades of beige. Auxiliary seats were dissembled in a convex division cabinet of burl amboyna, a Moluccan Island wood

A glass-quarter brougham with all-weather front, also on a Cadillac chassis. It was finished in straw yellow, with black moldings, chassis and upperworks. The interior was trimmed with a putty-colored cloth and the cabinetwork was done in curly ash in a modern design but without marquetry or striping. The auxiliary seats were forward facing and of comfortable proportions

A convertible coupe with disappearing top built by D'Ieteren Frères on the Mercedes supercharged sport chassis

Another view of the Mercedes convertible coupe, with top erected. This body was sent to New York for the Mercedes exhibit at the National Automobile Show, but was sold before that exhibition

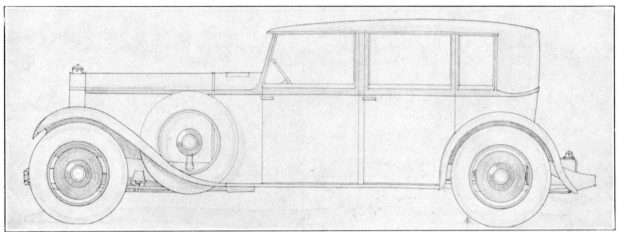

Design for a valanceless sedan-limousine on 145½-in. Packard chassis. Note that the doors are of practically equal width

The Vogue of the Vanishing Valance

By John Jay Ide*

IN FRANCE during the summer of 1927 there were brought out a number of 2-door, 4-passenger enclosed bodies, in which the doors ran down to the running-board level thus doing away with the valances that generally fill in the spaces between the running boards and frame.

This type of body was the result of an effort to weld into one harmonious whole the body and chassis, two hitherto more or less unrelated parts separated by the top of the chassis frame. The valanceless design was originally limited to the 2-door body as its earlier applications were on short chassis where a single wide door is more satisfactory than two narrow doors. During 1928 the idea of suppressing the valance made further progress abroad and is now being applied even in bodies mounted on the longest chassis. It is therefore no longer necessary to obtain adequate legroom for the rear passengers by providing wells or "foot baths" extending below the frame level on each side of the driveshaft.

---

* Care of Guaranty Trust Co., 3 rue des Italiens, Paris.

It is predicted that American coachmakers in their search for "original" and "novel" ideas will soon borrow this European conception and thus put themselves still further in the debt of their foreign colleagues. Indeed at the recent New York show Dietrich exhibited a body on a Franklin chassis, frankly based on a design by Snutsel, the well known Belgian body builder, in which the doors ran down below the frame and bulged out over the running boards and in which the rear wheels were enclosed in covers.

For the information of American clients and body designers there is illustrated the valanceless idea applied to the "Sedanca," a town car having a fixed roof over the rear compartment but a folding top over the driver who is further protected by windows. The Sedanca was originated by Barker of London and has been copied in England, on the Continent and, with slight changes, in America by Le Baron, Fleetwood and others. In the Sedanca shown here, the designers Thrupp & Maberly of London have coped successfully with the difficult problem of avoiding an appearance of undue heaviness of the doors below the belt line,

A Rolls-Royce, with Thrupp & Maberly "Sedanca" body in which the doors have been carried down to the running board, avoiding the customary valance

sometimes caused by their added depth. It is unfortunate, however, that the low window-sill level and deep cutout of the rear doors prevent the windows from being opened completely. The spare wheels conceal, at least partially, the potentially ugly line at the bottom of the cowl where the body is dropped below the frame level. In 2-door bodies on short chassis this line is often masked by large toolboxes sunk in the front mudguards.

EQUAL-WIDTH DOORS ESSENTIAL

There is also presented here a design for a conservative sedan-limousine, with vanishing valance, applied to a Packard chassis of 145½-in. wheelbase. An important point in this design is that the doors are of equal width at least to within the permissible limit of visual error. There is nothing so shocking to the eye even slightly affected by balance and symmetry as the current practice of designing bodies with doors of obviously different widths, frequently followed by a rear quarter window of yet another width. Imagine the effect of a facade of a building designed along these lines! Of course the excuse for such an unbalanced arrangement is that the bodies are mounted on wheelbases too short to allow doors of equal width unless the division behind the front seats projects into the rear compartment. As intimated above, the principal problem in the valanceless body is to avoid an appearance of undue heaviness below the belt line. Care must also

be taken to allow room for the rear-door windows to drop completely.

The small rear-quarter windows can swing out by being hinged at the front, an idea conceived by William Brewster and which affords good ventilation without drafts. Or, the window can be divided into two sections, each upper and lower half dropping into its own channel thus permitting the entire opening of the window despite the wheelhousing. The first use of this idea in a permanently closed body was in a sedan-limousine built by Kellner for the writer on an Hispano-Suiza several years ago. It is suggested that the rear seats of the present design be made adjustable by pulling them forward on a track, thus automatically changing the angle of the backs. This presupposes two central arms instead of the single arm now becoming generalized.

In closing this article it is desired to emphasize the importance of clients of custom coachmakers insisting upon adequate headroom. Because many chassis are now reasonably low, absurdly squat bodies are not so much the fashion as was the case two years ago. In any body used for touring, the distance between the rear part of the undepressed cushion and the ceiling should never be less than 37 in. The writer knows personally of a number of serious accidents caused by the heads of the rear passengers striking the roofs of bodies designed for smart appearance but not to give the occupants reasonable comfort.

New Phaeton Design, by Hooper, on Rolls-Royce Chassis

A DECIDEDLY new design for a phaeton is represented in this body by Hooper & Co. (Coachbuilders), Ltd., of London, on the Rolls-Royce Phantom chassis. It will be noted that the top of the body has a definite drop toward the rear, harmonizing with the oblique setting of the doors. Another interesting feature is the fact that the top folds within the body length, thus giving an effect of unity to the design

seats for which buff "Vaumol," a soft leather, is used. Especially wide armrests are provided for both seats, which are fitted with pneumatic upholstery, affording the acme of comfort. Rigid side curtains which open with the doors are housed, when detached, in a special compartment in the front seatback. A secondary Auster windscreen, with apron, completes the protection for the rear-seat passengers. Triplex is fitted in both the

A new phaeton design by Hooper & Co. in which the top of the body has a definite drop to the rear and the doors are set, in consonance, at an oblique angle. The top folds within the body length, giving an effect of unity to the design that is not generally accomplished when tops fold beyond the end of the body

that is not usually associated with folded tops. The rear occupants when seated are thus protected by the false body line formed by the folded top; they are "inside," the body and not outside, which is the impression frequently suggested by sporting cars.

The decorative scheme of the car is carried out in buff, pastel green and polished aluminum. The buff of the body panels is repeated in the trimming of the

secondary and front windscreens; the latter is of the one-piece type, hinged at the top, and is provided with two wipers. The instrument board is especially designed and is illuminated by the Hooper masked lighting system. Tools are accommodated in the steps and valances, and in the tail is a commodious compartment for additional articles. Polished-aluminum wheel disks are used in accordance with the current mode.

Group of Bodies by Carrosserie Henri-Labourdette

A 4-passenger "conduite intérieure," mounted on the 8-cylinder Ballot chassis. The front seats are adjustable and the tail is arranged to receive a small trunk, or hand bags

Torpédo "du Mans," with triple raised deck, mounted by the Carrosserie Henri-Labourdette on 15-hp. Lorraine chassis. Note the low-hung, sporting effect of this car, with the modish radiator screen, wheel disks, special running board and tread

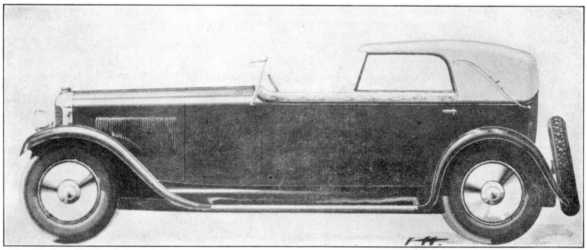

The "Jockey Club" cabriolet designed by Carrosserie Henri-Labourdette for the 32-hp. Minerva chassis. The "Plein-ciel" roof construction permits it to be opened completely or partly, so that the passengers on the rear seats are sheltered. The body rail is of carved walnut. The sloping glasses of the division slide, but the door windows lower. The auxiliary seats are both forward facing

The Four-Seater Coupe in England

By H. J. Butler*

THE fully enclosed body having two closely coupled seats and a single wide door on each side was a prominent feature of the last Olympia Show. Since then it has increased in popularity and some of the leading British manufacturers have made a standard model of it. The majority of the bodies built are fabric paneled and many are of Weymann construction.

The typical 4-seated coupe has a slight or full sloping single-panel windscreen. The door is from 36 to 40 in. wide and is hinged on the forward pillar. The side quarters are usually plain, for few are fitted with windows beyond the door, but dummy outside joints

seat without sliding the front one forward, especially if the door is more than 36 in. wide, but much depends on the size of the chassis and the amount of room taken up by the steering. These bodies are mounted on chassis of varying horsepower, consequently the seating comfort is apt to vary considerably, especially with regard to that of the back seat.

The ideal job is when the chassis is long enough for a comfortable 4-seated body to be mounted, so that the line of the back of the body does not extend beyond the rear axle; also so that the seats are a sufficient distance apart so that no floor wells are re-

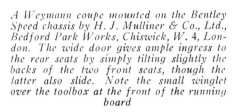

A 4-seater coupe that has been standardized by Humber, Ltd., Coventry, England. This "sports" coupe is mounted on the 6-cylinder, 16/50-hp. chassis, and is fitted with Triplex glass throughout. A sliding roof is also fitted for a small extra charge

A Weymann coupe mounted on the Bentley Speed chassis by H. J. Mulliner & Co., Ltd., Bedford Park Works, Chiswick, W. 4, London. The wide door gives ample ingress to the rear seats by simply tilting slightly the backs of the two front seats, though the latter also slide. Note the small winglet over the toolbox at the front of the running board

are frequently employed to decorate these plain side quarters. At the back there will be a trunk or luggage container covered with fabric to match the body panels, behind which is fitted the spare wheel. In some instances, the luggage container is built into the body and there may be access to it from the inside. Some of these models are called "sporting" or "sportsmen's" coupes and, as an added attraction and selling point, a sliding roof may be fitted. A sliding roof works to the utmost advantage, because the section of movable roof is both light in weight and small in area. Also a body so provided emphasizes the sporting character of the car, the fabric paneling also contributing to the same end.

The front seats will be similar to those of a saloon, that is mounted on slides, and, in order that easy access may be provided to the rear seats, each bucket seat has a hinged back which is tilted forward over the cushion when required. With the driving or passenger bucket seat in its normal position and the back hinged forward, it should be possible to get into the back

quired. Floor wells may be dispensed with if the distance from the back of the front seats to the back of the body is from 36 to 39 in. but if less than 36 in. it is advisable to insert floor wells. These are built below the floor some 6 or 7 in. deep and on each side of the cardan shaft. They may be parallel or wedge-shaped in plan and sufficient space must be left at the sides to provide a safe landing. The best type of floor well has a sloping footboard at the forward end which will be partly overhung by the front seat. The bottom of the front seat is often cut away or hollowed out so that more toe space is provided.

Regarding the design of the back seat this is usually 17 in. wide from front to back and made stationary or arranged to tip as one unit. This single-unit tipping seat was fitted in the two straight-eight Hillman coupes that Major Segrave took with him as tenders for his record-breaking attempt at Daytona. These 4-seater coupes were also Weymann bodies, but the most remarkable feature was perhaps the fact that they were fitted with left-hand steering in order that they might be better adapted for driving on American highways. When the back seat tips the rear compartment is then

* 46 Hart Grove, Ealing Common, London, W.5., England.

available for carrying luggage when a full complement of passengers is not being carried. There are also many coupes which may be classed as "occasional four," rather than "full four seaters." If in the former category, then the back seats will usually consist of two separate folding flap seats with padded back rests to add to their comfort. With the full 4-seated coupe, the back seat will often be wide enough to accommodate three in an emergency. Additional comfort may be afforded by fitting an elbow rest on each door for the front-seat passengers, and a similar convenience at the ends of the back seat.

A Weymann coupe mounted by Darracq Motor Engineering Co., Ltd., on a 14/45-hp. Talbot chassis. It has a sliding roof shown partly open and the front seat is wide enough to accommodate three adults. (See view below.) The back is hinged to give easy entrance to two occasional seats in the rear. The body is sheathed entirely in a black coated fabric and has a cream-colored molding. The interior is trimmed with a brown furniture hide

"Sportsman's" coupe as made by Wolseley Motors, Ltd., Adderley Park, Birmingham. This body is of Weymann construction and is mounted on the 16/45-hp., 6-cylinder chassis. A typical color scheme consists of red fabric for the main panels and trunk, with black upperworks. It is trimmed with a soft red leather

At the right is an interior view of the Talbot coupe shown above. The inside height is 45 in. and the width across the front seat, 48 in.; the method of adjusting the rake of the back of this seat is also shown. Tip-up seats are used in the rear. A closer inspection reveals the offside seat in the folded position and the fact that the back light opens outward

Interior of "Austin Seven." Seats two adults in front and two or three children or a third adult on the back seat. The exterior panels are metal to the waistline, above which fabric is used. The windscreen is of Triplex glass, but a "de luxe" model is also made with all windows of Triplex

HIBBARD & DARRIN as *"Automobile Architects"*

Designing for the Industry now Transcends in Importance This Firm's Original Work of Building for Private Clients

THE firm of Hibbard & Darrin is today unique in its position in the automobile industry. This firm is now practising as automobile architects with a clientele drawn from three distinct classes: (1) Leading automobile manufacturers in various countries; (2) important coachbuilders in several countries, and (3) private clients. It is noteworthy that designing for the industry has grown in importance far above the original work of building for private clients.

Hibbard & Darrin was established to carry out the conception which was in the minds of Thomas L. Hibbard and his associates when they formed the firm of Le Baron, Inc., in New York in 1920. It was their intention to act chiefly as

Airplane view of the Hibbard & Darrin berline for the Renault Eight chassis

automobile architects. In other words, to design the entire vehicle so far as its exterior appearance was concerned. This plan was carried out for a short period in America, but the reception of designing ideas by the industry was so limited that it shortly became necessary for the firm to establish its own body-building connections to carry out the wishes of individual clients. Mr. Hibbard and Mr. Darrin conceived that Paris would be more receptive to the original aim, and launched boldly forth in the establishing of a practice in the classic center of coachbuilding in France. At first their practice was chiefly confined to the foreign colony, but their designs soon attracted attention, not only of the European car and

Designs by Hibbard & Darrin for the New Renault Eight

←≪

A cabriolet coupe for the Reinastella chassis. Seats three passengers, baggage being carried in the tail

≫→

A berline for five on the Renault Eight chassis. Note the slanting door window; no ugly gap is left when this lowers

←≪

A "conduite intérieure" for seven passengers. A special window regulator lowers the front-door window without gap at front

body builders, but also came to the attention of motor-car manufacturers in the native land of the designers. Thus prophets—if abroad—are not without honor, even in their own country, if the paraphrase may be permitted. One of their designs attracted so much attention at the Paris Salon that it was adopted in 1927 by the Cadillac Motor Car Co., and with slight alterations is still being used by this Company.

Hibbard & Darrin have been acting as consulting automobile architects for numerous motor-car manufacturers including: General Motors Corporation in the United States, Daimler-Benz in Germany, Armstrong-Siddeley in England, and Renault in France. They have also been appointed consulting designers for a number of similarly prominent coachbuilders in various countries, the latest engagement of this type being for Barker & Co. (Coachbuilders), Ltd., London, one of the oldest coachbuilding firms in the world, having been established in 1710. In using the Hibbard & Darrin designs this firm not only puts the Barker nameplate on their bodies, but underneath, the Hibbard & Darrin name.

The new Renault Eight is a striking example of the new policy of the automobile manufacturers to place the general exterior design of their cars in the hands of specialists. Illustrations on the preceding page show that without changing the familiar Renault appearance, Hibbard & Darrin have altered the proportions in such a way as to present on this chassis models of sporty and low appearance, without sacrificing interior comfort. All of the standard models on the new 32-hp., 8-cylinder Renault chassis, the Reinastella, were developed by Hibbard & Darrin. A striking feature of the design of these Renault closed bodies is the slanting windshield. This type of windshield has been made practical for production by a new development by

Messrs. Southern and Darrin, for which patent has been applied for in various countries. This permits the window light of the door to lower without leaving the ugly gap that has heretofore been customary when sloping windows were used in doors. This is accomplished by an inexpensive and simple device which will be described in an early issue of AUTOBODY. The invention has been adopted in production by Renault, Armstrong-Siddeley and several other European manufacturers who wish to take advantage of the present vogue of the slanting windshield; it is being put into production by several American firms.

The success of Hibbard & Darrin is not based merely on designing ability, but is the result of a combination of experience, organization and experimentation. Their designing ability, we need say nothing of, as the work is known all over the world. Regarding their organization, they have an entire building situated at the Étoile, in the artistic center of Paris, in which they employ numerous designers, sculptors and draftsmen for the interpretation of their creations. Working for a world-wide clientele and with the important automobile factories of Europe and America, the scope and character of their work is necessarily extremely broad. Probably the greatest factor in their success in the creation of workable and practical designs has been their large experimental facilities. Hibbard & Darrin built last year over a million dollars worth of samples in special bodies, and even large manufacturers do not generally have the organization necessary for similar experimentation.

These designers have developed a number of special molding treatments which have been patented in Europe where better protection is afforded for designers than in America. Copying of designs which has been so prevalent in the United States is not practical abroad when the new designs are registered.

Weymann-American Will Expand Activities

Weymann American Body Co., of Indianapolis, has arranged for closer co-operation with the successful English Weymann company and an expansion of the activities of the American company. Managing Director E. G. Izod, of Weymann Motor Bodies (1925), Ltd., arrived from England early in March to visit American automotive plants and especially the Indianapolis works of the Weymann American Body Co. He brought with him some specialists from the successful English plant so that in the future the output of the American factory will conform to the standards of the best English practice. Before sailing for England on the *Majestic*, May 10, Mr. Izod effected an extremely important step in the progress of the Weymann body in the United States by securing the appointment of John Graham as president of the Weymann American Body Co. Mr. Graham was one of the founders of the Holbrook Co., custom-body builder of Hudson, N. Y., and for more than 20 years has enjoyed the reputation of being one

New President of Weymann-American

of the finest builders in the United States. The combination of Mr. Graham's extended experience in high-class bodywork and that of the English company in the organization, design and manufacture of Weymann bodies now assures to America the opportunity of securing Weymann bodies of the highest class. In England, the Weymann constructions have made extraordinary progress under the direction of Weymann Motor Bodies (1925), Ltd., and the close cooperation that will now prevail between the English and American organizations will assure the same standards of workmanship, design and efficiency as obtain in Great Britain where Weymann bodies are built for many of the highest grade chassis.

H. Leigh Whitelaw has been elected chairman of the board of the Weymann American Body Co. He was trained as a production man in the American Radiator Co., and is now vice-president and general manager of the American Gas Products Corporation; also a vice-president of the American Gas Association and of the Gas Heating Boiler and Furnace Association.

U. S. Post Office Department, Office of the Purchasing Agent, Washington, D. C., will receive sealed bids until June 11, 1929, for 250 mail-truck bodies of 202-cu. ft. capacity; 150 mail-truck bodies of 215-cu. ft. capacity; 400 mail-truck bodies of 91-cu. ft. capacity. The Department also reserves the right to negotiate with the accepted bidder on the 91- and 202-cu. ft. bodies for the construction of a shorter cab, having sliding doors on the outside and a sliding door in the partition back of the driver, if the change does not involve an increase in the contract price.

Three Bodies by Farina on Italian Chassis

A pleasing all-weather, cabriolet-type town car on the long Lambda "8" Lancia chassis

"Conduite intérieure sport" for four passengers on an 8A Isotta-Fraschini. Note the interesting bonnet louvers

A cabriolet, with deeply rolled belt, built by the Stabilimenti Farina, of Turin, on Fiat's 525 chassis

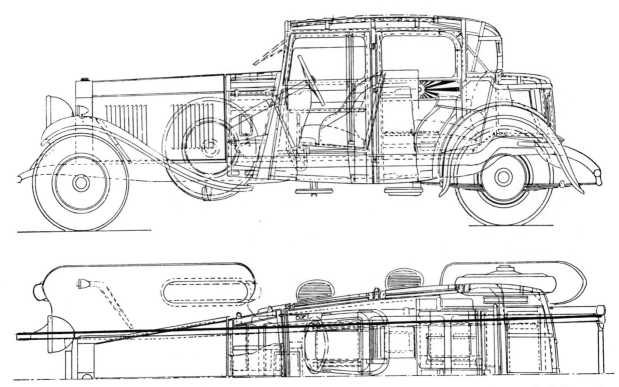

Prize-winning drawing in the British design Competition No. 1. A close-coupled Weymann saloon on Rolls-Royce chassis by James Luckett. An unusual feature is the use of hinged cowl panels, underneath which tool boxes are provided

British Design Competitions

BIRMINGHAM designers won the lion share of the awards in the British design competitions, sponsored jointly by the Society of Motor Manufacturers and Traders, the Worshipful Company of Coach Makers and the Institute of British Carriage and Automobile Manufacturers. According to *Motor Body Building*, Competition No. 1 was won by James Luckett, 60 Hugh Road, Small Heath, Birmingham, with a de-sign for a Weymann close-coupled saloon on Rolls-Royce chassis. Second prize in this competition went to Frederick James Read, 45 Mansel Road, Small Heath, Birmingham, for a semi-Weymann body on 30-hp. Lanchester chassis. Like the preceding body, this had metal lower panels, but a sunshine roof and a running board of the air-float type. A novelty was a whisky-and-soda set housed beneath the rear seat.

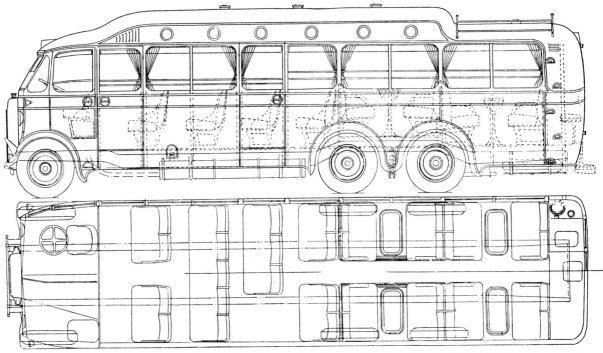

Prize-winning coach design in the British design Competition No. 2. This drawing, by Alfred William Lyons, is for a "forward-control, 32-seater saloon coach" to be mounted on a Thornycroft FC chassis

V

Deluxe Delivery Cars & Motorcoaches

This 1930 American Austin custom town delivery car by Hildebrand
elegantly made its rounds on the streets of New York for sixteen years.
The 75-inch wheelbase was ideal for floral delivery in the theatre
district on crowded First Nights.

Smart Delivery Cars

A special body by Huber on Willys-Knight chassis for Jay-Thorpe, Inc., of West 57th Street, New York's "rue de la Paix." This car, intended for small-package delivery on a 30-mi. route, is effectively finished in gray and black. Exterior panels are of aluminum. The interior is lined with mahogany-stained Haskelite on the sides, and with fabric leather on the ceiling. Delivery is from the front, a tip-up seat being provided for the attendant

A de luxe "town car" by Bender on White Model 158 chassis for Thurn, a dressmaking shop east of Fifth Avenue in the fashionable Fifties. A special feature is the removable polished-aluminum roof section over the driver; this is stiffened by transverse ribs and when in use is fastened by large thumbscrews at the inside rear and outside front corners. It makes a neat continuation of the roof line and harmonizes with the other bright metalwork of the front of the car. There are "Bright Bumpers" at front and rear. Access is by key only, through the wide door at the rear

This smart delivery car is on Walker Electric chassis but has been made to simulate a gasoline vehicle. The Champion Auto Equipment Co. built a fleet of these bodies for Stewart & Co.'s new Fifth Avenue store

In the Commercial-Body Field

Mack Trucks, Inc., is now offering this light, fast-delivery car on three standard wheelbases, 138, 158, 168 in. Besides the panel body, three other types are mounted on this 6-cylinder chassis: A covered express, an open express and a platform body

An attractive delivery body built by the Huber Wagon Works for one of New York's leading jewelry-and-silverware firms. This body is paneled inside with walnut-stained plywood and outside with aluminum. The body is mounted on a White chassis and has a loading space 67 in. long, 50 in. wide and 50 in. high. Pillar lamps, chromium-plated hardware and other de luxe equipment is used for this body, the lower portion of which is painted black. The letter panels and the saddle panels of the bonnet and cowl are finished with aluminum lacquer. The molding and fender treatment is interesting, and unusually large hubs are provided for the wheel disks

A new "town car" ambulance offered by Sayers & Scovill Co., of Cincinnati. This Worthington invalid car, designated by the manufacturers as the "Aristocrat of Invalid Cars," is equipped with an 8-cylinder motor and mounted on 154-in. wheelbase. There is a removable roof section for the front compartment and the doors are provided with windows so as to give the driver complete protection in inclement weather. No applied moldings are used, all being pressed into the panels. The chassis extends to the end of the body, thereby avoiding overhang and making it practical to bolt the body across the rear frame member, in addition to the usual side attachment. Inside dimensions are: Length, 84 in.; height, 50 in.; width at belt, 53 in.; width at floor, 42 in.; floor to ground, 31 in. Interior is trimmed with walnut panels and Spanish leather. The floor is of inlaid-rubber sheeting. Equipment includes Thermos bottles, electric fan, heater and the usual medical accessories

A Belgian Motorcoach for Portugal

A de luxe long-distance motorcoach mounted by the well-known Belgian firm of Jonckheere Frères which has plants at Beveren, near Brussels, and at Gand. This coach is of the latest type with inside parcel racks, and recessed seatbacks on which are mounted ash receivers. This 6-wheeler is intended for operation out of Lisbon, and as it is for long-distance service, a toilet room with running water is installed at the left rear corner, and auxiliary baggage-carrying capacity is provided on the roof

Bus-Body Production Increased Last Year

PRODUCTION OF BUS BODIES increased about 20 per cent in 1929, and was the best year in this industry since the peak periods of 1925 and 1926. Last year 8,864 bodies of various types were produced, according to the annual survey of *Bus Transportation*. The number of city-type buses built remained about stationary but there was a noteworthy increase of inter-city coaches, and the production of school buses represented a peak record for this type. The production in the important groups was as follows: School buses, 3,425; intercity, 3,031; city types, 2,337. Only six double deckers were built and there was a marked decrease in new sightseeing and hotel coaches.

For the 5,368 common-carrier buses, the most popular body size continued to be the 29-passenger model which constituted about 25 per cent of the city buses and nearly 35 per cent of the intercity production. The 21-passenger model was next in popularity, 691 inter-city units being built as compared with 254 in 1928, and 590 city units as against 597 in the previous year. The 25-passenger size maintained a good increase in intercity units but gained only slightly in the urban group. The 33-passenger model made an important jump in the number of intercity units, from 82 in 1928 to 239 in 1929, and also did fairly well in city service, increasing from 93 to 165. The great gain of the 29-passenger was in intercity service, from 851 in 1928 to 1,050 last year, but for city service the units built declined from 780 in 1928 to 584 in 1929. This loss in the city group might be accounted for by the appear-

ance of 202 new bodies of 39-passenger capacity, the tendency in city work being toward the large "street car" types, though the 21-passenger model is holding its own in this field. Many bodies of this seating capacity are being built with extra-wide aisles so as to carry up to 40 passengers during the peak-traffic period, the extras being carried as standees.

School bodies were reported by 55 manufacturers and the production reached the record total of 3,425, an increase of about 50 per cent over 1928 and exceeding comfortably the 1926 production of 3,091. The most popular body size in this group was the 30-passenger model which jumped from 324 units in 1928 to 1,264 bodies last year. Other popular body sizes were the 20-passenger model with 509 units, the 25-passenger with 311 units, the 40-passenger with 291 units, the 35-passenger with 176 units, and the 50-passenger with 137 units. No other sizes reached an output of 100 units, but there were 97 bodies built of 55-passenger capacity and 54 of 65-passenger capacity.

The total number of buses now in regular operation in the United States is estimated at 92,500, of which about 42,000 are school buses, 35,640 are operated by the regular motor carriers, 11,256 by electric-railway companies and subsidiaries, 1,454 by steam railroads and subsidiaries, and approximately 2,150 by other users. The total investment in rolling stock is estimated at $450,000,000, and in terminals $110,000,000. Gross revenue of $322,000,000 was received by buses, last year, and 10,835,000,000 passenger-miles recorded.

Practical Method for Developing the Wheelarch

By Norman D. Brown *

THERE are numerous ways of developing the wheelarch theoretically, but in practice these have been found to give poor results, usually ending in the body looking too squat or short or giving the appearance of an indifferent turnunder at the rear. These defects can be remedied by using the method illustrated herewith in which the side, plan and section views are shown in bold lines. A scale is drawn at the bottom of the diagram by projecting a line from some convenient point *a,* such as where the shut line intersects the datum line, to any point on a line projected from the intersection of the wheelarch and the turnunder of the back of the body. Connect this point *b* to the datum line where

the side turnunder at the top of the arch *F* graduating into the normal turnunder at the bottom *G,* as this has been found to give a better line when finished; this only applies to the rear portion from the center to the back.

Mark three or more points on the mudguard contour as may be necessitated by its shape shown as *A, B* and *C.* This gives the lines *A, B* and *C,* in side plan views. Then draw *X, Y* and *Z* in the side and section views; work out in plan the lines *X, Y* and *Z* which are proportionate turnunders. Where the lines *X, Y* and *Z* in plan cut *A, B* and *C,* will be found three points for the rear contour of the arch. Project down on the side view, obtaining the finished line at the rear. For the

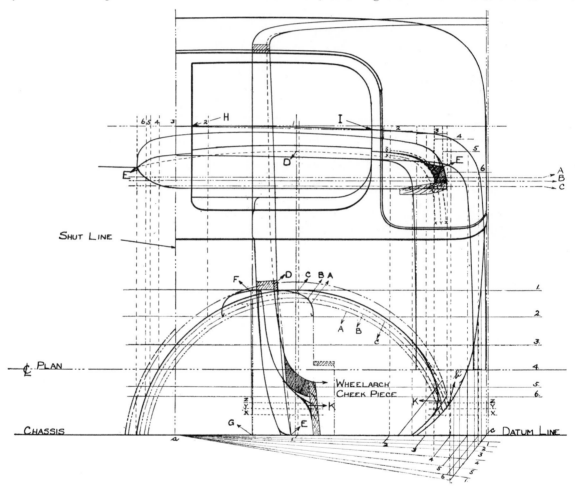

the back turnunder commences, *c.* Then draw the lines 1, 2, 3, 4, 5 and 6 in side view. Where these cut the back of the body project them down to the scale line *bc* and join to *a.* Where lines 1, 2, 3, etc., cut the wheelarch, project them down to their respective lines in the scale and draw back parallel lines to *b* and *c.* Square these lines up to the plan; then in plan, taking line 4 for example, draw a horizontal forward until it cuts the other line 4. From this point measure in the side turnunder on line 4 in the section view. This gives one point through which the arch will pass in plan. Do this with the remaining lines and it will give the arch outlined in plan. It is important to allow ⅛ in. extra on

arch in section view, measure the distance in plan from the outside and repeat on the section view. For a fixed quarter light, the inside of the arch is easily arrived at by carrying down the inside line of the rear-quarter pillar and running it around parallel to the outside of the arch. Repeat the inside line of the arch in plan and the complete wheelarch is finished. In plan view, draw the line *HI,* which is a straight line, from the back of the rear standing pillar to the front of the quarter pillar. For a drop quarter light, the inside of the arch may be parallel to the glass run, plus the distance from line *HI* to the outside of the plan. By this method the inside of the arch assumes the shape of the side sweep.

To save timber the arch can be of bent ash and marked out from the line *DE.* This line is drawn from

*Body draftsman, 48 Montpelier Rise, Golders Green, London, N. W. 11, England.

the inside top to the inside bottom of the arch. The shaded portion of the arch is marked out from part of the remainder of the bend and glued and screwed on. This saves the timber as the width of the bend can be kept down to a minimum. The block *K* is added to complete the contour of the arch. The main advantage of using a bent arch lies in the fact that it is much lighter and stronger and can be marked out from a bend, 4 in. wide by 1 to 1½ in. thick, instead of having to cut the whole arch out of solid timber and joining at the center, which is more expensive and weaker because of the short grain.

Motor-Truck Bodies for *Retail Delivery*

By Samuel Simon*

REPLIES to a questionnaire sent to members of the Retail Delivery Association, covering the specifications of their package vehicles, indicate that practically all large merchants are using body equipment built to their own special design and to suit their individual requirements as to details, dimensions and appearance. . .

Goodwill Value of Handsome Vehicles

Most merchants who operate a delivery service appreciate the great publicity value of handsome vehicles bearing their business name. The delivery equipment of a modern department store should have an individu-flecting the character of the firms they represent. Although this may involve some sacrifice, from a utility and cost angle, the trend to greater beauty continues.

Trend to Greater Beauty Continues

The full de luxe panel and the "ritzy" town-car delivery types present a most striking appearance on the street, but it is generally agreed that their initial cost and lesser carrying capacity, as well as the driver problem involved in their operation, exclude their use for regular department-store delivery work, although in a few cases I have noted the addition of one or two ultra-de luxe units by some stores for use in conjunction with

De luxe and "semi-de luxe" types of delivery cars. At the left is a de luxe town-car type, mounted on White Model 60 chassis for a Fifth Avenue clothier; it is aluminum paneled, and the roof over the driver is removable for the town-car effect in pleasant weather; the windshield is chromium plated and shatterproof glass is used throughout this compartment. This body for De Pinna was finished in Valentine's Gymnite Green, with gold lettering, the wheels and belt molding being in gray-brown. At the right is a "semi-de luxe" package body, mounted by Fitz Gibbon & Crisp for a department store on Mack BL chassis. The body is 114 in. long, 55 in. wide and 60 in. high. The main panels are of Plymetl and at the rear there is a curtain above the tailgate which has a flush-type hinge. The driver's doors are arranged to swing back and fasten against the sides in warm weather. The upper panels are finished in Gymnite Green, and the lower panels and wheels in gray-brown; ivory striping is used

ality in appearance that is immediately recognizable, and at once associates the store with the vehicle in the mind of the person seeing its motor equipment on the streets. Commonplace, ordinary-looking units create unfavorable, or at least negative, impressions, whereas good-looking vehicles set up favorable reaction in the minds of the potential customers on the street, creating inestimable goodwill value to the store in question.

There are still a large number of department stores that are operating body equipment that was designed with utility and low maintenance as the prime objectives, beauty being subordinated to practicability. Screen- and curtain-side bodies, although quite practical, have little merit from the standpoint of appearance, and in my opinion will eventually give way to units with more eye appeal, and which at the same time retain the essentials of efficient and economical delivery.

We are more "style conscious" today than ever before, and business houses have sensed that delivery cars of handsome appearance have substantial value in re-

their regular fleet. This, no doubt, is for the advertising value involved, and steps up the tone of the store in the eyes of the public. In some cases these vehicles are reserved for use only in the finer residential neighborhoods.

Demand for "Semi-de Luxe" Jobs

Recently there has been a demand for what might be called a semi-de luxe delivery that retains as far as possible the advantages of the strictly utilitarian job with that of fine exterior appearance, and without involving too high an initial investment or too great an outlay for maintenance. This type of body is of full panel construction, with graceful flowing lines that harmonize with the lines of the chassis and become in effect a part of it, instead of being a box-like affair with severe straight lines, built without regard to chassis appearance and merely to serve as a receptacle for carrying merchandise from store to customer.

Good design can accomplish the desired harmony between body and chassis, without involving too great expense or too great sacrifice from the utility standpoint. The drivers' vestibule of this semi-de luxe panel body can be arranged with either full-height or half-height doors, and if preferred, left side of vestibule

NOTE—Excerpts from a paper entitled "Construction and Design of Motor-Truck Bodies for Retail Delivery," presented at the 14th annual convention of the Retail Delivery Association at Cleveland, O., Mar. 20, 1930.
* Secretary and treasurer, Fitz Gibbon & Crisp, Inc., manufacturers of commercial bodies, Trenton, N. J.

A Modern, De Luxe Furniture Van

A de luxe furniture van, with double doors and flush-hinged tailgates at the sides and rear. It was built by Fitz Gibbon & Crisp on Mack chassis for the Flint & Horner furniture store, 66 W. 47th St., New York. This van is 19 ft. 6 in. long, 7 ft. 4 in. wide and 7 ft. 6 in. high. The panels are of aluminum and are finished in Nitro-Valspar Rubicelle, deep, with gold striping and lettering

At left, interior view of the Flint & Horner furniture body, showing square wheelhouse pockets and flush-hinged tailgate and the complete interior lining. In the center view is shown the driving compartment with three individual bucket seats and an instrument board with all the accessories of the modern delivery vehicle. At the right is a front view of this body, showing the ventilating quarter windows and the special illuminated glass sign in the peak

A three-quarter rear view of the Flint & Horner furniture van, with the right-side double doors and flush-hinged tailgate open. Note also the special deep belt moldings which act as rubrails

This fleet of de luxe furniture bodies was built by the McCabe-Powers Auto Body Co., of St. Louis, for the Lammert Furniture Co. The bodies are mounted on 2½-ton Autocar chassis and are 17 ft. long, 7 ft. 6 in. high and 7 ft. 6 in. wide. Aluminum paneling was used in place of steel because of the ease of fabrication and lesser weight of the aluminum

can be built in solid with but an imitation door. These doors can be arranged to swing back and fasten against side of body, a convenience many drivers will appreciate in warm weather, and one that speeds up the entrance and exit of driver or helper; at the same time, doors are available for full protection in inclement weather. Width of these doors should be ample for entering or leaving the body with an armful of packages. Rear of this body can be arranged with full double doors, or half doors and tailgate, or curtain and tailgate; all without breaking the symmetry of the job as a whole.

DRIVER VISION AND COMFORT

Driver's seat should be arranged with careful consideration for the comfort of driver and so laid out that good vision is obtainable in all directions. A certain standard of dimensions can be worked out covering the distance from steering wheel to back of seat; under steering wheel to top of cushion; height of cushion to top of glass in windshield and distance from top of cushion to side window-sill line. If properly worked out, these dimensions will assure comfort and vision for practically all drivers. Helpers' seat can be arranged to fold out of the way so that entrance can be easily made into body from driver's compartment. Folding iron gates or sliding screens can be arranged across front of body behind driver, if desired for protecting load against theft.

LOADING BINS OR HINGED RACKS

Loading bins can be applied to inside of body, or a division rack can be permanently hinged to side and swing out of the way, if not used. This permanent

fastening eliminates the possibility of driver removing rack and its attendant loss or breakage.

A domelight is usually placed on an angle at front head piece and reflected toward the inside of the body, with a switch within easy reach of driver. Tailgate is metal lined, and equipped with a special hinge that eliminates space between gate and body when in the down position and provides a flush, clean-looking, exterior appearance.

The flooring should have lap joints, and be made of tightly fitted dry stock to assure cleanliness. Inside of body should be lined with slats or panels that are easily removable to facilitate repairs; this lining also promotes cleanliness of interior.

METAL-SHEATHED PLYWOOD FOR PANELS

The main exterior panel of bodies of this type can be of laminated wood, covered with metal, which is highly satisfactory for this class of work, assuring a smooth-appearing panel, free of waves, and possessing considerable strength. Lower rear corners of body are rounded and of metal, over a heavy wood post which will prevent many dents that are apt to be received at this vulnerable spot.

Chrome plating is being universally used on exterior hardware, and non-shattering glass is being demanded for complete driver protection. A 1-piece, plate-glass windshield, arranged to swing out, with automatic wiper and metal "cadet" visor above, will be found most satisfactory.

Non-skid step treads are advisable at the driver's door. Three leather straps, fastened to the upper part of the body on the inside, will be found useful for carrying

A new and larger Speed Wagon body of the semi-de luxe class now replaces the former Speed Wagon Junior on Reo's Model 15 chassis. Note the cabriolet-type front, the graceful contour of the roof and the rounded rear corners. It has ten more cubic feet of space inside than its predecessor and is paneled with natural-finish plywood to the belt line, above which slats are used

This Fremont town-car delivery body, mounted on Reo's Model 15 Junior chassis, was exhibited at the recent Progress in Transportation Shows. It was finished in a combination of orchid and yellow and is in line with the present tendency toward distinctive delivery cars for high-class shops in metropolitan districts. Note the coach lamps and the windows in the bulkhead

rugs, etc. Battery should be located in an easily accessible position for changing or watering. Likewise the tool box should be in a convenient location. These are details that are often overlooked.

The ideal location for the gas tank is under the chassis at the rear, but in some cases this location is preferred for carrying the spare tire, and in that event, the tank is placed in the usual position under the driver's seat. Where tank is under chassis at rear, the spare-tire can be carried in the front-fender well or can be fastened to left side of the body, although this will in many cases block the entrance through the driver's left door.

FURNITURE VANS ARE IMPROVED

Vans for transporting furniture are also being built with exterior appearance as a principle consideration. Some fine de luxe units are seen on the streets and because of their size command unusual attention. Practically the same detail of finish is carried out on these vans as on the smaller de luxe panel bodies. Double side doors with side tailgates are provided on both left and right sides, as well as rear, and made as flush as possible with main panels of the body. The panels are welded into 1-piece sections, eliminating moldings, covering the joints and forming large, clean panel areas that lend themselves admirably for effective lettering.

FLUSH TAILGATE HINGES

The side and rear tailgates are using hinges that eliminate space between tailgate and body. This is especially desirable for furniture work. Rear corners are rounded to achieve a de luxe appearance. If desired, an illuminated sign can be installed on the peak over the driver. Front, rear and side marker lights in various color combinations are applied which present a striking effect when illuminated at night. A deep peak over the driver's vestibule is utilized to carry part of the load.

Driver's cab can be arranged with an upper and lower berth, if desired, for sleeping quarters on long runs. Wheelpockets on bodies of this type are squared off on the inside instead of being left radial. Tie rings are fastened to the inside panels for lashing load. Pads are usually applied to sides, front, rear and peak of the body, and in some instance pads are made to cover the floor as well. Side and rear doors should have provision for keeping them open while being loaded.

PAINTING OF THE COMMERCIAL CAR

The matter of satisfactory paint finish is still an important question with fleet operators. The conventional oil-paint and varnish method is no more satisfactory on a motor-truck body than it was on passenger cars. Lacquer manufacturers have been working steadily to produce a lacquer that would provide a durable finish for truck-body work. On an all-metal, exterior surface without loose moldings this can be done satisfactorily, but on composite construction there is great difficulty in maintaining good adhesion to a wood surface. Some of the leading lacquer manufacturers are now producing a material that has substantially more elasticity than previous materials of this type and it is claimed that this will not peel or chip. However, to secure this elasticity, the deep luster produced for polish had to be sacrificed. The composition of this type of lacquer is such that it cannot be given a rub finish. Some operators are asking for a clear-varnish coat over the lacquer, apparently finding it difficult to reconcile themselves to a semi-dull finish.

Seating of English Motorcoaches

BY R. H. MORTER*

A diversity of seat types are used by motorcoach builders in England. At present the highbacked, type of seat is in favor for all-weather and saloon coaches. The top of the squab is as high as 22 in. off the top of the cushion, and is fully sprung; a flush-folding glass-topped table is usually recessed in the back of the seat, to open at a convenient height; if required, above this a mirror is fitted which, besides being a necessary part of the equipment from the feminine point of view, also detracts from the height of the seatback.

These seats are generally made in pairs, often with a fixed aisle armrest and sometimes with a small folding armrest in the center. The fixed center armrest is only used when the aisle is offset and the seats are arranged in pairs down on side and as single seats on the other side. This layout of seats is only used, however,, in the highest class long-distance coaches, being more or less forced upon the coachbuilder by reason of the regulation 90-in. overall width. The smaller type coach seat is used where both seating capacity and comfort are needed on short-route service vehicles. As these have necessarily to be placed closer together the backs of the seats are either well sloped or given a turnunder with a well radiused bottom, and sometimes fitted with a sloping toeboard below.

The spring-back seat, that is, with the back supported by two $1\frac{3}{4}$ x $\frac{5}{16}$-in. spring-steel "irons," is made up in a number of shapes with various names applied to them by different manufacturers, such as "bucketed seat," "semi-bucket seat," "'C' type seat," "swept-back seat," etc., are used mostly on city buses where seating accommodation is of more importance than extra comfort. The spring-steel supported backrest has been introduced in the London service omnibuses but has not, as yet, become, the general rule.

PRESSED-STEEL SEAT LEGS

Seat legs have undergone a change for the better, the pressed-steel shaped leg having almost entirely displaced the old-type flat-steel or angle-iron frame; a few legs have been introduced incorporating a sloping toeboard. Air-bag cushions and squabs are used on high-class jobs and various thin steel curved spring seats are on the market but none yet has superseded the coil-spring cushion frame which seems the only type suited to hard wear and service.

Fittings on the seatbacks have become more or less standardized and usually consist of a mirror and one or two ash trays. Grab handles, cellulose painted or celluloid covered, are universally fitted on the gangway side of the seat backs. For the trim of the seats, genuine leather is preferred to leather cloth, but the prevailing material is moquette, a carpet-like, closely woven material made up in innumerable fancy patterns. The seat backs are invariably covered with hair-carpet or rep.

---

* "Regels," 65 Berkeley Road, Kingsbury, London, N.W. 9, England.

Pickwick's New "Duplex" Day Coach

The new Duplex day coach designed by Dwight E. Austin and now being used between San Francisco and San Jose, Calif. This coach has a capacity for 53 seated passengers and as in the case of the Pickwick Nite coach and the preceding Pickwick Observation-Buffet coach, the driver sits in an elevated position and is thus provided with exceptional vision. There is a central aisle intermediate the two seat levels, with maximum headroom of 85 in. and a minimum of 72 in. over the rear baggage compartment. There is a toilet room on the left side just aft of the driver, and an emergency door at the left rear corner

The new Pickwick Motor Coach Works at El Segundo, Calif., one of the beach towns near Los Angeles. Nite and Duplex day coaches are built in this factory which was opened a few months ago under the direction of Dwight E. Austin, vice-president and general manager, and designer of the Duplex coach, the Nite coach and the Pickwick Observation-Buffet and other coaches used by affiliates of this important organization

The power plant of the Duplex coach, weighing about 1,800 lb., can be removed and replaced in 20 min. The power plant is rolled out of the front of the coach after loosening four bolts and disconnecting the gasoline and electric lines, which are on a single assembly. A new unit is then rolled in and secured in place

Interior of the Duplex coach which is built entirely of aluminum alloys and steel, and insulated throughout against heat and cold. This view shows the seats in the upper compartment. These reclining seats are of Pickwick design, made chiefly of duralumin, and trimmed with a mohair plush of modernistic design

The general overall dimensions of the Duplex coach are as follows: Length, 32 ft.; height, 9 ft. 10 in.; width, 8 ft.; wheelbase, 246 in.; over hang, 10 ft.; road clearance, in center between front and rear axles, 16 in. The weight of the coach unloaded is 17,000 lb. and the passenger load is estimated at 8,000 lb., or a total of 25,000 pounds.

COMBINED CHASSIS-AND-BODY STRUCTURE

Like the Nite coach, the Duplex is an all-metal construction in which chassis and body have been combined. The principal structural members are 7-in. steel channels which extend along the lower outside edge of the coach. These are tied together by 14 various cross members and form a foundation to receive the body construction and chassis units. These heavy channels on the outside of the structure also form an extremely solid guard rail to protect the coach from accidents. Three additional channels of steel and duralumin run the entire length of the coach above and below the windows. The uprights are of pressed steel, connected at the bottom to the 7-in. channel and at the top to duralumin carlines.

The inside and outside sheathing of the structure is of duralumin, insulation being placed between this double-sheet wall. The central aisle, 20 in. wide, is built above the lower floor level and is made of a ⅛-in. duralumin plate running from the motor compartment to the rear-wheel housing. The headroom over the aisle is 85 in. except over the baggage compartment where it is 72 in. The drive shaft and other mechanical equipment going to the rear axle are carried under this aisle. From the aisle, uprights are carried at intervals connecting with the roof. These with the compartment partitions and braces make a type of honeycomb construction that is exceptional for its rigidity.

BAGGAGE STORED IN COACH

The baggage compartment behind the rear axle provides 284 cu. ft. of storage space, accessible by 30-in. doors on each side. These doors have double-latch door locks, and signal switches operate pilot lights in the driving compartment if the doors are not properly latched. At the extreme left corner aft of the baggage compartment is an emergency door, 24 x 70 in., with automatically unfolding steps. The main passenger entrance is on the right side just aft of the front wheels where there is an air-operated door, 26 in. wide by 68 in. high.

The driver's cab is on the upper level and may be reached either from the interior or from the small outside door on the left-hand side. His elevated position and the narrow corner pillars give greater vision than is enjoyed by most motorcoach drivers. There are two observation seats for passengers at the right of the driver. The floor of this compartment is well insulated to prevent heating from the motor and there is a large ventilator on each side of the front panel. The power plant comprises a 150-hp., 6-cylinder Sterling engine and is removable from the front in the same manner as provided for the Nite coach. The power plant can be taken out and a new one rolled into place in 20 min. Just aft of the driving compartment a lavatory is installed, equipped with a Sands' marine closet, a porcelain wash basin and paper-towel container. On certain runs, it is expected that a buffet will also be installed in these coaches.

THE SEATING ARRANGEMENT

The seat accommodation is for 53 passengers, all of vhom are carried on Pickwick patented reclining chairs,

with the exception of five on the rear lounge, two observation seats in the driving compartment and two folding seats in the vestibule. There are only 18 seats on the lower level, leaving 35 of the choice upper-deck seats. Another feature of the general arrangement is that only 16 seats face the rear, the remaining 37 passengers face in the direction in which the car is traveling. The individual reclining seats are of Pickwick desgn and construction. They are constructed chiefly of duralumin, are quiet in operation and are deeply upholstered in mohair. A mohair trimmed armrest is also provided for the aisle-seat passenger.

ALL WINDOWS SAME SIZE

Draped curtains are provided at all windows which are of the Pickwick sliding type constructed of steel and Bakelite channels. All windows are exactly the same size, are interchangeable and can be replaced from the outside. Portable tables fit into special brackets in the compartments and can be used for card playing, dining service, etc. In addition to the sliding windows, there are eight roof ventilators. Heating is provided through 12 hot-water radators, utilizing the water from the motor-cooling system and if necessary the heat from the exhaust pipe; thermostats are installed to prevent overheating of the motor or the coach. Fuel equipment includes two 50-gal. gasoline tanks.

The Truck Industry Prospers
BY ALLEN WEEKS

MOST truck manufacturers in the Middle West are extremely busy. Whether you believe that general business conditions are fair, good or poor, the truck business is better than it has ever been. In a recent tour through the Middle West, I found the production departments of the truck manufacturers in the same tension as these departments usually are in the automobile plants—an unusual condition in the commercial-car industry.

One of the large manufacturers inaugurated some time ago the selling policy of rating accurately each chassis. Truck salesmen had formed the habit of over-rating—an easy selling habit to acquire. The truck buyer, however, finished as a loser when he bought a truck and considered its pay-load capacity to be unlimited. Now truck salesmen are "transportation engineers," know the limits of their models and have been taught by factory representatives how to adapt the line to various requirements. Truck manufacturers are keenly interested now in the results obtained by their customers and have trained salesmen to apply the manufacturer's experience to the users' problems. Truck buyers evidently appreciate this co-operation.

President Hoover's request that Federal, state, county and city building programs be speeded up has already helped the truck industry. Ohio opened bids in March for 335 trucks to replace the same number that were allotted to the State when the war surplus was parceled out. At that time, truck manufacturers felt this shortening of their market, but are now rejoicing that the period of replacement has arrived. Orders and inquiries now in hand by the various truck manufacturers indicate that a steady sales volume may be expected during the coming months. In spite of spotty business in various lines, truck business is good and this year promises to be better than any previous one. In 1929, between 800,000 and 900,000 units were sold. This year, the sales bid fair to top this mark and land in the brackets between 900,000 and a million.

VI

Body Design Art & Engineering

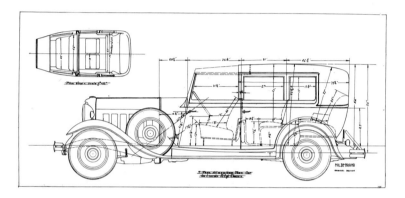

Coachbuilders were expected to provide completely dimensioned engineering drawings for client approval prior to construction. This roomy Rollston all-weather town car on Lincoln V-12 chassis was drawn by Hildebrand in 1931.

Color and Body Design

Color Should not be Merely Decoration but an Integral Part of the Design, Contributing to the Planned Silhouette of the Car

By Francis D. Willoughby*

COLOR has had always an important part in the automobile and present offerings show the tremendous increase in the use of bright and attractive shades as compared with the conservative darker colors of coach blue, maroon, black, and green, that were the standards of the early days and of the vehicle, prior to the automobile.

In recent searches for color treatment, car manufacturers and paint-and-lacquer companies, have turned to bird plumage, minerals and nature's big storehouse of flowers, for color blends which have produced some shades that were hitherto unthought of, for this purpose.

In the matter of combining the use of colors to properly portray the design features of the body, and the whole car and, conversely, in the designing of the body features toward the type of color treatment to be applied, I feel that the ultimate has not been reached and that there is much left to do.

Too much in the past have we designed contours, offsets, reveals, and moldings to form a balanced mechanical picture and a good "eye line" and then have selected color to decorate the job. The proper use of color families, and combinations have a definite purpose, should have governed perhaps the designer's hand in connection with the ideas for which the design is created.

The "Flash" Effect

I feel there has been too much attention paid to intimate or minute effects of the exterior lines, moldings, etc., of the car, with not enough attention to the bolder picture effect that should be the basis of the eye appeal.

The elements of beauty also should not be those of static beauty as of the car standing still (with the possible exception of the showroom floor) but as of the car in motion. The factor of control today in design for the exterior should be the portrayal of motion dressed as attractively as possible. This means the use of only the bolder and stronger lines, and the proper accentuation of such lines to "give the flash effect" of the main motif, properly set into relief by colors—fine hairline striping has no place in the "silhouette" or "flash" effects.

Also, only convention and history are the reasons why body upperworks should be black. Solid-panel backgrounds of one color, with the picture-frame and silhouette effects in a contrasting color, have an entirely new usuage in our idea. Black in lacquer finish is now one of the most attractive colors for this purpose, especially when combined with offsets of other colors such as silver, gold, orange or green.

Originality and Artistry Required

To obtain the ideal of this thought in design—the elimination of the intricate and small details of the exterior, and the inclusion of bolder accentuation of the motif of the car design—there is required greater skill in the design layout. It thus demands a simplification of ideas but a greater originality in conception. Under this idea the sweeps of the panels, the turnunder of the sides, the roof crown, the molding

lines, the proportion of the reveals and all items that enter into a mechanical design, plus the color-design conception, must be correct in detail and relation. They must replace, through their sheer beauty of simplicity and perfect relation, the attempt to attract through an artful trick-up of fancy panels, moldings without a purpose and color and stripes added as "decorations."

In other words, the entire scheme of the eye appeal of the car exterior should be thought out thoroughly, and expressed by the designer all the way through to the very finish in color treatment.

Interior May Be Finely Developed

On the other hand I would put into the interior all the fine beauty of detail and intimate character that is to reflect the personal home of the owner. Added to the appeal of a comfortable luxury of deep and restful-looking cushions and backs should be portrayed the attractiveness of fine detailed work accurately and precisely done. This can be expressed in simple or elaborate fashion and include touches of period effects as may suit the whim of the owner.

There is not a thing within the interior of the car that is not within intimate nearness to the occupant and therefore there should not be a thing that will not serve its place, in the whole scheme to please. Here again the correct effect cannot be produced with cheap or homely fabric decorated with fancy hardware to lend it "class," but each part in detail should be properly worked together to produce a complete picture.

Ideas Exemplified in Salon Exhibits

The bodies exhibited by the Willoughby Co. in the current Salon of four distinct types contain an effort, with some limitations, to show these things. Into them has been put the conception of color treatment when making the designs. Perhaps one of the most striking examples of this is the Lincoln "town sedan" in which two shades of green have been used on the exterior and interior. Their complimentary arrangement in connection with a simple exterior treatment of lines has the intention of carrying out to a degree, the ideas that I have presented. This model has been selected by the customer as the basis of a new design from the lines of which some of the regular production at its plant is being built.

The Packard "sedan-limousine," in a bold way and with the sportif effect, combines a cracker-buff and blue combination with extreme contrast. The Franklin town car, with a combination of tan and mulberry and black, shows a departure from the previous conventions in the use of the darker and lighter colors. The Lincoln limousine, with two tones of gray supplemented by carrying the upholstery color to line out the reveals that frame the vision into the interior, exhibits a large job of exceeding height and length where the attempt is made to reduce the appearance and size into a pleasing exterior treatment. In this again the conventions that have surrounded a car of this kind are being left alone and a new thought has been attempted.

* President, Willoughby Co., custom body builders, Utica, N. Y.

Derham-Lincoln

Modern Art — and the Modern Motor Car

By William H. Emond*

FREQUENTLY heard during National Show week were such remarks as: "They all look alike to me," or "After you have seen about four exhibits you have seen the whole show." These and similar comments unquestionably reflected the reaction to the general appearance of the cars. The poor salesman at the show who could not point out a wide belt molding, a curved front face of the corner pillar and a spliced-out drip

was an extension-top phaeton, usually called a touring car; today that picture is the sedan. The 2-passenger car is a roadster or a coupe. Nobody ever calls them automobiles. These three types, with some variations as to the number of doors, comprise the great bulk of American automobile production and it is these three types, with special emphasis on the sedan, that reveal the "deadly similarity" in body design.

Fig. 1 illustrates the use of long narrow rectangles for effect of elongation and speed

molding, all in combination, on at least one of his cars, felt as if he had no automobile to sell provided he believed, as many do, that constant repetition spells fashion.

Paul Thomas at the S. A. E. semi-annual meeting, from the outside looking in, complained of "slavish copying" and a "deadly similarity." In an address before the Metropolitan Section, Amos Northup, from within, while apparently agreeing with Mr. Thomas on the main issue, discreetly refrained from open criticism, but one could hardly follow his suggestions and be accused of copying anything now discernible. Mr. Thomas was openly critical while Mr. Northup merely suggested. In an article on Detroit appearing in "Outlook" and "Independent," of Feb. 13, Matthew Josephson writes: "The figure of the new motor car was a great improvement over that of recent years but all of the major companies had adopted the same style and given their cars similar eyes, hips and square foreheads." He then goes on to explain how this came about, but is slightly off as to facts.

Three Main Body Types

The so-named sedan is the typical American family automobile. When the word automobile was mentioned fifteen or more years ago, the picture in mind

Mr. Thomas in his address mentioned "Modern Art" as applicable to exterior as well as interior design. Mr. Northup lightly touched upon its use in connection with interiors only. Mr. Thomas's criticism of passenger accommodations were hardly applicable to present-day well designed bodies and his suggestion of rearward-facing intermediate seats is not an arrangement that a prospective purchaser would tolerate. Nevertheless, Mr. Thomas if taken seriously (and this is decidedly worthwhile) has given us much to think about: Fashion; Modern Art.

A Proper Field for Modern Art

Mr. Thomas observed that many people think fashions are set by the manufacturer and thrust upon a sheep-like public. In prosperous years like 1928, so far as the automobile industry is concerned, this is largely the fact. It takes a little jolt of adversity, or prospective adversity to awaken the industry from the serene complacency for which the past boom year is responsible. The study of public taste and preference is a difficult matter when attempted in advance of exhibition. What the public will accept is a hazardous guess in any line. However, certain trends in present taste are quite apparent and should be of assistance. Modern Art in its true artistic sense exhibits certain distinct character-

*Consulting body engineer, Box 308, Syracuse, N. Y.

istics. Its proper influence on interior design is acknowledged. Why not, as applied to closed cars on exterior design as well?

APPLICATION TO EXTERIORS

One of the characteristics of modern decorative design is simplicity and a preferential use of straight lines and angles. Mr. Thomas said that large, square windows make an ordinary sedan look static and lumbering. This is true if the emphasized rectangles approximate the square, but not where the length is much greater than the height. Moreover, all angles need not necessarily be right angles. Even in a flat front design a slanting shield, and quarter in harmony therewith, would dispose of the static effect.

The above observations apply for the most part to that portion of the elevation design above the belt, usually referred to as the superstructure. Thank goodness, we are still streamlining the main body and blending it more or less successfully with the hood surfaces, except in a few instances where the designer thought he

So far as closed bodies are concerned it is difficult to design a superstructure to comport with this idea. A slanting V-front and the use of a sine-curve for developing surfaces back of the master cross section are about all that can be done and this type of car would only be suitable for road use. The sine-curve not only suggests speed to the eye and mind but actually accomplishes something in reducing skin friction and eddies.

SKETCH UTILIZING THE SINE-CURVE

Without attempting to design a wholly practical body but to show the theoretical application of sine-curve development to a closed speed car, still employing fenders for protection against splashing but shaping and disposing them in such a way as to offer the least possible resistance to wind pressure, a study sketch is offered. The sine-curve in this study, Fig. 3, ends at point X on the elevation and the several horizontal sections, and the master line *A* is rounded in from X to the center line as a concession to expediency. If the sine-curve development, allowing room for two passengers on a rear seat,

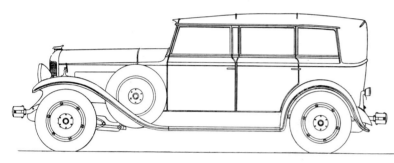

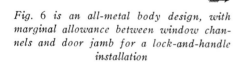

Fig. 2 shows the elimination of static effect by a change from rectangles

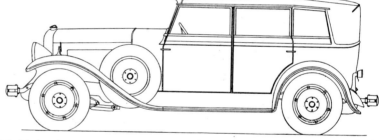

Fig. 6 is an all-metal body design, with marginal allowance between window channels and door jamb for a lock-and-handle installation

had to do something to earn his pay and could think of nothing but queerly disposed fancy moldings and broken panels.

SUPERSTRUCTURE WORTHY OF DESIGN

The superstructure is, after all, an important element in a pleasing design. Thus far it has mostly been treated only as an extension of the lower or main body surface with some holes punched in it for doors and windows. Why not treat it as a superstructure, keeping it light in weight and giving the car a smart and speedy appearance, by rolling in the main body at the belt on a development from the cowl and hood, thus preserving the streamlining up to the superstructure? To be sure something in this line has been attempted on one or two production cars in this country; although a vast improvement over conventional closed-body design and meeting with popular favor, the results still preserve much of the old clumsiness and top-heaviness. In Europe they are doing it much better and have been for some time.

Mr. Thomas suggested a further development of the streamline principle to express more adequately in design the element of speed. Mr. Northup in his remarks concerning the treatment of the front end apparently has a similar thought.

were continued to the center line, the surface would develop a keel as it approached the center and the overall length would be totally impractical for anything but a racing model.

It is interesting to note that the proportional development of the various sections by triangulation produces a sine-curve as far as X on every section, precisely as would happen if each section had been developed from the circle. This means that whatever virtue the sine-curve possesses in eliminating eddy drag is distributed over the whole surface.

ROADSTERS NEARLY ALL LOOK ALIKE

Open-car models offer many better opportunities for variety and distinction in design than the closed models; and yet it is in this field that Mr. Thomas's complaint of deadly similarity is most emphatically applicable. American roadsters all look alike except for a few fancy moldings and applied gadgets. To be sure, the standard American roadster is a good-looking car, but they do not all need to look alike to be attractive; and while the present style is admittedly smart and suggestive of speed, much more speedy designing is possible with a rational use of the sine-curve both in plan and elevation. From the master section forward the ideal shape would, of course, be parabolic, but so long as fenders have to be treated as gadgets in the assembly line, not much more can be done with front-end development than is suggested by Mr. Northup.

PHAETONS MIGHT ALSO BE IMPROVED

Phaeton models as now offered in sales-rooms present a greater variety in design than roadsters, yet here again the differences consist mostly of the cutting-up of side surfaces into variously shaped panels by the use of moldings. It apparently has never occurred to American designers to speed up the lines of the main body by leaving a long straightaway distinctly outlined,

the case of a certain car not needing a radiator cap that felt obliged to put on an imitation cap. This was done, not to add an artistic touch but because the public thought the car did not look like an automobile without an imitation radiator with a cap on it. Another instance is to be seen in some recent broadcast advertising where a certain make of car, calling attention to its marvelous accomplishments in inspired designing, mentions not less than four periods of ancient decorative art and incidentally drags in an extremely modern interpretation of an antique vase. All this in one series of cars. The

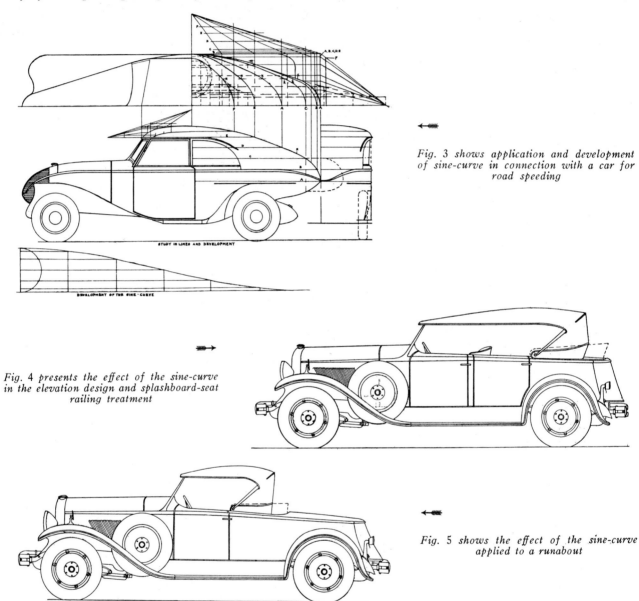

Fig. 3 shows application and development of sine-curve in connection with a car for road speeding

Fig. 4 presents the effect of the sine-curve in the elevation design and splashboard-seat railing treatment

Fig. 5 shows the effect of the sine-curve applied to a runabout

treating the seat rails as parts of a superstructure with an incidental splashboard effect that allows a clean-cut main body development to carry the picture. This style of body is attractive and perfectly practical, yet nothing of this character is being offered to the American buyer today.

It is by no means a certainty that a series of cars, practical, comfortable and comporting with the Modern Art movement would make an instantaneous hit with the public. Mr. Thomas is more optimistic in this respect than most of us feel. As an example, one member in the discussion following Mr. Thomas's address, cited

question might be put as to whether the ad writer is right in his estimate of public intelligence.

Again, Walter Mitchell in his article in the February issue of AUTOBODY gives us a glimmer of an idea as to what the wind would do, but he evidently favors the use of gadgets and fancy moldings. He likes the spliced drip molding, presumably because of what the wind would do; but in this case it isn't what the wind would do but what the water could do that should stimulate the mind of the designer. We might add more gadgets by placing a gargoyle at each end of the drip. The advertising expert could then make reference to another period of architectural design—the Medieval Renaissance. Mr. Mitchell may be a good example of average public taste.

COMPLETELY STREAMLINED CARS

Every good designer knows that the ideal motor-car design would eliminate fenders and streamline the whole car surface over and between the wheels, extending the overhang, front and rear, sufficiently for a contour that would reduce wind resistance to a minimum. Everyone knows that this type of car would not fit in with present parking problems, therefore would be totally unsuitable for city use. What might approximate the ideal and still be practical for all purposes under present conditions has been previously mentioned. More straight-lining and streamlining, less old-style coachwork detail, lightening of superstructure both as to appearance and actual weight, better outlook from closed bodies as part of the superstructure-lightening process. All these features would be strictly in line with Modern Art development and notwithstanding doubts heretofore expressed, one might venture the prediction that such designing would easily hit a note of fashion.

A CAR FOR EACH USE

Mr. Thomas touched upon designing that would be distinctly appropriate to the particular use to which a car is to be put. Here is a field where the possibilities have hardly been scratched. The 2-car family is with us in the hundred thousands. We are hearing much about the 3- and 4-car family. Why not exploit the 5- and 6- and more-car family? In the days of horse-drawn vehicles every well-furnished private carriage house had an appropriate style of vehicle for every distinct use: At the shore or country place, a victoria for afternoon driving and general use; a family station wagon, a station omnibus or wagonette for meeting a party of week-end guests; large and small body breaks and a tandem cart for steeplechase, hunt or polo match,

and so on; for city use, a brougham for shopping, the theatre and getting about; a cabriolet for driving in the park; a runabout for son; a gadabout for daughter and so on. It was as important to have the right vehicle for the particular purpose as to wear the fitting costume for the social function.

What do we see now, within and without the inclosure at a steeplechase, a polo match, a golf club or anywhere else for that matter? A lot of so-called sedans and limousines, fewer but quite numerous phaetons and roadsters, all in their respective categories looking alike except for size and a few splashes of color. How can a sporting event look like anything but a city traffic jam under such conditions? Where is the snap and go to this sort of exhibition?

REAL FIELD FOR CUSTOM BUILDER

It would seem to be within the custom-body designer's province to start a change in this condition and yet he is only struggling along in a sharp competition with the same old types, only recently adding to his lines two or three kinds of convertible bodies (popular in Europe only because the purchaser deludes himself into thinking he gets two cars for one tax) which do not work and never will work satisfactorily.

Herein lies the particular opportunity for the application of Modern Art interpretation to the uses and significance surrounding the problem in hand—the smart vehicle on smart lines—the staid and steady, more static—the outing and sporting types to look sporty and fast instead of merely tacking the word "Sport" to the catalog name of a hackneyed design—the attaching of names that are descriptive either of the character or purpose of the car instead of using traditional coachbuilders' names for vehicles not even remotely resembling their predecessors. The use, in a word, of simplicity and expression in design and the attainment thereby of attractive novelty.

Colors for Commercial Wagons*

MUCH attention has been given during the past year to the refinishing of delivery cars; with the increasing use of individual and striking color schemes in motor cars in general, the days of the old-time black commercial vehicle are about over. There are several things to be considered in providing an attractive and suitable color scheme for such vehicles. Much depends upon what the purpose of the vehicle is. Vivid red is a good color for a fire engine, but it would not be so good on a florist's wagon. Old-fashioned common sense will dictate the proper viewpoint to every owner.

Certain types of delivery wagons with closed bodies and severe body lines call for colors that will not accent the unattractive features of the design. In this connection, cold, dark shades of blue and dark chocolate browns are excellent colors. . . . Both the dark blue and the brown take silver, gold, cream, vermilion and orange as a trim or lettering color.

The attractive appearance of any colored object is accomplished by close attention to detail. Visibility is an asset to attention value in this type of vehicle and, as such, warrants careful consideration in using the secondary or accent color to good advantage. Shop keepers in all sections of the United States are com-

mencing to appreciate the appearance value of their delivery cars. Shades of orchid, violet, rose and delicate blue tints have been adopted generally by the florists as symbolic of their trade. Each florist has been able to use secondary and tertiary colors in such a way as to assure individuality for his own vehicles and in this way he has been able to establish trademark value for his wagons.

Garish colors for business vehicles are now *passés*. We have begun to agree with the early Egyptians that harshness and lack of harmony offend, but that brilliance and richness can be effected in good taste. Early colorists studied nature for their color schemes and learned how to create subtle harmonies. Nature still teaches us. The attractive color grouping in the orchid, the subdued green and blue of earth and sky, the rare colorings of birds and fish, the hues of precious stones, all supply us with hints for the use of colors.

Laundry wagons look crisp and attractive in white, pale yellows, light blues and tints of green. . . . Blues may be used effectively on white or yellow base colors. White contrasts splendidly when used on blue and green, yellow or pale gold. Bronze is effective on pale greens.

The growing use of motor hearses has given rise to some perplexity as to what may be done with them in the way of color. Just because hearses have always

* Excerpts from an article by Howard Ketcham, director, Duco Color Advisory Service, 21 E. 40th St., New York.

been black or white is no reason they always should be, any more than just because fenders were black for a long time, they must remain black. One of the newest types of motor hearses seats about 30 people and carries the casket as well. Such buses may be lacquered in dark blue or one of the maroons and still be proper to the spirit of their use. . . . Men's and women's specialty shops are using properly combined colors to express the feeling of their services also. Many of them are tasteful and distinctive and seem to express the meaning of the vehicle. Browns and beiges, the popular colors of the year, predominate.

Making a Cowl, With Raised Panel, on the Artz Press

AT the plant of the Union City Body Co. at Union City, Ind., the Artz metal-stretching press has been used for the production of a variety of panels. Some of the panels it has been claimed could not be produced on a press of this type, but the Union

shows the steel sheet in position ready for stretching. In Fig. 3 the sheet has been stretched and the rise of the hydraulic ram has been stopped. While the sheet is in tension, the overlay and other irregular features are completed; with hammer and a wedge of wood the

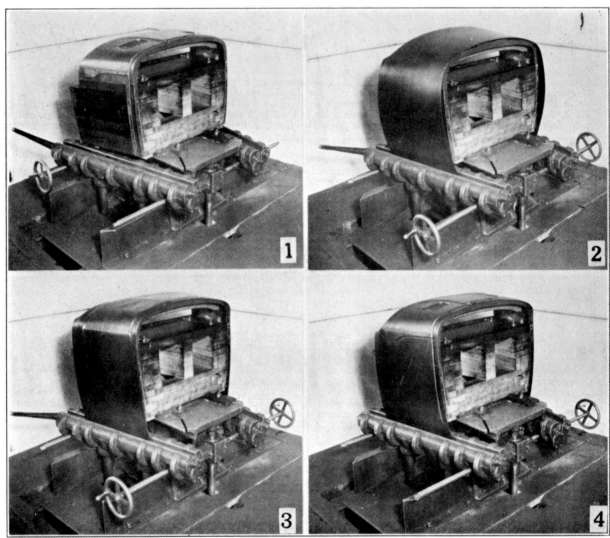

Fig. 1. *Composite wood-and-iron form for making a cowl with overlay panels, ventilators and hood ledge on the Artz press*

Fig. 2. *The ends of a 20-gage steel sheet are secured in the grippers and all is in readiness for the upward thrust of the hydraulic ram*

Fig. 3. *Cowl panel stretched, and ready for setting down the metal, with hammer and wooden wedge, around the overlays, ventilator openings, et cetera*

Fig. 4. *The cowl panel, with overlay, ventilator openings and hood ledge completed. It is now ready for removal and trimming*

City Body Co., with Roy Fullerton, superintendent of its metal shop as ring master, has been able to make the Artz press "perform," and practically every type of panel that was required in quantity has been made on this press. The accompanying engravings show the production on the Artz press of a raised-panel cowl with two ventilator openings on top, hood ledge and side molding. This cowl is made of 20-gage steel on a wood-and-iron form illustrated in Fig. 1. Fig. 2

metal is set down around the hood ledge, ventilator holes, molding and overlay. Fig. 4 shows these operations completed and the panel ready for removal from the press. After removal, the panels are trimmed and the ventilator openings cut out. This cowl of 20-gage steel is stretched and peened in less than 10 min. by the Union City Body Co. which has originated methods of making a number of difficult panels with the Artz press, under Fullerton's superintendence.

Further Notes on the Application of Dynamic Symmetry

By William H. Emond*

IN a previous article on the application of dynamic symmetry to automobile design, reference was made to the system of proportioning design by the use of area units—instead of line ratios—as having been used by the ancient Greeks. This was Hambidge's theory. Ernest Flagg in a recently published work on the Parthenon Naos laboriously proves that simple proportions were used in at least some Greek designing; and he goes out of his way to slap the Hambidge theory. A commentator has drawn attention to the fact that the proportions Flagg has so painfully demonstrated in connection with the Parthenon were used in planning the Great Pyramid. As a matter of fact all this was discovered years ago. There is no doubt as to the familiarity of ancient Greek designers with the properties of the root rectangles, and it would appear from some of Hambidge's analyses that the ancient Egyptians, from whom the Greeks got their start in geometry, had used area proportions in planning many architectural decorative details.

Individual artists, architects and mathematicians, acknowledging the perfection of Greek geometrical designing, propounded theories at various intervals in the past. Each labeled his alleged discovery of a sys-

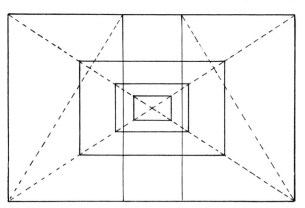

Fig 1 *showing development of rectangles by the line-ratio method. Note the disproportionate area of the central unit, when dividing the figure by perpendiculars on the diagonal*

tem and usually claimed that it was universally used by the classic artists. For most of us this last is difficult to believe. In fact it takes a deal of faith, in view of some of the more complicated of Hambidge's analyses, to believe in the universal employment by Greek artists of the system he has named "dynamic symmetry."

It seems easier to conclude that some of the Greek artists used area-unit proportions and others direct line ratios, and it is quite possible that each system had its advocates. Artists and human nature were likely much the same in 700 B.C. as today. Then it may have been the Statics vs. the Dynamics, as it seems to be now—with barbarians on the side lines sneering at both. If this were the year 700 B.C. and I were living in Athens, especially if automobiles were then being designed, I should certainly join the Dynamics.

* Consulting body engineer, Box 308, Syracuse, N. Y.

To illustrate the difference between compositions developed from ordinary and from root rectangles, let us examine Figs. 1 and 2. Fig. 1 represents an ordinary line-ratio rectangle with the long-to-short-side ratio of 11:7. This is the base-to-height ratio of the Great Pyramid, yielding in its turn the "golden mean" ratio between slope line and half the base. For comparison let us take Fig. 2, a root rectangle with a

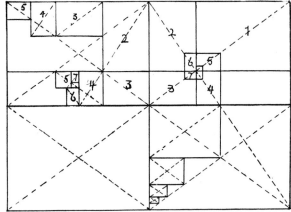

Fig. 2 *showing development of rectangles by area-ratio units. All rectangles in the upper left quarter have a definite area ratio. In the upper right quarter are shown a similar series of area-unit rectangles plotted in a logarithmic spiral; this growth by "dynamic symmetry" coincides with the plan of shell growth, such as exhibited by the chambered nautilus. In the lower right quarter are a series of rectangles developed by the line-ratio method, after the manner of Fig. 1; these cannot be coiled around an "eye" as in the "dynamic" series directly above, and hence the system typified by Fig. 1 is described as "static"*

height-to-length ratio of $1:\sqrt{2}$, drawn to the same scale. This $\sqrt{2}$ rectangle has been found peculiarly adapted to automobile designing.

In Fig. 1 an infinite number of rectangles similar to the master figure may be developed on the diagonals, but if perpendiculars are erected on the diagonals it is found that the master figure is cut into two equal rectangles at each end but there is left in the center another which is not similar and hence cannot be used for the generation of rectangles similar to the master figure. If the master figure were a root rectangle, the perpendicular on the diagonals would divide it into two, three, four or five similar figures, according to the root number. It is evident therefore that the 11:7 figure has its limitations as compared to a root rectangle.

In Fig. 2 it will be noted that the perpendicular to the diagonal of the $\sqrt{2}$ rectangle cuts the long side of the master figure exactly into halves, thus allowing its division into two equal complementaries which of course have the same properties as the master figure. This is where it differs from the 11:7 rectangle. If, as in the side elevation of an automobile, the design composition has such functional proportions of length to height as to make it possible to cover the area by adjacent master rectangles and their equivalents, each equivalent or reciprocal and the whole area will be proportional to the master figure.

Let us now examine briefly the functions of the $\sqrt{2}$ rectangle. After dividing Fig. 2 into two complementaries, then quartering by a horizontal through the center, we have four reciprocals of the master figure. In the upper left quarter are shown, generated on perpendiculars, a series of rectangles which are in random arrangement and reciprocal with the master figure, but diminishing in area ratios. In the upper right quarter of Fig. 2, a series of exactly similar rectangles have been generated, coiled around an "eye," the point of intersection of the diagonal and perpendicular. The possibility of this arrangement of a series of rectangles thus generated around the eye is the excuse for referring to this system as "dynamic." Using the eye for a pole, one may describe about this coil a logarithmic spiral, the plan of shell growth. In the lower right quarter of Fig. 2 are a series of rectangles developed after the manner of Fig. 1; if an attempt be made to coil these

rupted by functional details, but distinct in spite of all the interruptions; then the area of the whole superstructure, subdivided by uprights into separate areas of glass and opaque panels; later, the disposition of mudguards, moldings and accessories may be determined geometrically in accordance with the master plan. It is the nice proportioning of these areas and details that make the satisfying picture. It would seem from the general character of the problem that a method of obtaining good proportions should be based upon areas, rather than line ratios, for the best effect.

In the accompanying study of a streamlined "cabin" sedan, the whole height of body, from base line to top of roof, is the length of the shorter side of the basic rectangle, leaving the drop of the radiator shell below the base line of the body to be determined within a reciprocal proportion, treated as in excess. This is more in line with common practice.

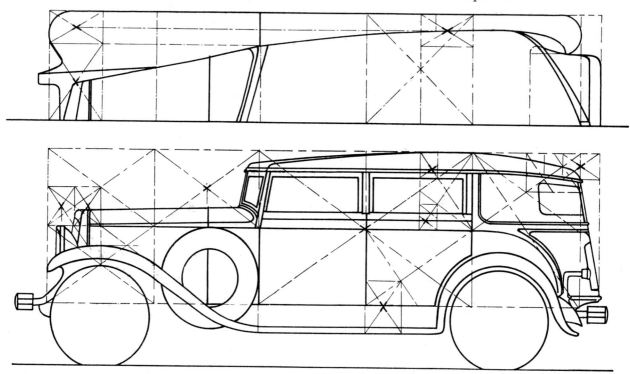

An interesting streamlined "cabin sedan" developed by the root-rectangle or area-unit method, sometimes referred to as dynamic symmetry. All of the rectangles shown in light broken lines are proportionately related. Note the unusual V-shaped rear of the superstructure and the built-in trunk at the rear

around an eye it will be found that it cannot be done; this series then, and the proportions thus obtained, are described as "static."

In a simple analysis of Fig. 1, after constructing the two end complementaries, if a series of rectangles on perpendiculars were coiled about the eye these rectangles would not be reciprocal to the center portion of Fig. 1; hence the only available method of proportioning is by line ratios as shown. On the other hand, in Fig. 2, all of the rectangles developed on perpendiculars with the diagonals are reciprocals; the larger rectangular areas may be subdivided easily and quickly, with the certainty that a line drawn either through the eye or the center will be coincident with the side of a rectangle in true proportion. Progress in the development of a design by this diagramatic method is fast and sure. In my opinion this is as good a reason as any for the adjective "dynamic."

In automobile designing, distinctly indicated area units are essential features of the composition. There is the main body and bonnet area, more or less inter-

The $\sqrt{2}$ rectangle with a long side of 70 in. has an indeterminate short-side dimension of approximately 49½ in. The square root of 2 being 1.414 the ratio of the short side to the long is as 1 : 1.414. The long side being 70 in., the short would thus be 49.498 in. The square root of 2 being indeterminate it will be better for the designer to construct the rectangle graphically rather than by scale. The dimension thus obtained is a perfectly practical dimension for the overall height of the main body, and for the proportioning of closed-car designs this $\sqrt{2}$ development is simple and satisfactory.

This body design has no static appearance whatever. It looks speedy, is speedy, and at the same time is built within a practical overall length for city parking. The superstructure is treated as a streamlined cabin. The V-front and V-back reduce wind pressure and eddy drag materially. The passenger compartments may be ample for five people and leave exceptional luggage space under the V-back structure. This part of the design is susceptible to a variety of treatments. In this case it is an imitation trunk.

A special body soundproofed to provide clear radio reception and quiet travel-comfort. The body was designed and built by Le Baron Detroit Co., and mounted on a Lincoln chassis

Insulated Automobile Body Provides Perfect Radio Reception and Improved Passenger Comfort

By Harvey B. Lindsay*

MUCH interest has been aroused in the possibility or probability of making special built-in radio sets standard equipment in high-class automobiles. Radio sets have been frequently installed in closed cars by enthusiastic radio fans, and provided novel enjoyment. But just as the automobilist of today wants the smoothest pull to his car, so he wants his radio clear and unspoiled. Any such innovation in the passenger car to be thoroughly successful must be thoroughly right, and to get it thoroughly right invariably means careful analysis of the essentials and correction of the faults that develop in the process of perfection.

This is clearly attested in the extremely successful results that have been obtained in a radio-equipped spe-

* President, Dry-Zero Corporation, 130 N. Wells St., Chicago, Ill.

cial body recently built by the LeBaron Detroit Co. In building this body it was realized that to get perfect radio reception while the car is in motion, road sounds and extraneous noise must be excluded to a degree not previously approached. LeBaron's chief engineer, John W. Votypka, started an investigation to ascertain how this could be done without adding any appreciable weight to the body. He found that the U. S. Bureau of Standards' sound laboratories in Washington had discovered that an extremely light blanket material—Dry-Zero—had shown great value in both sound-deadening and insulating (from excessive cold) the cabins of aeroplanes. Indeed, the Bureau's experiments and tests had been so conclusive that Curtiss and several other plane builders had used the Dry-Zero blanket with the greatest success in protecting their

 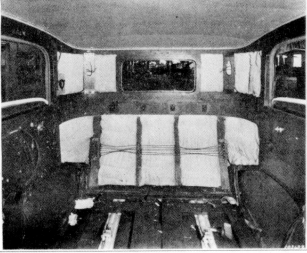

Interior of the special, soundproofed body, built by Le Baron Detroit Co. on Lincoln chassis. As shown at the right, a 1½-in. Dry-Zero blanket was attached between all frame spaces, as well as in the roof, floor and doors. Because of its softness, Dry-Zero makes a fine padding over the cushion springs and further soundproofs the body

passengers from the otherwise excessive noise.

In this special body on Lincoln chassis, the radio loudspeaker and controls are placed on the back of the front seat, in perfectly harmonized design, and so that reception would be excellent in all parts of the car. In insulating the body, a 1½ in. thick special Dry-Zero aeroplane blanket was installed in all "between-frame" spaces of the body against the inner surface of the outside metal; this even included the door panels. On top of the roof bows, a made-to-size Dry-Zero blanket was stretched, covering the entire roof. The floor also was carefully sound insulated with this material. When the entire job was completed tests were run with complete satisfaction. To determine the degree of perfection reached, comparative tests were run between this car and another not treated with Dry-Zero. The improvement was marked, especially in the complete quiet-comfort obtained and the clarity and perfection of the radio reception.

It is interesting to note that this treatment of the body also achieves two further results, due to the fact that this blanket material has the highest resistance to the passage of heat of any known commercial insulant. These are: (1) a marked degree of temperature comfort—for example, in the winter—is induced; and (2) under a hot bright sun, the radiating effect of the ordinary roof on the passengers' heads is largely checked. It is often not realized that inasmuch as radiated heat travels 186,200 miles a second, no amount of breeze between roof and passenger has the least effect on the radiation—it can only be moderated by a competent roof insulation.

This body is of imperative interest to the automobile industry. It has shown that radio can be as completely enjoyed in the closed car as in the drawing room, and has indicated the way to more complete passenger luxury. Incidentally, approximately 120 sq. ft. of 1½ in. Dry-Zero blanket was used, which weighed but 20 lb.—about one-seventh the weight of cork.

Blue Still Leads Automobile Colors

Blue continues to hold its place as the preferred summer color in the automobile field, according to the Automobile Color Index published by Duco Color Advisory Service. The rising movement recorded for blue since the middle of February has been sustained at the high level achieved in June. The standing of the various colors are given below, with corresponding figures for June, 1929, in parenthesis: Blue, 203 (256); black, 134 (73); brown, 100 (90); green, 93 (64); maroon, 49 (27); gray, 17 (79). Black is showing signs of resistance to the decline that began in April. Greens and browns have moved slightly upward. Interest in maroon has been declining since March. Gray is almost at the nadir but its avoidance in production work gives it a certain exclusiveness for custom bodies. Effort has been made to develop a stronger interest in gray by introducing a series of gray nuances in greenish, bluish and brownish tints.

The vogue for bright colors appears to have reached the saturation point for the present. The current trend is toward dark, serene color values, clear and rich in depth.

The Calendar

NATIONAL ASSOCIATION OF MOTOR BUS OPERATORS..Sept. 18-19
  At Chicago
MOTOR AND EQUIPMENT ASSOCIATION
  At Cleveland.................................Nov. 10-14
AUTOMOBILE SALONS
  At Chicago..................................Nov. 8-15
  At New York...........................Nov. 30-Dec. 6
  At Los Angeles............................Feb. 7-14
  At San Francisco.........................Feb. 21-28
NATIONAL AUTOMOBILE SHOWS
  At New York...............................Jan. 3-10
  At Chicago................................Jan. 24-31
FOREIGN SHOWS
  At Paris, France..........................Oct. 2-12
  At London, England.......................Oct. 16-25
  At Brussels, Belgium......................Dec. 6-17

An 18-passenger parlor coach, built by Morley Motor Bodies Ltd., of Sydney, for the Australian National Airways, Ltd., the air service established by Messrs. Kingsford-Smith and Ulm, the men who flew the Pacific two years ago. This body weighs about 3,000 lb. and is mounted on a Fargo Freighter chassis, which was extended 2 ft. The body paneling is of 18-gage aluminum and the cowl of No. 20 steel. The finish is Australian lacquer—aluminum to the elbow rail and blue for the superstructure, the canvas deck being painted in light blue. The folding steps and roof baggage rail are nickel-plated. Note the use of horizontally sliding glass in the windows. Two mail boxes are fitted into the back, under the rear seats. Except at the rear, the seating accommodation is by seagrass-and-cane-trimmed chairs. The framework of this coach includes an interesting group of woods: The main frame is Australian spotted gum and blue gum; the pillars are blue gum and New Zealand beech; roof bars, Australian coachwood; wheelarches, Japanese oak; through rails, tying pieces and roof, Queensland bunya; floor, 6 x 1-in. Tasmanian oak, screwed and leaded; interior panels, Queensland maple. Other interior trim is of brown leather to match the cabinet work

Slanting Door Windows that *Lower without Gap*

REFERENCE was made in the July, 1928, issue of AUTOBODY to the McAdam patent for a "closed automobile body" with sloping front-door windows, and about a year later, in the June, 1929, issue, to some bodies built by Hibbard & Darrin and Brewster & Co., the front doors of which had slanting windows that lowered without gapping at the front edge. Both body-building companies, through their designers or employees, filed applications for patent on this construction but it was found that Josiah W. McAdam, of Vancouver, B. C., had preceded them with an application dated Mar. 25, 1927. U. S. Pat. No. 1,671,433 was granted to Mr. McAdam on May 29, of the succeeding year.

Eliminating the gap of slanting door windows was accomplished by the simple procedure of using parallel

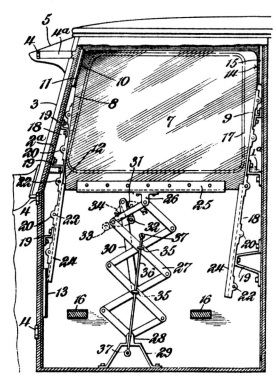

One of the constructions suggested in the McAdam patent for the purpose of eliminating the "blind spot" and providing a slanting door window that would lower without gap. This construction utilizes an inclined track with rollers, but parallel inclined channels were also envisioned by the patentee

sloping channels and is practical where the slope of the door is not too great. The accompanying patent drawing shows one of the constructions contemplated when Mr. McAdam applied for his patent. Mr. McAdam had in view also the elimination of the "blind spot" at the front corner of the body. Four of his eight claims specified an enclosed automobile body "having relatively narrow inclined front-corner posts, an inclined anti-glare windshield supported by the corner post, etc." The forward part of the front door and the window opening had a corresponding inclination. The unitary window pane was a parallelogram with horizontal upper and lower edges, and inclined front and rear edges for which corresponding guides were provided. In several

of his claims, inclined tracks with anti-friction rollers were specified. In the actual practice, merely guides have been used.

Several old body builders have reported the use of slanting door windows early in the history of the automobile industry, but we have not heard whether any of these were constructed in such a manner as to cover the principles of this patent. Some of the other aims specified by the inventor have been accomplished without encroaching on the McAdam claims. Non-glare windshields have been provided by setting the glass at a slight angle but retaining vertical pillars, and specially constructed corner posts are being built which provide clear vision. The use of slanting corner pillars and slanting front-door windows that lower without gapping is therefore a matter of convenience or optional design, rather than necessity, in the attainment of clear vision at the front corners.

The McAdam construction, however, facilitates the attainment of clear vision and eliminates the necessity of the "fake" construction sometimes employed when a slanting upper front-door pillar is used with a rectangular glass. One preferred construction suggested in the patent provides for a door with a front pillar vertically disposed below the belt, which is desirable from a constructional standpoint; the rear door pillar is vertical throughout its length. As the McAdam principles cover the easiest and neatest way of constructing non-gapping, slanting door windows, the important sections of the eight claims of the McAdam patent are reproduced below:

MCADAM PATENT CLAIMS

1. An inclosed automobile body having rearwardly inclined front corner posts and wind shield, front doors having window openings, the front edges of said openings corresponding to the inclination of the corner posts, a unitary window pane mounted within each door and having a front edge inclined from top to bottom thereof, and means for sliding the window upwardly and downwardly in a path corresponding substantially to said inclination.

2. An inclosed automobile body having front corner posts of minimum width as viewed from the driver's seat and inclining rearwardly from the hood to the top, front doors having the upper portions of their front edges correspondingly inclined and having upper window openings whose front edges are close to and parallel with said inclination, a plate glass window mounted within each door to be moved upwardly and downwardly to closed and open positions respectively, said window being in the form of a parallelogram having inclined front and rear edges, guiding means engaging said edges to cause the window to move in a path substantially parallel to the corner posts, and toggle levers for actuating the window.

3. An inclosed automobile body having relatively narrow, inclined front corner posts, an inclined anti-glare windshield supported by the corner posts, front doors having their upper front edges correspondingly inclined and hinged along said edges, the upper hinges being secured to the visor, said doors having window openings in their upper portions, provided with correspondingly inclined front edges, tracks mounted within the door in advance and in rear of said openings and arranged substantially at the same angle as the front of the openings, a plate glass window mounted to slide up and down between the tracks, said plate having parallel horizontal upper and lower edges and parallel inclined front and rear edges to correspond to the tracks, and means for raising and lowering the windows.

4. An inclosed automobile body having relatively narrow inclined front corner posts . . . tracks mounted within the door in advance and in rear of said openings and arranged substantially at the same angle as the front of the openings, said tracks having spaced openings formed therein, anti-friction

rollers mounted in the openings, a plate glass window mounted to slide up and down between the tracks, said window having inclined front and rear edges to contact with the rollers, and a series of toggle levers mounted beneath the window and operable from the inner side of the door to raise and lower the window in a line substantially parallel to the inclined front corner posts.

5. An inclosed automobile body having relatively narrow, inclined front corner posts . . . tracks mounted within the door in advance and in rear of said openings and arranged substantially at the same angle as the front of the openings, said tracks having spaced openings formed therein, anti-friction rollers mounted in the openings and projecting slightly beyond the inner faces of the tracks, side flanges formed on the lower portions of the tracks, a plate glass window shaped to slide up and down between the sets of rollers, said window being engaged by the side flanges when lowered and by felt padding when raised to prevent rattling, and means operable from the inner side of the door to raise and lower the window.

6. An inclosed automobile body having relatively narrow inclined front corner posts . . . said tracks having spaced rollers mounted therein and side flanges on their lower portions, a plate glass window having horizontal upper and lower edges and parallel inclined front and rear edges to contact with said rollers, the upper and lower terminals of the front edge and the upper terminal of the rear edge being bevelled, upper and lower stops mounted in the door to contact with said bevelled terminals to arrest the window in uppermost and lowermost positions, and means for raising and lowering the window in an inclined direction and for holding the same in intermediate positions.

7. In an inclosed automobile body, front corner posts inclining rearwardly from hood to top, said posts being of minimum width as viewed from the driver's seat, front doors having the upper portions of their front edges inclined and having window openings provided with correspondingly inclined front walls located relatively close to the inclined front edges of the doors, the upper portions of the doors from the bottoms of the window openings up being transversely thinner than the lower portions of said doors and the outer edges of said inclined walls being rounded to reduce interference with vision, windows mounted within the doors and having front and rear edges inclined similarly to the corner posts, means for raising or lowering the windows, and means for causing the same to travel in a direction substantially parallel to the inclined front walls of the openings.

8. In an enclosed automobile body, front corner posts inclining rearwardly from hood to top, doors having the upper portions of their front edges and the front walls of their window openings correspondingly inclined, window panes mounted within the doors and having horizontal top and bottom edges and inclined front and rear edges corresponding

substantially with the corner posts, guides engaging the front and rear edges to cause the panes to move in said inclined direction, transverse supports arranged in the door beneath the panes to support the same when lowered, a flanged strip carried by the lower edges of the panes to rest on said supports, and manually operated toggle mechanism located beneath the panes and connected to the flanged strips to elevate and lower the panes.

We understand that the Murray Corporation of America has acquired the rights to the McAdam patent.

The Calendar

New Jersey's Motor Buses carried more passengers last year than its trolley cars. The drift to motorized transit has been increasing in recent years, but in no populous state has this transformation been so rapid as in New Jersey. Most of these motorcoach passengers were carried by Public Service Co-ordinated Transport, one of the largest operators of motorcoaches in the world.

General view and interior of the rear compartment of Pierce-Arrow's new town car in the "Salon" series. It has a V-type windshield, transformable front, the modish radiator screen, chromium-plated beading around the bonnet louvers, across the louvers themselves and on the chassis valance on each side of the step light; bright-metal tire covers, 5-in. single-bar bumpers and another touch of bright metal in the stainless-steel framing of the windows. The interior also has numerous interesting features: Plain-stretched upholstery with leg and head rolls; flush-type ash receivers in each quarter and separate cabinets for toilet accessories; clock built in division header; concealed auxiliary seats; interesting hardware; wood trim in dark mahogany of special shape on division and door friezes; lambskin or plush rug; leather "scuff" panel instead of carpet on the doors. On another model, an umbrella was concealed in a special compartment of the right front door and there was a flush-type ash receptacle on each side of the instrument panel

Wind-Tunnel Tests on Reo Royale Sedan

By C. M. Templeton

WITH the advent of smooth hard-surfaced high-ways and fast, yet safe, automobiles it is not uncommon for the average motorist to drive at speeds ranging from 50 mi. per hr. upward. Undoubtedly, a considerable amount of power is used in overcoming air resistance at these speeds, but can the actual loss be determined? Can this factor be reduced by change of design without resorting to such unusual treatment that the public might term it "freakish"? To give definite and concrete data on this subject, tests were made by the engineering-research staff of the Murray Corporation of America, in conjunction with the design of the new Reo cars, and with the co-operation of the aeronautics department of the University of Detroit.

The first step was to make up two accurate quarter-scale models—one of the 1930 Flying Cloud Sedan of 124-in. wheelbase, which was a conventional type of car, and a model of the proposed new Royale sedan of 135½-in. wheelbase. The Royale design incorporated a new-type fender, a "vee" radiator with a rounded

Fig. 1. *Wind-tunnel test of the new Reo Royale sedan, compared with 1930 Flying Cloud sedan. The quarter-scale models were suspended in the manner shown to give an effect similar to that produced when the car is passing over the road. The tests showed the aerodynamic design of the Reo Royale—the inverted lower model—to be approximately 12 per cent more efficient*

top, slanting windshield with a rounded front-header treatment and a new-type back panel incorporating a rear splash apron in novel manner.

These models were suspended in the wind tunnel as shown in Fig. 1, with the lower one inverted. This method of suspension gives an effect similar to that produced by the full-sized car passing over the ground or road. Tests were made at air speeds ranging from 30 to 80 mi. per hr. in 5-mi.-per-hr. steps. It was found that the resistance varied uniformly as the square of the velocity. Calculations showed that, at 80 mi. per hr., 60.2 hp. was required to overcome the air resistance of the 1930 Flying Cloud model and 52.5 hp. in the case of the new Royale design. The amount of power absorbed by air resistance was rather startling, but the fact that the Royale design, although much larger, was approximately 12 per cent more efficient was highly encouraging. This increase in efficiency may be interpreted in terms of additional speed or economy. Fur-

thermore, the changes in design previously mentioned also materially increased the beauty of the job. The test proved that it is well worthwhile to study the effect of the air flow about a car in conjunction with new designs.

The next step was to learn more about the movement of the air and the resulting pressure and suction re-

Fig. 2. *Movement of the air about the Reo Royale sedan is shown in this photograph of an oiled-and-lampblacked plate, placed on the longitudinal center line of the model. The position of the model and plate in this test was horizontal, so as to prevent distortion, by gravity, of the lines of flow*

gions. Therefore, an aluminum plate was attached to the new model at the longitudinal center line of the car as illustrated in Fig. 2. With the plate in position, the model was mounted in the tunnel on a suitable stand so that the aluminum plate was horizontal and parallel to the line of flow in the tunnel. The horizontal position of the model was necessary to prevent distortion by gravity of the lines of flow. The plate, previously enameled a dull white, was covered with a paint made of kerosene and lampblack, and when the air was turned on the kerosene flowed, due to air friction, scouring channels in the lampblack. These channels are an indication of the condition and direction of the air flow around the body. Flow diagrams of this type were obtained for air speeds of 50 and 80 mi. per hr., respectively.

From a study of the air-flow pattern in Fig. 2, it can be seen that the air flow in the region back of the body

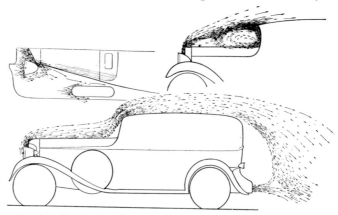

Fig. 3. *Sketch showing the air flow around the Reo Royale sedan. Note the disturbance of the air flow by the bumpers, headlamp and spare wheel in the fender. The sketch in the upper right-hand corner shows the eddies produced by the protruding header of the 1930 Flying Cloud sedan*

is exceedingly turbulent. This turbulence in the form of suction forces and eddies is the cause of the major part of the air resistance of the body. The lines of flow at the back of the body indicate approximately the shape required to produce perfect streamlining at the rear. The disturbance of the air due to the bumpers can be clearly seen from the line of flow. The flow at the windshield is affected somewhat by the "boundary layer." This layer is caused by the friction of the plate which is producing some of the lines of reversed flow close to the windshield. The correct flow at the windshield is similar to that shown beginning at the black spot and flowing smoothly over the top. The flow at the radiator is that which would be produced with the radiator shutter closed. With the shutters open the lines of flow would be entirely changed at the front of the cowl. The flow here as at the windshield is somewhat affected by the boundary layer produced by the plate. This layer is the cause of the outward lines of flow. Without the plate and hence the absence of the boundary layer, the lines of flow would be closer to the vertical and as shown in the sketch (Fig. 3). The plan form of the hood is better than its elevation. However, the lamps, brackets and spare wheel disturb the air flow and neutralize the benefits obtained from the streamline-plan form. An exploration of the air flow around both models was also made with the use of fine silk threads. The results of this test are shown in the sketch. In this test the flow around the windshield was exceedingly smooth in the case of the new design. The flow around the windshield of the 1930 model was turbulent and actually reversed by the protruding header.

The engineering research staff is continuing with other tests which can not be discussed at present. From the work described above it is evident that there is much to be done by means of scientific research to reduce the large percentage of power now required to overcome air resistance.

Weymann American to Build Metal-Paneled Weymanns Here

JOHN GRAHAM, president of Weymann American Body Co., who it will be recalled was the guiding hand of the Holbrook Co. for a great many years and one of the pioneers in the custom-body field, has given us the following information with respect to the activities of the Weymann American Body Co. at Indianapolis:

A body has been developed which is paneled with metal, instead of fabric as heretofore, and which still maintains the Weymann principles, the engineering features and advantages of the Weymann body as regards light weight, silence and comfort in riding.

We anticipate that the trade will be interested in considering the new metal-paneled body for production manufacture. To meet this demand, we are preparing to collaborate with manufacturers by building samples and by engineering for the production of these bodies in the manufacturers' own plants or their production sources of supply. This can be worked out most advantageously as the metal-paneled Weymann, in production, can be built at a cost competitive with the compositive body and without making it necessary for the body manufacturer to revamp his methods of production.

One of these metal-paneled Weymanns was exhibited on a Duesenberg chassis at the Chicago Salon and received most favorable comment, not only from the manufacturers but from the public in general.

I appreciate that in the past considerable resistance was experienced on account of the fabric covering, because most of the public demanded a highly polished exterior, but with the development of the metal-paneled body this resistance is eliminated and there is no restriction so far as design is concerned. The Weymann metal-paneled body appears no different, to a layman's eye, than a composite body and yet it embodies all the essential advantages of the Weymann construction.

The Weymann American Body Co. will still maintain their manufacturing and engineering headquarters in Indianapolis.

Franklin Adopts Clear-Vision Pillars for Series 15 Cars

Franklin has joined the group of cars that are providing true clear vision for motorists. This important safety feature for present-day traffic conditions has thus taken another step in the march of progress. Three or four years ago, many front corners were as wide as 4 or 4½ in., around which it is impossible for the eyes to see. The Campbell Clear-Vision corner post was designed to come within the interpupillary distance and thus make it possible for the motorist to see pedestrians or cars approaching from cross streets. All of the production cars have since narrowed their corner

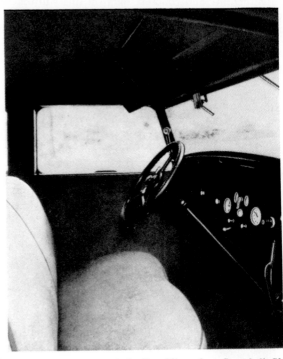

The narrow corner post of the Franklin sedan. Campbell Clear-Vision corner posts are now standard on all the closed models of Franklin Series 15 cars

posts, but many do not yet come within the critical dimensions for giving the driver perfect vision. This has been worked out scientifically in the Campbell Clear-Vision corner post and on an economic manufacturing basis. These posts are now standard on several important lines of production cars. Practically all custom cars now provide clear-vision driving. Although in the custom field, the volume does not warrant tooling up for the production of pressed steel or forged units, the blind spot is eliminated by the use of narrow cast pillars, usually of manganese bronze or a high-strength aluminum alloy.

Martin-Parry Corporation has reduced its capital from $2,280,000 to $1,000,000, thus permitting the creation of adequate working capital, as well as the payment of a liquidating dividend of $4 a share to holders. The management is being concentrated in York, Pa., and the activity of the company will henceforth comprise the manufacture of windshields and other automotive parts. **F. M. Small,** who has been president of the corporation, was elected chairman of the board to succeed **John J. Watson,** resigned. The board of directors was reduced from eight to five and now comprise Messrs. **F. M.** and **J. E. Small, W. A. Keysworth, W. C. Beitzel** and **V. K. Keesey,** all of York, Pa. The resigning directors were John J. Watson, Walter R. Herrick, William T. Dewart, Sir Ashley Sparks, Douglas McKay, Henry Hopkins, Jr., and C. G. Cottee.

VII

Motorcar Design of the Future

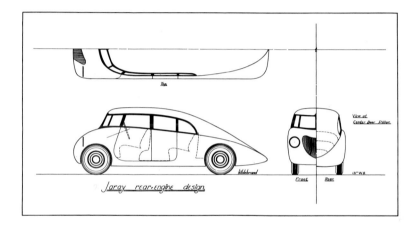

One view of the future, from 1931—a rear-engined "teardrop" limousine designed by George Hildebrand for the Jaray Streamline Corporation of America, which had patented its aerodynamic concepts in 1927.

Motor-Car Design of the Future

By Amos E. Northup*

IT will be my endeavor to try to foresee what really may happen to motor-car design in the future, combining with each development a reason for departing from the usual practice.

Unified Concept for the Car

First let us consider the view-point of designers in other fields. May we take for example the architect. He develops the ensemble design; the foundation must be in exact relation to the house, just as the house must blend with the landscape. The complete design is developed around some one, central idea. Just as the finished project must be a unified whole, each small unit is designed to be a part of this whole and is necessary to its beauty. It is unthinkable to have the foundation and house each designed by different architects, the landscaping by a third, and expect the result to present a correct and pleasing appearance.

It is only logical that the same treatment be applied to automobile design. Just as the foundation and the house must be in perfect relation, so must the chassis, the foundation of the body, be in perfect relation with this body. There should be no apparent dividing line between these two parts of the whole. Furthermore, the lines that are used in the fenders must balance lines in the body, the proportion of glass opening must be determined in its relation to the length of the body, the height of the dash is controlled by the height of the body. From a different angle, the lines terminating the radiator, cowl and top must all be in accord, each worked out in respect to its relation with the other. From these, the width of the hood, cowl and windshield assembly are developed. Just as the chassis must be a part of the entire picture and not a separate unit, so must each of the details be developed to fit into the picture of the whole, each necessary and adding its touch to the perfect creation, nothing superfluous or out of harmony.

Chassis Should Be Changed

In order to achieve better proportions, first of all, between the foundation and the body, there will have to be a change in the chassis. This I firmly believe will be the front-wheel drive, which permits the entire design to be made lower. By lowering the body and by eliminating the side aprons (which are not only unnecessary, but which prevent harmonious design) the entire picture will be changed. But it will be changed to most perfect advantage. At this stage can we really create the exact relation of the foundation to the house, producing a whole in as perfect relationship as can the architect. Even as viewed by the laymen, there is a great advantage in producing a car much lower. With the present demand for speed, with cars gliding around curves just as fast as if the road were straight, driving will certainly be much safer.

Flat Radiator to be Abolished

Pleasing design must be developed with a true relation of all lines both in plan and elevation. For this reason, I do not think the radiator of the future will be flat on the front surface. At present all lines in plan end abruptly at the radiator, which absolutely

NOTE—A paper entitled "Treatise on Future Body Design," presented before the Metropolitan Section of the Society of Automotive Engineers at New York, Nov. 15, 1928.
* Chief Designer, Willys-Overland Co., Toledo, O.

prevents continuity of sweeps. A shape to the radiator other than flat, both in plan and elevation, will create an impression from all angles that will be much more pleasing. It is my contention that the entire front assembly appears too mechanical. The present mounting of the lamps, the front apron, and the front of the fenders certainly do not enhance the appearance of the car. They should appear integral with the car, to be built as a part of it rather than as separate units. I sincerely believe that by closer cooperation between motor-car designer and chassis engineer, our future cars will each have more of an individual appearance than at present when at a certain distance it is difficult to distinguish their identity.

Comfort, Then Beauty

Increase in tread has been foreseen; its universal use is bound to follow. Every salesman is aware that today his sales efforts and sales talk must be directed along the line of beauty and comfort. Performance is established; it is a prerequisite. But we are agreed that nothing, not even beauty, can be substituted for comfort. Since this increase in tread will enable the designer to make the rear seat wider and much more comfortable, and at the same time not detract from the beauty of the car, but enhance it, it will surely be universally adopted. With a motor car well proportioned, pleasing in lines, and ultra-comfortable, a goodly share of sales resistance will be reduced.

Better Vision for Driver

Another point of vast importance is clear vision. We have been solicitous for the ease and comfort of the passengers. Let us consider ease and comfort for the driver. To drive with ease and safety, the driver must have wider range of vision than at present. Even though he is alert, many times cars come within his range of vision suddenly and without warning. This is a faulty feature of the design of the car, and is the cause of many accidents. There are several points to consider in the treatment of clear vision in its entirety. Naturally, we think first of the front pillars. There has already been a great forward movement in this regard. Special "clear-vision constructions" have been developed. Beyond this consideration is the width of the windshield, also the width of the front door. The need for vision directly to the left of the driver is imperative, and the practice of designing a wide door, thus moving the door pillar out of the driver's range of vision must become popular.

Since we are dealing with safety in driving, let us not forget to emphasize the danger of the usual practice of three riding in the front seat, as it is at present designed. The driver is not free to operate as quickly as he should; he is not in a position to meet an emergency. This seat will be constructed, as time goes on, to actually accommodate the driver and two passengers. As attention is drawn to this danger, dimensions will be worked out that will aid in comfort and safety.

Interior Should Be Restful

Just as the exterior of the motor car should present a unified appearance, so should the interior, although each gives an entirely different impression. The exterior creates the impression of beauty in speed, dash and power, as contrasted with the purpose of the interior which tends to beauty in quiet, comfort and restfulness. Design of the exterior has progressed much faster than that of the interior.

I might even venture further by saying that within my experience as a designer of motor cars, we have been using the same styles of trim either plain, plaited or tufted—a little deviation on the door trimming, but that's all. In my files I have interiors of eight and ten years ago and with the possible exception of the headroom and a few minor departures, one could scarcely tell whether it was a 1928 design or 1918. The need of the interior is, as stated before, to create a feeling of repose and comfort. It may surely be luxurious and artistic, but it must be conducive to restfulness. Of necessity this will eliminate anything of ornate design, and embody plain artistic treatment.

Modern Art Will Be Used

Modern art, with its straight lines and planes, will without a doubt be used in the interior of the automobile. Not only the style of trimming, but the hardware, the garnish molding, in fact, the whole atmosphere will be changed by its use. This new treatment can be produced reasonably and there can be no objection from the standpoint of manufacturing, if properly handled. The public coming in contact with this new trend in art will sooner or later demand it to be carried out in motor-car interiors. As long as it will serve our purposes to a good advantage and is decidedly a step forward, we should not wait until it is demanded. We should anticipate this demand and at the same time help ourselves solve the problem of advancing the interior design.

Many will take exception to my firm ideas concerning the interior. However, I will substantiate my convictions with sound reasoning. Let us consider the treatment of our home; each room serves a purpose; but as we are seated in that room, whether it be library, solarium, living room or study, we are not conscious of its conveniences or necessities. If we require one certain thing, it is within reach or vision, but as long as we do not need it, it is obscure. Subconsciously we are assured of its presence and can rely on it, but it is not obvious. It does not distract our attention, but is so worked into the scheme of the room as to be a part of it, and instead of detracting from the beauty of the room just because it is useful, even perhaps mechanical, it adds to the general effect by its treatment.

Improve the Instrument Board

Any one object or group of objects which stand out boldly can not help but detract from that general desired effect. It tends toward distraction and agitation rather than restfulness, quiet, peace, and comfort. We must not overlook the rather firmly established fact that the car interior should produce these very feelings. We take great trouble to produce just these in the rear compartment. But the driver, above all occupants, should be considered. Why not have the instrument board so designed and placed that he is only remotely conscious of it, yet he is assured of its presence when he needs it? It should by no means be covered or hidden, nor should it be outstanding. It should be artistic rather than mechanical in appearance. The car itself is a mechanical conveyance, yet that fact should not even be apparent. Naturally, my views eliminate the aeroplane-type instrument board, but incorporate a panel so designed as to be a part of a carefully worked out, restful interior, rather adding its touch to the picture as a whole than detracting in the least. It serves a double purpose, its mechanical and necessary one, along with its aesthetic one.

Changes in Body Types

It is always hazardous to venture a prophecy. However, I will offer a few thoughts on future body types. I do not believe the roadster will ever pass out of demand, but some new thought must be put into this model to make it more accessible to enter the rumble seat, and also furnish real protection for passengers in that seat. There have been some contrivances on the market, placing a canopy over the rumble seat, but this is only a makeshift. It is next to impossible to enter the rumble seat when this top is in place. My thought would be to have one top to cover both compartments. When the top is raised it will give the appearance of a touring model, which will be far more convenient than the additional top as used today. When the top is lowered, it will create just as sporty an effect, if not more so than the present roadster. At present this idea is only in the experimental stage, but it should meet instant approval by both manufacturing and sales divisions. By producing this model it would necessarily eliminate the phaeton as a standard type.

The sunshine car as exhibited at the Paris Salon, both in 1927 and 1928, seems to have registered an approval in Europe but the American public, I am quite sure, will not give this type the same acceptance. The collapsible sedan, which is now offered by several of the custom-body builders, will undoubtedly be more suited to the demands of the American clientele. This type will give a wider range of vision with the top lowered than any sunshine top yet developed. This latter type has a distinct advantage in being more rigid and maybe a trifle easier to open, but the general design and style, both when open and when closed, certainly is in favor of the collapsible sedan. It is design and style that determines the popularity of a model.

Modify the "Coach" Model

The present "coach" model will undoubtedly be due for a change within a short time. If more thought is put to the model, a much more pleasing design will be the result. Up to now, it has been "How reasonable can we build this model?" Of course, this point cannot be overlooked, but we must also hold in mind that we must constantly improve, and by doing so, invest it with more style and more comfort, thus creating a larger demand. Exterior design will be changed to be more conducive to comfort by making the door wider than at present, which will afford easier entrance to the rear compartment, without any discomfort to the driver's companion. Up to now this fact, alone, has been a decided sales resistance to this type.

Then, too, more comfort can be built into the front seats. They can be made wider and made adjustable forward and backward to allow for variance in the reach of the driver. It is quite possible, no matter what the price range, to build into that car the two vital items, that is, style and comfort. In the foregoing treatise are several predictions relative to future design, which may be summed up in the one idea: Style and comfort must be uppermost in all motor-car design.

The Questionable Profits of *Pure Novelty*

An Advertising Man's Pleadings That the Ground Gained in Body Design Be Not Lost on Account of an Excessive Pursuit of Novelty

By Walter Mitchell, Jr. *

NOVELTY is acceptable as a competitive weapon only so long as it does not flagrantly violate the principles of real beauty. Yet the latter happens so frequently in the field of body design that any practical method of guarding against it would be desirable. Examples of unbeautiful novelty were fewer in number at this year's Show than before, but the few were individually more raucous.

"Eye Comfort" and Profits Related

In the interest of certainty for the manufacturer's profits and of comfort for the public eye, some of the undisputed principles of good design (that which is certain to please the public) should be summarized in print for the benefit of confused automobile executives and jaded body designers. Perhaps some one able designer will have public spirit and patience to do this. Even better, I believe, would be a composite of sugges-

beautiful. An equally valuable set of cautions may be deduced from designs of novelty models, most of them intended to be ultra sporting—mechanically good cars

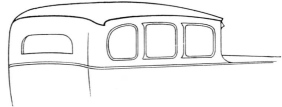

The roof finish of this fabric body suggests a gutter treatment that is possible with either metal or fabric rear quarter

whose sales were stunted by their homeliness. (A cursory survey of the past three years reveals only one such model, a roadster, that sold in large enough volume to repay the investment in dies and fixtures. As is well

"Airline Effects" Applied to Some Recent Custom Designs

Fleetwood-Cadillac   Holbrook-Duesenberg

tions from the foremost designers in the industry, compiled under the guidance of AUTOBODY, and somehow thrust into the presence of all company executives who have the approving of designs. No one will expect it to inspire genius or guarantee outstanding works of art. If it served only to prevent atrocities it would save many thousands of dollars.

Simple Factors Determine Approval

Average public taste could not be so notably uniform if it were not determined by simple factors. If this be granted, it should be possible to discover these factors

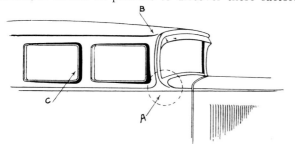

Sketch showing: (A) Three way split of the molding on the cowl; (B) up-turned front end of gutter; (C) a possible window-reveal treatment emphasizing the front rather than the sill edge

by observing the points of similarity in those models that have pleased the public well and faithfully—the ones whose popularity has lasted because they were truly

*1724 I St., N. W., Washington, D. C.

known, sales for most "freaks" show a big start, and then a quick drop.)

It will probably be obvious to any reader that the deductions below are the products of someone with the advertising viewpoint and not those of an experienced body designer, that I lack the perspective of long years spent in designing wheelbarrows, buggies and hansom cabs. As a reader of AUTOBODY I have always been pleased with the editor's liberal policy of letting the outside in occasionally to take a whack at our industry. Only a continuance of his openminded policy would account for the use of this material.

The "Flow of Air" Principle

After examining past models, here is the principle which seems to me most significant: "Lines emphasized in a body design should not do anything the wind couldn't." Though this idea may be wrong, yet the reading could be worthwhile by generating an idea in the course of refuting this one. I do not mean the same thing as "streamline," that good old term which has now died and gone to the dictionary. That word properly refers to the surface of the body only; and has long since become an undisputed axiom. This principle relates to the moldings and high lights which today carry the sole responsibility for distinguishing one make of car from another. It is not at all a new principle, but frequent violation shows that it is not taken seriously. Those designs which have been most favored by the public are the finest examples of obedience to this principle, and *vice versa*. Do not search for a deep explanation. The layman's eye simply likes things that are graceful and flowing.

No flow of air or other liquid butts head on into another stream at right angles without affecting the course of the stream attacked. Should not such a practice be avoided in body design? Manufacturing facilities have so improved in the last two years that it is possible at no added expense to avoid practically all such breaches.

MOLDING AND FRONT-PILLAR LINES

Note the large number of designs where the belt molding splits at the cowl and sweeps in unbroken line up the front body pillar and across the windshield header and down the other side. In two important makes, this line has been split three ways, the third branch sweeping across the cowl in front of the windshield. The comments that I have heard, both from the public and motor men, favor this type of design over that where the front pillar sprouts independently and unheralded from the cowl panel.

Notable also in this connection is the swept molding across the Auburn hood, which seems to suggest the route being taken by the wind current sweeping over the front fender. In contrast to this is a sweep sometimes used in custom work which starts from the radiator cap in a long curve ending at base of the body, opposite the front body pillar. This seems like a direct defiance of the path of wind currents, except in models where extra wheels are carried in fender wells. Moreover, no model has ever been popular that featured an exaggerated coach-pillar line brought out merely by an applied molding, and lacking the return curve at the base of the pillar which lends it the finished appearance of "pushing

Mitcl

Lines emphasized in a body design should not anything the wind couldn't.

* * *

Why not emphasize the front edge of a wind reveal instead of the sill edge, thereby suggesting t idea of a strong front presented by each window fram to the passing wind?

* * *

The former right-angle intersection of drip a rear-quarter-window moldings is now gracefully join in most successful designs.

forward on its own account." Yet the practice is not yet abandoned.

Almost two years ago one of the minor manufacturers avoided a butt-end contact between the gutter and front body pillar by bending upward the last three inches of the gutter, causing it to blend into the line across the windshield header. The present method of making body-pillar and header cover panels should make it possible to do this in production without extra expense, yet I do not find that anyone has adopted it.

BELT TREATMENT

Some sort of emphasis on the belt line, either by molding or high light, is so obvious that it is neither possible nor desirable to avoid it. In handling this problem it

Gardner

Some new models illustrating the pleasing effect of using symmetrical belt panels

Hudson

Studebaker

will be found that the most successful models have
either abided by the "air rule" propounded above or
have relieved the belt line by a treatment that was
frankly symmetrical and artificial. This tendency
showed strongly again at the Show just closed. Models
by Auburn, Chrysler, Gardner, Hudson and Packard

Marmon

(open) with perhaps some others, have found this device
acceptable to the public. Whenever this symmetrical
panel has been used above the "main line" belt molding, it has been necessary to define the ends of the panel
by lines which swept up from molding to pillar in the
front, and down from the pillar to belt in back; this is
what the air current would probably be doing. In every
case where a variation was attempted the result was
unsatisfactory, emphasizing a direction which air currents could not possibly be taking, and resulting in a
car which looked higher and in some cases, awkward.
It destroyed the optical illusion for which the designers
were striving. Note by a study of these designs that
any such belt panel above the main belt line will have
concave ends, if properly designed.

None of the "offset" belt panels have proved exceptionally successful, especially one case of a rather wide
panel which ceased unaccountably just aft of the rear-
door hinges (on a well-known sedan) and therefore
appeared to have been stopped "by order of the rear
fender."

Effect of Artists' Drawings

Whether it be admitted or not, I believe that advertising artists have done considerable to speed the advent
of better motor-car design. The artist often painted
more of what he had been hoping for, than what he
saw. I have wondered whether an advertising drawing originally suggested the use of a swelled panel to
secure a length-of-car high light, in place of a belt molding. With the greater prevalance of trained designers
in the automobile industry, the influence of advertising

artists amounts to less than formerly, but still offers
two or three good instances.

Artists' drawings of late have frequently employed
shadows swept forward from the rear fenders, in a
curve which lingered roughly parallel to the apron for
a time; then again tended upward "in sympathy with"
spare wheel or front fender. This dip of air currents
along the side of the body was rather pleasing and
something which I had believed would sometimes be

Gardner

picked up and consciously used by a designer, probably
in the form of embossed panel work. In November,
just after rough drafting this discussion I found the
idea used on a certain model for the Salon; a short
time later, the Flying Cloud "Mate" appeared with this
quirk utilized in a manner on which I have heard a
large amount of favorable comment.

Study of Air Currents

In connection with this it would be interesting and
possibly helpful to try a plan developed at Langley
Field for experimental studies on airplane design. Over
the surface to be studied small arrows were mounted on
friction posts or pins, tight enough not to be jarred
from position by vibration, but loose enough so that
they would be blown into position parallel to the air
currents when the machine was in motion. At the end
of the flight the exact nature of typical air currents
could be drawn to scale from the direction of these
arrows. Perhaps this has already been tried. If any
reader of Autobody conducts experiments along this
line I should greatly appreciate hearing of the results.

Windows Reveals

Observation of window-reveal treatments on popular
cars vs. languishing models confirms the rule not-to-do-
anything-which-the-wind-couldn't. Here it might better
be called the "bag o'wind" principle. Many window
treatments, especially those with a semi-circular rear-
quarter window, give the impression of a bag dragged

Durant

along in the wind with its mouth to the front and open.
When one rear corner of the rear-quarter window is
given the appearance of a sharp corner, the layman's
imagination is immediately relieved. He sees a place
for the wind to escape. Obviously the upper corner
is the one to be curved in order to "pull down" the back
of the body. It is hardly necessary to name the good
and bad models which are referred to in this connection.

Here I would like to venture an idea that cannot be
reinforced by observation of past models. It is customary to emphasize the sill edge of windows by a
wider step in the reveal treatment—for no apparent

reason except that it is architectural practice in houses (which customarily stand still). I cannot discover that it adds greatly to beauty or dignity, and it certainly does not contribute to the idea of motion. Why not emphasize the front edge of each window reveal, even going so far as to "trail off" a double-reveal treatment into none at all at the rear of each window or of the group? It offers to the imagination the idea of a strong front presented by each window frame to the passing wind.

IMPROVING DRIP-MOLDING LINE

Ever since the advent of ball-back design, the rear ends of gutters have been a sore and homely point, generally one at which a vertical molding back of the rear-quarter window and the rear-edge deck molding formed a right-angle intersection with the gutter. It is notable that in most of the successful new designs the gutter bows gracefully, swings downward and

Reo
Illustrating the dip of air curves along the side of the body emphasized in one of the actual exhibits at the National Show

blends in with the belt line. In some other models the gutter stops abruptly in the middle of an open space, which the wind would never do. In only one model has it been tapered off to a trailing point, the obvious, graceful solution.

With the type of stamping and welding practice now in general use the vertical molding back of the rear-quarter window is unnecessary; is retained only by habit. It is better omitted, and some models have done so. Another quirk in rear-gutter finish, suggested by a fabric body designer, is shown by a sketch.

THE QUESTION OF PROPORTION

One other principle might be suggested for discussion by the designers who write this handbook—namely, the matter of proportion in bulk, the point along the length of the car at which the greatest cross section should occur in each type and model, the point of maximum height, the relative height where the maximum width should occur. A careful study of these points has been one of the major factors in the success of two of the prominent designers in the body field to-day.

In other words, is there something equivalent in body design to the "golden mean" in the dimensions of a rectangle. It requires an artist to arrive at conclusions and limits on such a question, but I believe there is something to be gained by the study and discussion of it for the benefit and education of the executives who judge the designs. The point of greatest height and greatest cross section in practically all of the new models lies one and one-half to two feet ahead of the point where it did three years ago. Yet new models continue to appear in which something is gravely wrong.

The public sees it and does not buy them. Somewhere money is lost on amortization of dies and fixtures.

One artist suggests that there is some optimum proportion between the various areas in the conventional profile view of a design. That is, a ratio of hood to body, of side panel to super-structure, of roof quarter to rear quarter. A mathematical study of these areas on successful models might reveal some interesting ratios, but because of the fine scorn which designers usually hold for mathematics, it will be hard to find anyone to make the study.

JUDGMENT ON NOVELTIES OFTEN WRONG

Many a good product from the designers has gone down to defeat because of the demand for novelty from the sales and engineering executives. It is time that the designers club together to do a little pre-selling which will enable these men to recognize a profitable design, one of which the public will not tire in a few weeks. One of the principal realizations it would bring is the point that nothing radically new can be done to the basic elements of the body without loss of grace or beauty, until such time as a radical change in the whole plan of fender and hood design can be made pleasing; and this is not apparently an immediate contingency.

The novelty of the immediate future must come in finesse and the handling of small detail, a careful advance toward more perfect beauty rather than a mad pursuit of yearly novelty. Several manufacturers seem to be reaching the rather logical conclusion that "the public would rather have imitations than atrocities" in automobile design.

There is still need for a conservative educational manual, not over "three feet deep," and physically small enough to fit in the trim-tailored executive coat pocket.

Hupp's new Model "S" roadster departs from the conventional in lines and color treatment. Sweeps give the forward part of the car a much higher effect than the rear, suggesting the angle of an airplane fuselage while the mudguards simulate the flow of air emphasized by the coloring of the body. The cowl extends about 8 in. back of the instrument panel and the rear edge of the doors have a sweep in harmony with the sporting design. The rear of the body is extended to cover most of the fuel tank and beadings converge at the center. The roadster lists at $1175, f.o.b., Cleveland

The Calendar

S. A. E. SUMMER MEETING......................May 25-29
    At French Lick Springs, Ind.
A. R. A. CONVENTION AND EXHIBITION...........June 18-25
    At Municipal Auditorium, Atlantic City, N. J.
NATIONAL ASSOCIATION OF MOTOR BUS OPERATORS..Sept. 18-19
    At Chicago

New Basis for Future Automobile Designs

Scientific Research Will be the Keystone in Determining Future Body Design and Assuring Sales Appeal. Reaction to Designs Differs Among Various Classes of People

By Julio Andrade*

IT seems to me that there should be a wide distinction made between that art, the aim of which is to create masterpieces for the glory of art—for the enjoyment of a few, for the gratification of the artist's emotions—and that art, the aim of which is to sell as much as possible of its products to the general public for the financial progress of a particular industry.

What Does the Public Want?

An artist in the first classification does not have to consider the tastes and likes of the people. In fact, he considers his work an absolute in art and it is for the public to value it. However, the artist engaged in industrial activity should consider mainly what motor-car buyers like, and give it to them. But the artist or designer of any kind does not know much about the taste of the masses; he acts upon an emotional impulse, not upon a rational solution; his taste is to him an absolute in design; if he likes it, everybody should like it.

The fact is that nobody knows much about what people like. One often hears an executive exclaim: "This or that is what the people like." But he forgets that "the people" include races, classes, ages and regional groups, and are not like an individual. Often the individual himself does not know what he would like. It seems to me that the problem of finding out what the public wants or is apt to want pertains to social sciences, that is, to the anthropologist, psychologist or sociologist, not to the designer or executive.

In the Realm of Science

Though it is true that there is not a man in the country prepared to give such guidance, there are scientists engaged in similar work who after research, tests and statistical work—for this is the basis of any such study—could supply us with more information than we could collect in our blind, whimsical way of working. By this, of course, it is not meant that the public will do their own designing, for they do not know what they like until they see it. Besides we cannot expect ideas from them. To give an illustration of how scientific research of this kind could be used in our field, consider the front-wheel-drive car. Two makes at least will be on the market soon. If they are a success, we shall develop an opinion as to why they sell. Other manufacturers may start producing front-wheel drives and will feature those characteristics which in their opinion are the cause of success. They may or may not be successful. If the first front drives are a failure from the sales standpoint, we shall probably not have front-wheel drives for a long time to come, but this will not be a conclusive proof that people do not want automobiles of this type. Well conducted tests, scientifically planned in the salesrooms throughout the country, would give us a more logical and rational answer.

It seems then that the immediate problem is to find out, first, why did this or that model sell, and second,

what will the public be apt to like next year. We take for granted these days that a car sells mainly on its beauty and think of beauty as an absolute, but all those acquainted with the industry for the last five or ten years will remember some cars that were well built and thought to be beautiful that brought failure to their manufacturers. We know also of unattractive looking cars, from our point of view, that brought tremendous success to their manufacturers.

I do not doubt that good appearance is the most important attribute in a car today, but beauty is relative and exceedingly elusive of definition and control. Its

Interior of the Chrysler "77" Crown sedan showing the tendency toward the application of modern art in automobile interiors. Note the treatment of the door friezes and the modernistic reading light. The door fittings and other metalwork also have the straight-line decorative treatment

enjoyment is purely an emotional phenomenon. What looks good to us, today, may not seem so tomorrow. What is beauty to us may not appeal to the European, to the Asiatic, to the South American or to different classes in our own country. Our beautiful blondes are not so much admired, as some may think, among the African negro or the swarthy Arab.

Other Factors than Design

I have always thought that the success of a certain automobile of medium price that experienced a great increase in sales in the autumn of 1927—generally attributed to the intrinsic beauty of the models—was brought about by several circumstances. Aside from the unquestioned excellence of the design, there was the fact that the announcement was made at the psychological moment, when we had just finished admiring another automobile of rather high price, announced a few months before, which had created a furor and had

---

* Body-designing department, Murray Corporation of America, Detroit.

left in many people the desire to own a car that would look something like that one and would be within their income. Other reasons, of course, were that the car was well advertised and built by a reputable company. The same designers turned out shortly afterward two other cars which in their estimate were better looking than that successful one, but their sales were a failure compared with the first one.

In the spring of the following year, that is only a few months after the successful car was announced, another company bought one of these cars and had it copied line by line with the aid of templets. The company made the best car it ever made, but the car did not sell. That company is now out of business.

STYLE FORECASTS

If scientific data were obtained as to people's likes and expectations with respect to automobiles, it would then be possible to predict with some certainty the design of the future. With the information available at present and judging by some scientific findings in the development of other arts, it does not seem likely that we shall have radical changes in the appearance of automobiles without radical changes in their use and mechanism. The automobile has followed more or less the same artistic evolution as other useful objects. What prompts their creation is a physical necessity and not an aesthetic pleasure. In the beginning all efforts are concentrated on the perfection of the main object of the invention. Once this is accomplished, as it has been with the automobile, we start to beautify its appearance and pay more attention to comfort.

DESIGN CONFORMS TO CONSTRUCTION

Before the first cars were made it would have been impossible to predict their present form, but it would not have been so difficult at the beginning to predict the shape they attained, because in the design of a useful object like the automobile the designer is much influenced by the form of an existing object that most closely approaches the purposes of the one to be invented. As a result of materials and the mechanical construction, certain necessary shapes develop which become the basis of future decorative treatment.

As improvements in construction become necessary and the number of uses increases, the shape has to follow a similar transition, though retaining most of the old characteristics. For instance, applied moldings were at the beginning a necessity in the construction of bodies. In the refinement of its shape a play with moldings developed and they were placed to the best advantage for the balancing of the surfaces; their shapes and sizes were shuffled for a more pleasing appearance. But today, when moldings are not a necessity, they still remain as the standard of decorative motifs of the body. Offsets and depressions with molding characteristics belong to the same order. Because of manufacturing improvements, the designer today is free to use practically any ornamentation he pleases, but few would become reconciled to it because having grown up with the progress of the automobile, we have developed a taste for those characteristics that have been so much a part of them.

EFFECT OF PRICE ON DESIGN

It is possible that if a scientific research were made, as proposed above, that designs would have to be divided into about three classes, low-, medium- and high-price car designs which would indicate in what price category the cars belonged. It is obvious that the higher the price of a car, the more individuality it should possess. Mainly because the price of an object bears a rather direct relation to the number of prospective customers. It is safe to render high-class merchandise original as it will be bought by a relatively small number of people, having more affinity of taste than the general public. If we were now to consider, as seems logical, that a buyer will exhibit the same taste when he buys a car as when he buys another object, we would think that the prospective customer of a low-price car does not want originality or individuality in his car if that would make the price he paid for it evident from its design. He would like his car to be as undiscernible as possible from popular higher price ones. It must not be forgotten that a decorative motif used for the first time on a low-price car will be associated with that class of car by designers and manufacturers, thereby making it undesirable for use on high-price cars and thus isolating even more the low-price car. It is possible that attempts at originality in this field are not only wasted, but detrimental.

CLASS TASTES DIFFER

Accepting the hypothesis that the wealthier classes have a more refined taste than the others, as a result of the environment in which they live, they would appreciate design from a different point of view than those of more primitive tastes. The former classes recognize the appropriateness of decorative motifs with the use of the object and these are enjoyed mainly for their aesthetic merits.

For those less imaginative and artistic groups, design must be associated with some definite symbolic significance; it must have a meaning. For instance, two or three years ago, when it was the style to decorate the radiator cap with outstanding ornaments, most of them had a direct significance. Where these ornaments did not have this direct symbolism, it was chiefly the result of the fact that the abstract name of the company or that of its president could not be repeated in plastic form. But in most instances had the company's or the president's name been Cat or Goat, a cat or goat would have been installed on the top of the radiator shell. Observing this practice from the standpoint of the public, I would say, but without anything to prove it, that the owner of the higher price cars would not enjoy such ornamentation, but others would be delighted after the salesman explained to them the connection between the ornaments and the president's name. There are races and classes that do not enjoy ornamentation without a direct significance.

SENSIBILITY TO MINOR CHANGES

Another item on which research and tests could throw some light is the great expense and time given to minor details and insignificant changes made on new models. It must be realized that we are dealing with a relative matter. Experts in the industry will notice minor details incorporated in any car. A door window, for instance, whose corners had a radius as small as $\frac{1}{4}$ in. and drawn to a depth of 2 in. would attract the attention of the observing designer by its looks and that of the engineer and metal man by its difficult metal draw. But would the customer notice anything different?

All those engaged in a business in which success depends on pleasing the public will eventually adopt more scientific methods. Our traditional conception of cause and effect may be fundamentally wrong in some instances. Certain methods might have brought successful effects, but we cannot be sure that the same methods will bring success again.

Body Session Considers the *Car of the Future*

Motor Car of Ten Years Hence Discussed at S. A. E. Annual Meeting

THE appearance of the motor car ten years hence was the main theme of Capt. H. Ledyard Towle's address before the body session at the annual meeting of the Society of Automotive Engineers at Detroit on Jan. 19. He said that it was useless to talk to engineers about body designs for this year or next; in the main they would follow the usual practice of seeing what the leader had and then duplicating it as nearly as possible on their own chassis. He thought that the industry had passed through the stage of merely making things work and that it was now largely concerned with making its creations beautiful.

Certain basic principles of fundamental design must always be followed, but it was often advisable to get an outside point of view, hence he decided to develop his talk along lines that were strictly outside the original topic assigned. He said that we are now living in an age that might later be called the "American Renais-

One has only to note our fashions in apparel to see what has been done in simplifying design, line and color. Consider today's fashion in women's dress, compared with the old days when everything seems to have been done to distort the woman's figure. Nowadays the fashion simply covers the figure without trying to change it in any way. These are all basics which we shall have to achieve with the motor car, as well as with men's attire.

Aerodynamic principles are being applied to automobile-body design which will increase performance per horsepower, and in a few years, we may find the engine and transmission units at the rear of the machine. Today, everybody is immersed in tomorrow's immediate problem. It is the thing close by that worries us. Tomorrow's car will perhaps be much like today's, but the ideal way to design a motor car is to think what it will be five or ten years hence.

Design, patented by Guillaume Busson who won the "Coupe de l'Originalité" at one of the recent "Concours d'Élégance" in Paris. This design embodies some of the pre-

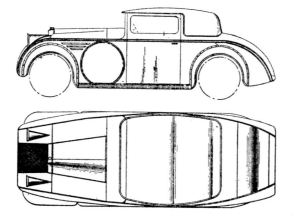

dictions made for the car of the future. The whole car is enclosed in a "shell"; fenders, aprons, radiator and lamps are incorporated in the shell, instead of being treated as separate units

sance." This movement was observable in many industries. Architecture and furniture have felt this new influence and it is even observable in railroad-car construction. New York buildings have taken on an entirely new aspect since "set-backs" were ordered, when they exceeded a certain height with relation to street width. The result has been to produce more beautiful and more useful buildings; it was found that where terraces had been created the offices on those upper floors were rentable at a higher price.

Things which function perfectly seem beautiful to us. We admire the greyhound or the Arab stallion because they seem made to do their particular work. One might liken them to the roadster in the automobile industry, or perhaps to a racing car. An elephant and a tractor or truck may also have their own inherent beauty and that is all they need, because they do specific things. That is something to think about when one is drawing moldings up and down, hither and yon, all over the body without thinking what those moldings should do, if anything.

Today's automobile bodies have been so designed that all cars look a great deal alike. There is no reason for this except fear, the fear of spending money in dies the public will not accept. That fear should not exist because the public will take what is given if it understands why it is being done. If one simply says, "Here it is. How do you like it?" the public hesitates to answer because offhand it does not know, but if one explains why this or that was done, it will find an acceptance. If one tells why these new mechanisms are called "free wheeling" or "synchro-mesh transmission," the public will take them but not if one simply says, "free wheeling" or "synchro-mesh transmission."

There is no use discussing the motor-car design of today because everyone can see it, but the motor car of the future will be quite different. If one observes the animals that walk or run over the earth, one will discover that practically all motive power is at the rear. Some experimental work has already taken place in providing engines at the rear of the automobile and many designers think that this is one of the future developments for motor cars. It has already been tried out in a preliminary way, but certain difficulties must be overcome.

The automobile is merely a refined buggy, as yet. Hoods are so long and seats so low that a seventh sense is necessary to know where the right front fender is and where the curb that you cannot see is. Also, those funny, big lamps that are now out in front of the car will have to be put inside and be made to turn with the wheels so as to show the way when turning corners. It costs money to push these lamps along. A certain new car which had larger lamps put on it, was found to be 5 mi. slower at top speed; needless to say, those lamps were removed. Front fenders are at present air catchers. In the future they and the wheels will be hidden and become a part of the car; then we shall have forced-draft ventilation and never need to open a window.

Road Speeds Suggest Altered Contours

Road speeds are now 45 to 50 mi. per hr., on the new super-highways they will be 65, 75 or more. This indicates the probability of the adoption of the teardrop body, i.e., one that is big and round in front and slopes away at the rear. This conforms with aerodynamic design as evidenced by the airplane wing. The latest "queen of the seas," the *Bremen*, looks like any other liner above the water line in front, but below it is blunt in front just as in the teardrop design and fades away at the stern because it has been found that there is less resistance in the water with this design. In other words, the developments point to a complete reversal of the present outline of our cars.

In the upholstering of our motor-car bodies one finds the same old plaits but if one goes outside this industry, one finds that in the furniture field a decided change is taking place. This furniture which seemed so queer a year or so ago is finding greater acceptance as we become accustomed to it and some of these chairs are extremely comfortable. On the other hand, radiator screens which are now so popular are not really sound design. No reason exists for them except the copying of European road-race experience and these conditions do not apply for the ordinary use of motor cars. Radiator screens are one of the things that will come and go. Slavish copying of what one sees at the shows is not good designing. It will be recalled that a few years ago one car appeared with a curved tiebar for headlamps; today there are many such on our cars.

The color of automobiles is a subject of much argument. Every man, in his own mind, thinks his opinion is as good as the next man's. There is only one way to find the color for cars that will sell and that is to ask the dealers what the public will buy or wants. A questionnaire among thousands of boys who belong to a recently formed "craftsman's guild" revealed that the majority were in favor of dark colors; specifically they favored; (1) dark blue; (2) maroon; (3) green; those who favored red or bright colored cars were in the minority. The public tires of red before it does of dark blue because of the greater wave-length frequency beating upon the retina of the eye. People also tire of the same color, hence the need for some bright colors at the proper time and on the proper models. Automobile colors right now reflect the mood of the people and the effects of the business depression.

Discussion

A lively discussion, ably directed by L. Clayton Hill, ensued over the hypothetical rear-engined car with teardrop body, and also touched upon defects of present-day cars and bodies. David Beecroft asked if color could really give an effect of greater speed or lowness. Captain Towle responded with the results of a height test at the General Motors' proving grounds where black-top sedans were declared by company officials to be lower than white-top sedans although the latter were actually about ½-in. lower because of less tire inflation. With reference to the speed effect, he suggested that if the design permitted, the top and back of the car be painted in a dark or "far" color such as blue, and that a bright or "near" color, such as orange, be used for the middle and front of the car. This would give the car the feeling of leaping ahead, but of course, much would depend on the basic design of the body.

Modern Fitments Will Remain

With reference to the trend to dark colors, Chairman Hill stated that the colors of automobiles would always express the times a nation was experiencing. In the matter of modern-art motifs, he felt that these would continue to be used for interior fitments as they were a reflection of the present period and would remain as long as these motifs were to be found in other contemporary art such as architecture and interior decoration. They were not so happy, however, for the exterior of automobiles. One reason was the desirability of reducing wind resistance. In the last decade ordinary road speeds have risen to 45 or 50 mi. per hr. and on good highways 60 to 70 mi. were not unusual. Hence aerodynamic design was becoming of increasing importance, if manufacturers desired to get the most out of their cars. At present, he said, "Mama and Papa" generally ride over the axle, and with only about 36 in. above the cushion; the rear seat must be moved forward for these speeds, or perhaps the whole body, if the engine is to be placed at the rear.

More Room with Engine at Rear

Herbert Chase pointed out that if the engine be placed at the rear, it is not necessary to provide additional length there because it can be positioned horizontally, as is done on one of the present British cars, and then occupies no more room than the trunk. The steering wheel of today's car is approximately in the center of the car and thereby limits passenger capacity; if the space between the axles and the outside of the running boards of a Ford chassis were available for passengers, it would accommodate as many passengers as can now be carried by the normal Lincoln.

City and Highway Driving Different

G. Betancourt took exception to the idea that all cars should be streamlined to attain maximum performance on the open highway. There were two general types of driving to be considered: City and highway driving. The majority of cars were used in cities where the protection afforded by bumpers, brakes, etc. and quick acceleration were more important than wind resistance. To develop a car for maximum highway performance, it would be necessary to appeal to the 2-car family. The car that represented a happy medium was, he thought, the design to be aimed at. Placing the engine at the rear injects new steering problems in going up hill and the passengers would presumably be placed far forward in such a car. In present-day traffic, passengers feel much safer between the wheels, and as most of the time the cars carry only two passengers, they are already in the ideal position on the present driving seat.

Index

(Italic page numbers denote illustrations.)